NEW PROCLAMATION

NEW PROCLAMATION

Year C, 2003–2004

Advent through Holy Week

SUSAN K. HEDAHL

JOHN S. MCCLURE

FREDERICK A. NIEDNER

FOSTER R. MCCURLEY

HAROLD W. RAST, EDITOR

FORTRESS PRESS

MINNEAPOLIS

NEW PROCLAMATION
Year C, 2003–2004
Advent through Holy Week

Cover and book design: Joseph Bonyata

Illustrations: Tanya Butler, *Icon: Visual Images for Every Sunday,* copyright 2000 Augsburg Fortress.

The Library of Congress has catalogued this series as follows.
New proclamation year A, 2001–2002 : Advent through Holy Week / Francis J. Moloney . . . [et al.].
       p. cm.
  Includes bibliographical references.
  ISBN 0-8006-4245-7 (alk. paper)
      1. Church year. I. Moloney, Francis J.
  BV30 .N48 2001
  251'.6—dc21   2001023746

New Proclamation, Year C, 2003–2004, Advent through Holy Week
ISBN 0-8006-4249-X

The paper used in this publication meets the minimum requirements of American National Standard for Information Sciences — Permanence of Paper for Printed Library Materials, ANSI Z329.48-1984. ∞

Manufactured in Canada
07   06   05   04   03   1   2   3   4   5   6   7   8   9   10

CONTENTS

The Season of Epiphany
John S. McClure

The Season of Lent
Frederick A. Niedner

HOLY WEEK
FOSTER R. MCCURLEY

PREFACE

Now *Proclamation* continues the time-honored Fortress Press tradition of offering a lectionary preaching resource that provides first-rate biblical exegetical aids for a variety of lectionary traditions.

Thoroughly ecumenical and built around the three-year lectionary cycle, *New Proclamation* focuses on the biblical texts, based on the conviction that those who acquire a deeper understanding of the pericopes in both their historical and liturgical contexts will be motivated to preach engaging and effective sermons. For this reason, the most capable North American biblical scholars and homileticians are invited to contribute to *New Proclamation*.

We have asked the contributors to follow a similar pattern in their presentations but have allowed them to alter and improve that pattern in ways they think might be more helpful to the user. For example, one of the authors in a previous volume began each discussion of the Sunday lections with the Gospel rather than the First Reading, since it is assumed that most users preach on the Gospel reading for the day. In other instances, some authors have occasionally chosen to combine the interpretation and response to the texts into one section rather than separating them into two distinct sections.

In general, *New Proclamation* is planned and designed to be user-friendly in the following ways:

- *New Proclamation* is published in two volumes per year, designed for convenience. The present volume covers the lections for the first half of the church year, Advent/Christmas through Holy Week, culminating in The Great Vigil of Easter (Holy Saturday).
- The two-volume format offers a larger, workbook-style page with a lay-flat binding and space for making notes.

- Each season of the church year is prefaced by an introduction that provides insights into the background and spiritual significance of the period.
- The application of biblical texts to contemporary situations is an important concern of each contributor. Exegetical work ("Interpreting the Text") is concise, and thoughts on how the texts address today's world and our personal situations ("Responding to the Text") have a prominent role.
- Although the psalms ("Responsive Reading") are infrequently used as preaching texts, brief comments on each assigned psalm are included so that the preacher can incorporate reflections also on these in the sermon. The psalms, for the most part, represent the congregation's response to the first reading and are not intended as another reading.
- Boxed quotations in the margins help signal important themes in the texts for the day.
- The material for Year C is here dated specifically for the year 2003–2004, for easier coordination with other dated lectionary materials.
- These materials can be adapted for uses other than for corporate worship on the day indicated. They are well suited for adult discussion groups or personal meditation and reflection.

It is important to keep in mind that the Gospel is the formative principle of the lectionary and that most sermons are based on it. From the First Sunday of Advent to Trinity Sunday of each year, the Old Testament reading is closely related to the Gospel reading for the day. However, from the first Sunday after Trinity Sunday to the end of the year (Christ the King), provision has been made for two patterns of reading the Old Testament in the RCL: (1) paired readings in which the Old Testament and Gospel readings are closely related, and (2) semicontinuous Old Testament readings that are not necessarily related to the Gospel.

We are grateful to our contributors—Susan Hedahl, John McClure, Frederick Niedner, and Foster McCurley—for their insights and for their commitment to effective Christian preaching. We hope that you find in this volume ideas, stimulation, and encouragement for your ministry of proclamation.

HAROLD W. RAST

THE SEASON OF ADVENT

SUSAN K. HEDAHL

The common word *advent* is used to designate the first season of the church year. Its Latin etymology indicates the "arrival" or anticipated "coming" of someone or something. Like many seasons the church celebrates, Advent has vague and multiple origins. Early lectionaries and church councils show that Advent was observed as early as the sixth century, when it was in Gaul a penitential period in preparation for the celebration of the Nativity. In particular, as sermons from that period show, it was a season of fasting and almsgiving. It was then six weeks in length, but its duration continued to shift until settling into its current four weeks.

For many the celebration of Advent brings both *texts* and *images* to mind. Advent's texts are not abstract or hypothetical; they include familiar faces, names, songs, and actions. Always the Advent proclamation is filtered and nuanced by this original cast of those who set the stage for the arrival of the baby Jesus. Images of Advent have varied origins. Some are derived from biblical texts and others by association through their regional, historical, and ethnic reenactments. There are Advent wreaths, calendars, logs, the color blue, the increasingly darkened skies, and often the happily messy production of the Christmas story at its end, performed by free-spirited children and directed by worried adults!

> PERHAPS THE GREATEST GIFT OF ADVENT, IF TAKEN SERIOUSLY, IS THAT WORSHIPERS AND SEEKERS MAY ENCOUNTER AN INVITATION TO LOOK AT OTHER GIFTS THAT ARE UNEXPECTED, WEIGHTED WITH MEANINGS THAT BLESS AND CHALLENGE.

What does it mean to proclaim Advent today? In the environment of America's secularization of Christmas, Advent is as liable to being lost as a child in a shopping mall. It is a short season, and many are simply frustrated by the effort to synchronize what they wish to experience in church with what they see outside of it during the month of December. Perhaps the greatest gift of Advent, if taken seriously, is that worshipers and seekers may encounter an invitation to look at other gifts that are unexpected, weighted with meanings that bless and challenge. The Advent season presents those who listen and watch with interpretations of time and space and with the relationship of the divine and the human that leaves us blessed and baffled. One pastor said to a group that had gathered for worship at an important time, "Never underestimate the importance of just showing up!" All Advent asks of believers is that they show up! To all who are willing to celebrate Advent's unfolding, there is much that may be experienced although not necessarily explained. But then what fun is a mystery if it is "explained"?

The texts of Advent set the stage for us as we attend worship—curious, thinking we know all of this anyway, wondering if something new is going to be revealed. What do we hear? The voices of history through the prophets and chroniclers of the past whisper urgently, "Your Savior is coming to you! Pay attention to the signs!" The voices of those who play major biblical Advent roles show us, in part, that the Savior is about to arrive as the texts witness to their thoughts and feelings through dialogue, prophecy, and song. The names of the characters who herald the Savior's approach have been announced. But there is more. As we look toward the future, to Christmas and beyond, the texts let us know that Advent is not just an advance notice of an arrival, but that arrival and its meanings stretch into the future with the final fulfillment of all things in the Savior. Advent, paradoxically, leaves us in as much a sense of anticipation as it initially began.

The themes of Advent texts offer preacher and people the full array of God's intentions toward humanity with the coming of Jesus. *Repentance,* a strong note sounded by the prophets and John the Baptizer, call for a changed life as one of the imperatives that emerges from the birth of Jesus. With this theme, worshipers are most in touch with the church's historical understanding of the purpose of Advent. *Hope* also sounds through many of the Old and New Testament texts, as a reminder to those who suffer and those who can alleviate their suffering, that God is a God of justice and will use many means to accomplish that justice. And another theme that calls for thoughtful preaching is *righteousness*. This Jesus is the ultimate expression of God's righteousness and the righteousness that comes to each of us as a gift from God.

Advent reminds us that time is not exactly what we thought it was, as we witness the fulfillment of a prophecy that extends to the entire created order. More than ever today, in a world order that continues to shift with the struggles and hopes of the nations, Advent sets before us all—believers, seekers, and nonbelievers—a Savior who brings hope, judgment, healing, and peace to all. Against the kaleidoscope of change, we are all still called to anticipate and give thanks to the eternal God who enters graciously, lovingly, and continuously into time—our time—and speaks the incarnated Word of Jesus as the sign and meaning of new life for us all.

Selected Reading

Auden, W. H. "For the Time Being: A Christmas Oratorio." *Collected Longer Poems.* New York: Vintage, 1975.

Hedahl, Susan. *Places of the Promise.* Lima, Ohio: C.S.S., 1990.

Jones, Cheslyn, Geoffrey Wainwright, and Edward Yarnold, S.J., eds. *The Study of the Liturgy.* New York: Oxford University Press, 1978.

Sayers, Dorothy L. *The Man Born to Be King: A Play Cycle on the Life of Our Lord and Savior Jesus Christ.* Grand Rapids: Eerdmans, 1974.

FIRST SUNDAY OF ADVENT

NOVEMBER 30, 2003

REVISED COMMON	EPISCOPAL (BCP)	ROMAN CATHOLIC
Jer. 33:14-16	Zech. 14:4-9	Jer. 33:14-16
Ps. 25:1-10 (14)	Psalm 50 or 50:1-6	Ps. 25: 4-5, 8-9, 10, 14
1 Thess. 3:9-13	1 Thess. 3:9-13	1 Thess. 3:12—4:2
Luke 21:25-36	Luke 21:25-31	Luke 21:25-28, 34-36

Readings for this first Sunday in Advent set the stage for the season with their tones of remembrance and a sense of urgency for the future. These texts remark on God's power and presence through the various textual forms of prophecy, pastoral admonition and prayer, thanksgiving and hope. As a group, the readings are remarkable for their sense of the personal: Old Testament prophets and psalmists express not only lamentation for sin and warnings of future conflict but also great confidence in God's justice and loving intentions for creation. The pictures of a creation in turmoil at the advent of God actually demonstrate the real bedrock of God's concern for humanity and the establishment of God's reign forever.

FIRST READING
JEREMIAH 33:14-16 (RCL, RC)

Interpreting the Text

Jeremiah's prophetic career was marked by constant political upheaval and religious turmoil. With the destruction of Jerusalem in 587 B.C.E., Judah's leaders were forced into exile in Babylon. Jeremiah himself died in exile in Egypt. Today's reading is a portion of chapter 33, which was probably written by a postexilic author who uses Jeremiah's words of hope to further enlarge upon the promises of the reestablishment of David's lineage. The benefits of this new line of rulers, the "righteous Branch," include justice, righteousness, safety, and security for the people. Most importantly, this future fulfillment of a new reign, known by the name, "The Lord is our righteousness" (v. 16), is a symbolic renaming of Jerusalem, designating it as the embodiment of God's presence and promises as the one who makes of the people a righteous humanity through God's reign. Those in exile who found themselves under foreign domination without the necessary protections of daily life to flourish welcome these prophetic words of promise and hope.

Responding to the Text

For most American congregations, hearing this text addressed to those suffering actual physical exile from their land, experiencing a government in upheaval or destroyed, and the consequent loss of a safe spiritual home, seems remote from actual experience. Even so, in the early twenty-first century, there have been multiple experiences and fragmentary signs of what such exile might be like as people now encounter those events and circumstances that leave them feeling jeopardized and unsafe politically, economically, and spiritually. For Christians, the phrases "house of David," "lineage of David," and "Righteous Branch," provide a counterbalance and unwavering source of hope against contextual evidences to the contrary. God is in charge. The promise of the Savior, Jesus Christ, is heard in between the lines of history's unfolding and invites us to eager attentiveness.

ZECHARIAH 14:4-9 (BCP)

Like a drum roll announcing impending change and personages, this text begins, "On that day. . . ." This excerpt could be entitled "God Takes Jerusalem by Storm," for this last chapter of Zechariah describes God's final battle and consequent victory over all. Not only the God of Israel but also the God of the entire created order is proclaimed through the radical changes in the environment. God's final arrival and triumph is described in poetic terms, depicting how geography itself is rearranged as the sundering of the land prepares the way of the Lord.

The elements also change in such a way as to ensure sustenance and a stable environment: day is continuous, light is constant, life-giving waters flow—and all of these witness to the presence of God. The day of the Lord, promised and pending, gives Christians the assurance that God's witness to God's own self will not disappoint them: ". . . on that day the Lord will be one and his name one" (v. 9b).

RESPONSIVE READING

PSALM 25:1–10 (RCL);
PSALM 50 or 50:1–6 (BCP);
PSALM 25:4–5, 8–9, 10, 14 (RC)

Psalm 25 is a prayer for deliverance from one's enemies. The Hebrew text is in acrostic form (a different Hebrew letter opens each verse). The entire psalm is a stylized lament, beginning with a cry for God's aid and moving through a plea for help despite one's sin, expressions of trust in God, and a petition for defense and vindication before one's enemies.

Many Advent themes, such as God's presence, forgiveness, and protection in times of distress and uncertainty, permeate this psalm. The Advent theme of remembrance is also noted here, though not in the usual way, with the psalmist's plea that God forget human sin in the interests of further instruction in God's ways.

SECOND READING

1 THESSALONIANS 3:9–13 (RCL, BCP);
1 THESSALONIANS 3:12—4:2 (RC)

Interpreting the Text

This letter to Thessalonica, addressed to the Gentile Christians of that area, might well be the earliest known Pauline document. Appointed verses for this Sunday breathe the overall atmosphere of the entire pastoral letter. Paul's concern, love, and theological beliefs permeate the on-paper reflection of his relationship with the Thessalonian believers. The entire letter reflects a pastoral and corporate relationship that Paul hopes will continue in the future.

This Sunday's reading is based on two sources of information—Paul's established relationship with the Thessalonians and information he has received from his emissary to them, Timothy. Earlier in chapter 3, Timothy's report to Paul about the conditions in the congregation confirms Paul's remembrance of them.

Paul's understanding of the balance between his personal authority and that of God in Christ is shown here by the fact that, however he describes the Thessalonians or encourages them, his relationship with them is always a mediated one. In v. 9 Paul's thanksgiving for them is expressed simultaneously in his experiences of "the joy we feel before our God because of you." His feelings of love for them, as described in v. 12, also include the hope that "the Lord make you increase and abound in love for one another and for all." His admonitions to them to learn "how you ought to live and to please God" in 4:1 are derived from the fact that they "learned from us" how to do so. Finally, he reminds the Thessalonians that whatever they have learned about Christ, it is because of "what instructions we gave you through the Lord Jesus" (4:2).

What is the point of these consistent reminders of a new life in Christ for Paul and the Thessalonians? Just as Paul notes in v. 10 that he hopes that "we may see you face to face," so also the reason for all of this is specified in v. 13: that God will uphold the Thessalonians for the sole purpose of creating them "blameless" because of "the coming of our Lord Jesus with all his saints." In proclaiming this text, this strong eschatological framework is essential in understanding what motivates Paul's relationship with the Thessalonians.

Responding to the Text

The text raises many issues and realities for Advent consideration. As people attempt to locate the "reason for the season" in so many varied ways, one cannot miss the joys of personal and corporate relationality expressed in Paul's letter. In Christ and in the community of believers, we come closest to the joys of life in Christ at this final Advent. We come together not only as those who experience the sacred dynamics of such community, but as those who read them as a promise of things yet to be completed in us and the people around us.

This joy is created—sometimes under duress—by the realities that Paul emphasizes; mutual encouragement, instruction, concern, prayer, and leading a holy life. Undoubtedly, this text encourages believers to ask questions of God's intentions and purposes for them. Paul's words may prompt believers to consider the larger reason for Advent, to frame the season and its often short-term and forgotten satisfactions in a much larger eternal perspective.

Paul's words also show that life in Christ is not an individual effort alone but requires for its sustenance the support, responses, communications, and testing of a community of Christians. Such communities exist in many places. For some who worship together during Advent, there are daily reminders that they are also affiliated with other communities of Christians with whom it is not possible to be present in person, for whatever reasons. The hunger to look in person at the faces of loved ones can be acute. Paul's words to those who are absent from his daily life bear a special poignancy for the physical separations from loved ones that many feel at this time of the year. His words also show that relationships in Christ span many times and places and that the conversations of prayer in Christ bind them together. In a time of seasonal and sometimes personal bleakness, Paul's words sound a loving and steadfast note about the joyful reaches and possibilities of life in the Lord Jesus.

The Gospel

LUKE 21:25–36 (RCL);
LUKE 21:25–31 (BCP);
LUKE 21:25–28, 34–36 (RC)

Interpreting the Text

The Gospel for this Sunday must be read within the entire context of Luke 21 as it represents a portion of Jesus' overall description of God's local, cosmic, and personal expressions of judgment and redemption at the dawn of God's appearing. There is a breathless quality in today's Gospel. It paints God's return in all its sensuous aspects. People will see, hear, and feel the expressions and signs of God's approach. Sights, sounds, and events will all point to the advent of the Lord. But the conundrum is this: Are these reliable and true signs that relate to the coming of the Lord? In studying and preaching on this text, it is especially important to note the allusions, quotes, and references to both Old Testament and New Testament materials represented in this section. Here Luke's cross-referencing of other sacred texts is theologically significant.

The sections of this chapter specified in today's lectionary include portions of what is an entire chapter of Jesus' eschatological sayings. Verses 25-28 describe the coming of the Son of Man; vv. 29-31 offer the parable of the fig tree; vv. 32-33 talk about the timing of the Son of Man's arrival; and, finally, vv. 34-36 form the conclusion.

There has always been a proclamatory fascination with these texts for both preachers and listeners. What is one to make of these references, their context, and the array of apocalyptic and eschatological discourse today? Actually, our contemporary context is little different from Jesus' time as people today also attempt to decipher the links among events and to interpret events and the role of God in, through, and even hidden in historical circumstance.

Popular religious literature continues to maintain a public place for apocalyptic kinds of literature, some of it fictional in nature and other forms of it that rely on types of biblical prophecy and interpretation. As a result, many sermon listeners bring a wide variety of interpretative grids to the hearing of Advent lectionary texts that are eschatological in nature. The proclaimer may wish to sort out the forms and approaches of such a biblical genre by holding up specific biblical texts as examples of the tradition and the various ways these have been interpreted theologically. (Clearly this is a task that may extend into adult education classes and more intensive biblical study.)

Perhaps one of the best ways to think of proclaiming such materials, however, is to understand them through the language and vernacular of the poetic imagination. Where factual and rational explanation cannot go, the poetry of faith can, and the drama of these passages may be a useful way to get at what Jesus is saying about God's return as the coming of the Son of Man is described.

In the first section of this reading, Luke spends a great deal of time on "signs" as preludes to God's advent. By way of preface, it is important to note that Luke has described earlier in chapter 21 a past cataclysmic event, the destruction of Jerusalem. He now moves to another even more significant plane of events, as yet to unfold, as the created order shifts definitively toward the coming of God's reign. These coming events or signs will show themselves in a shaking of the natural order of creation: sun, moon, and stars will exhibit changes (see Isa. 34:4) and the earth itself will produced "distress" and "nations confused" by the behavior of the sea and waves. What follows these signs is the actual coming of the Son of Man "with power and great glory" (v. 26). In other words, the beauty of the created order as humanity has always known it will be supplanted by the beauty and power of the Son of Man, though Luke goes no further in describing what that is like except to simply quote an earlier reference to this from Dan. 7:13-14.

In v. 28 Luke urges the believing witness of these things not to indulge in fear but rather to anticipate the good that is yet to unfold. In fact, these signs and the appearance of the Son of Man mean one thing: "Your redemption is drawing near" (v. 28). It is a significant note of encouragement for what could only be generally productive of sheer terror on the part of the onlookers to such radical changes.

The second section of today's text is the parable of the fig tree, vv. 29-33. Here the emphasis is not on the fact of the coming of the Son of Man, but the *timing* of it. In this parable we have not simply a parabolic lesson learned from the fig tree alone, but as Luke notes, "from all the trees" (v. 29). The lesson is simple and eloquent. If we can tell the signs of approaching summer from the behavior of the trees, then we can also read the signs of the nearing of God's kingdom. With this assertion, Luke does not offer a complex, esoteric barrier to discerning God's approach. Instead he urges the believer to take at face value the import of change, "these things taking place" (v. 31).

The difficult part of this second section has to do with v. 32, in which Jesus promises that "this generation will not pass away" until everything has been accomplished. To what or to whom was he referring? Answers are not given. Instead, the text leaves the proclaimer ample interpretive space in relationship to our time. Whatever the proclaimer decides, clearly the issue of time and timing are at stake in this section of the reading.

In vv. 34-36 Jesus admonishes the listeners to reflect their concern and care for the coming of the Lord in their daily life. This portion of the text reflects a number of other biblical references, both Old and New Testament, regarding the commands of how to prepare physically and spiritually for the Lord. What is of particular concern for the listener is the surprise nature of the return: Luke alludes to Isa. 24:17, in which human beings are trapped like animals in some kind of snare or pit. The analogy is apt for what it implies about surprise, realization of one's actual tragic predicament, pain, and inevitable suffering and death. Of significance is that the coming of the Son of Man will affect all of creation, not just a portion of it. According to Luke's interpretation, judgment is universal, not particular.

Responding to the Text

Advent is a paradoxical preaching season. It offers the realistic, even frightening sense of what God's coming close means. Yet, it also dares to speak of a more positive and joyful side of this time of the church year. Both are to be held in appropriate tension throughout the weeks of Advent proclamation.

This particular Lukan text coincides with that end-of-year sense of impending winter, as the days grow shorter and darker. A poetic version of that more difficult side of Advent is featured in W. B. Yeats's poem "The Second Coming." Yeats looks at an aspect of God's coming that is often overlooked, namely, a call to acknowledge what has happened in Christ and its meaning for the world. Much of this poem deals with the world's inability and refusal to accept the implications of Jesus' birth. When Yeats concludes his poem with the following words, there is a sense of judgment and accountability that none can deny:

> And what rough beast, its hour come round at last,
> Slouches towards Bethlehem to be born?[1]

It is this side of Advent, as featured in this Gospel text, that contradicts our generally gentle feelings about the approaching Christmas season. Instead, we have an emphasis on the thinking, responsible believer and the calls to mature and somber faith commitments that are prepared for anything that might happen.

This Gospel text also acts subversively in its proclamation. It has a strangely de-centering effect with its imagery. For as this text is commonly read in the seasonal American context of approaching winter, we are oddly reminded by the image of the blooming fig tree (and all trees) of spring and new life! Just when the world's situation is experienced as gloom and doom, it becomes infused with new hope and possibilities for the believer. We are told to look up and to expect our salvation!

What does it mean to be expectant? Certainly we think of the answer in Christmas terms: we expect the coming of Jesus

PERHAPS ONE OF THE GREATEST CHALLENGES OF ADVENT PREACHING IS THAT WE NOT ONLY HOLD THE TENSION OF THE DARK AND LIGHT SIDES OF THE SEASON TOGETHER BUT ALSO ASK HOW SUCH A GOSPEL TEXT REACHES PAST ADVENT AND CAN INFUSE US WITH EXPECTATIONS THAT MOVE US TO CHRISTMAS AND BEYOND.

in his birth at Bethlehem. But what does it mean for the believer to be expectant? Who are *we* waiting for and how? The question comes to a world that often waits for nothing and no one. Hopes and expectations have been disappointed or, for many, have failed altogether. Even as believers we may be haunted by the possibility that we wait for no one, that we have been forgotten or never considered in the first place; that generations have passed away with no signs (that we know of), and so what is all the excitement about?

Perhaps one of the greatest challenges of Advent preaching is that we not only hold the tension of the dark and light sides of the season together but also ask how such a Gospel text reaches past Advent and can infuse us with expectations that move us to Christmas and beyond. This is a reality that definitely catches our attention as we move increasingly into a world whose pluralism politically, religiously, and economically is bringing ever more significant questions as to how we live our lives and for whose sake.

Image for Preaching

Radical, even uncomfortable as it might be in its incarnational sense, what does it mean for the human heart to be pregnant with God? What phrases do our Bible, our liturgy, our faith tradition, and our hymnody describe as the expectant heart, carrying God within?

SECOND SUNDAY
OF ADVENT

DECEMBER 7, 2003

REVISED COMMON	EPISCOPAL (BCP)	ROMAN CATHOLIC
Mal. 3:1-4 or Bar. 5:1-9	Bar. 5:1-9	Bar. 5:1-9
Luke 1:68-79	Psalm 126	Ps. 126:1-6
Phil. 1:3-11	Phil. 1:1-11	Phil. 1:4-6, 8-11
Luke 3:1-6	Luke 3:1-6	Luke 3:1-6

FIRST READING
MALACHI 3:1-4 (RCL)

Interpreting the Text

This passage is known to many by virtue of its quotation in Handel's *Messiah*. The name of this last book in the English Old Testament means in Hebrew "my messenger." Its author is unknown. The book has two emphases: the problems in postexilic temple life and the coming of one who is the "messenger of the covenant" (v. 1). It is this one who will restore blessings to the people. This prophetic theme carried over into the New Testament. The reestablishment of blessing and God's presence will be prefaced by the particular work of the messenger, which is to refine and purify. Like the fire of the smelting furnace for metal or the soap of the one who prepares garments by scrubbing and reworking cloth materials for use, this messenger will take the materials as they are and make of them something even better. One commentator notes that "because of its unwelcome odors the fuller's plant was usually outside the gates of the city."[2]

> LIKE THE FIRE OF THE SMELTING FURNACE FOR METAL OR THE SOAP OF THE ONE WHO PREPARES GARMENTS BY SCRUBBING AND REWORKING CLOTH MATERIALS FOR USE, THIS MESSENGER WILL TAKE THE MATERIALS AS THEY ARE AND MAKE OF THEM SOMETHING EVEN BETTER.

Responding to the Text

The hearing of this text could be liturgically reinforced by a choir or soloist's presentation of passages from Handel's *Messiah* that quote Malachi. This text is double-edged in its message: God's messenger has significant and even seemingly harsh work to accomplish. That which is unusable, impure, or unworkable will be put to the test. The analogies describe elements of fire and chemicals that have the potential for creating something durable and of beauty or destroying that which is not serviceable and responsive.

Like the fuller, whose work was odoriferous and unpleasant, God's messenger is quite capable and willing to "get down and dirty" to accomplish the work of purification and salvation. No sphere of human activity, however problematic, escapes the messenger's scrutiny and hard work. This call to alertness and the nature of the promised work of the messenger are at odds with the happy, luxurious feeling of approaching Christmas. In Charles Dickens's "A Christmas Carol," the arrival of the messenger and salvation come only after Scrooge confronts the tragic and sinful realities that characterized his life.

Another possible path of proclamation draws meaning from the work of the fuller, which is to purify garments and prepare them for use. In both Old and New Testaments, much is made of wearing garments that are suited to the occasion and to the honoring of God. Such garments are commented on in the parables, the epistles, and in the book of Revelation. How are garments for special occasions reflective of the work of Christ, the messenger, in us? Do we allow the messenger the spiritual work of clothing us in suitable garments of the heart and daily deeds that reflect Christ's work in each of us?

BARUCH 5:1-9 (RCL alt., BCP, RC)

This excerpt is from a later work (somewhere around 200 B.C.E. or later) that contains a mixture of quotations reflecting a variety of sources such as Daniel, Isaiah, Job, Sirach, and Deuteronomy. Today's alternative reading concludes the work of this anonymous author. The notes of invitation and triumph are clearly sounded. As in Malachi, the advent of God's work is on the horizon, and the people are asked to prepare for it by doing two things: (1) exchanging metaphorical garments of sadness and distress for those of joy, and (2) positioning themselves in a manner that befits the anticipation of God's arrival—"Arise, O Jerusalem, stand upon the height" (v. 5).

The people are also asked to celebrate the reversals of circumstance that will signal the advent of their God. First, donning the garments that are "the robe of righteousness that comes from God" (v. 2) is linked to being renamed: "For God will give you evermore the name 'Righteous Peace, Godly glory'" (v. 4). Next, the coming of God will even change the created order, for that which is high will be low and the low will be made even with the high so that the people of Israel have safe passage (v. 7). Even the trees will cover Israel in shade and fragrance as a symbol of God's approach and favor (v. 8).

This text is rich with visual imagery, and the proclaimer can find links herein to the Advent themes of anticipation, redemption, and the signs of God's favor that come to Israel and to us through naming, clothing, and protecting of the faithful.

RESPONSIVE READING
LUKE 1:68-79 (RCL)

Luke 1 features two major faith songs: Mary's song (the "Magnificat") and the song of Zechariah, John the Baptizer's father. The latter song is all the more remarkable, for it features Zechariah speaking after he had been rendered mute by his conversation with the angel who announced John's impending birth to him. The song is prophetic. It concerns itself not only with the birth of John but John's mission, which is to announce the coming of a "mighty savior" (v. 69).

This song promises deliverance from enemies, fear, sin, darkness, and war. The God who makes promises not only keeps them but does so within the daily and often profoundly troubled and tragic venues of God's people. This is the God who comes into our hear-and-now with promises of "light to those who sit in darkness" and the One who will "guide our feet into the way of peace" (v. 79). In a world increasingly more vulnerable to the actions of others, this text announces that God is God and that, despite the tragedies that characterize human existence, God brings salvation.

PSALM 126 (BCP); PSALM 126:1-6 (RC)

In Psalm 126 the community makes petitions and gives thanks. The people's fortunes lie in ruins; they have their share of sorrow. But the key word in this psalm is "joy" (vv. 2, 5, 7). The rhythm of the psalm is also marked by a sense of departure and return. Joy returns when God restores Zion (v. 1), and joy returns when those who began to sow in sadness return with the harvest in a state of joyfulness (v. 6).

PHILIPPIANS 1:3-11 (RCL);
PHILIPPIANS 1:1-11 (BCP);
PHILIPPIANS 1:4-6, 8-11 (RC)

Interpreting the Text

Considering that these words of Paul come from a time of his imprisonment, it is remarkable that they express such a sense of thankfulness and joy. Paul's opening words are typical of letters of that time—naming, thanking, and reflecting on those to whom he is addressing his thoughts. The salutation names those from whom the letter comes, Paul and Timothy, and those to whom it is addressed, "the saints in Christ Jesus," noted along with the religious leaders of the Philippians, "the bishops and deacons" (v. 1).

The remainder of these verses are partly prayer and partly personal address on Paul's part. He couches his thoughts in the form of remembrance. His remembrance of them elicits from him prayers that are characterized by "joy" over how they are "sharing in the Gospel" (v. 3).

These verses are a mixture of what Paul is feeling, what he wants for the Philippians, and God's agency. His feelings for them are characterized by joy (v. 4), partnership as they share both in the gospel and in God's grace (vv. 3, 7), confidence (v. 6), appropriateness (v. 7), and longing (v. 8). He wants for them the spiritual benefits of "more knowledge and full insight" (v. 9); that they be

> PAUL IS BOTH BLESSED BY THE MEMORIES HE HOLDS OF THE PHILIPPIANS AND A CONSCIOUSNESS OF THE DECISIONS, ACTIONS, AND DIRECTIONS THEY MUST CONSIDER TO PRODUCE A "HARVEST OF RIGHTEOUSNESS."

found "pure and blameless," (v. 10) and that they will, as a result, yield a "harvest of righteousness" (v. 11). He invokes God's multiple benefits on them, noting those things of which Christ is a part: "the day of Jesus Christ" (v. 6), "the compassion of Jesus Christ" (v. 8), "the day of Christ" (v. 10), and finally the "harvest of righteousness that comes through Jesus Christ for the glory and praise of God" (v. 11).

Throughout these words, Paul is both blessed by the memories he holds of the Philippians and a consciousness of the decisions, actions, and directions they must consider to produce a "harvest of righteousness." Paul expresses a kind of urgency that extends beyond thanksgiving to a deep pastoral concern for their future.

Responding to the Text

Today many messages, even important ones, are sent via e-mail. By its very nature, e-mail tends to "cut to the chase," to state the subject more succinctly and quickly than a traditional letter. As a result, some now lament the seeming demise of the letter, sometimes called "snail mail." Philippians is certainly more like a letter than an e-mail message. Paul lavishes time, prayer, thought, and words on the Philippians. He is not embarrassed by his feelings for them.

This letter is addressed to a group. It frames his theological concerns in a corporate fashion. Underlying Paul's memories and prayers is a sense of urgency for the Philippians' spiritual well-being. The feeling in this passage shows that Paul has made himself spiritually vulnerable to the Philippians. Indeed, this opening statement from his epistle has the potential for embarrassing and making uncomfortable all who hear it. It raises questions for both ministers and all persons in any community of faith. Do we pray for one another? Do we allow ourselves to respond to one another with the depth of what Paul calls "the compassion of Jesus Christ" (v. 8)? Do we have spiritual concern for the way others live and relate to God? Are we willing to share with them in the unfolding of the gospel in their lives and ours? And finally, do we see our relationships with other Christians on the long trajectory Paul describes, which is the final "day of Jesus Christ" (v. 10)? Asking the individuals in a group to respond to the question, "How do you see God working your life?" will reveal the embarrassment and loss of practice we have all experienced in sharing those matters of the heart for the sake of Christ and God's people!

This text asks each of us if we are expressing true and sufficient pastoral compassion and care for one another in the Christian life that leads, finally, to the presence of God. In the Advent season, these are excellent things to ponder, given the nature of a season that is primarily concerned in secular terms with "window dressing."

The Gospel
LUKE 3:1-6

Interpreting the Text

This Sunday in Advent is dedicated to the person and character of John the Baptizer. In these opening verses of chapter 3, Luke, the consummate historian playwright, deliberately sets the historical stage with names, places, lineage, and relationships that contextualize the manner in which John receives God's word. Both Jewish and Roman rulers are listed. All of these form a constellation of political, social, and historic activities and movements around John (as we shall later learn), as he receives God's word, but indeed "in the wilderness" (v. 2).

This reference to the wilderness is significant. It is not only the place of John's reception of the word, but historically it marks that venue of God's significant actions with the Israelites throughout their history. Luke's placement of John "in the wilderness" situates him in a succession of God's messengers.

The content of John's mission is seemingly simple. He both preaches and baptizes. First, his proclamation is intended to prompt the listeners to receive a "baptism of repentance for the forgiveness of sins" (v. 3). This baptizing is different from our postresurrection practice. John's baptizing served as a sign of the cleansing of one's life as a prelude to returning to God via repentance. Luke fixes the theology of this type of baptizing by putting into John's mouth prophetic words from the prophet Isaiah in vv. 4b-6.

These words change our understanding of John's audiences. The words from Isaiah in some sense hark back to the pluralistic, historical scope of the opening three verses of chapter 3. Salvation, according to Isaiah and John who quotes him, is intended in such a way that "all flesh shall see the salvation of God" (v. 6). In other words, what John offers through his proclamation and baptizing is intended for all people and is universal in its scope. That Luke ascribes these particular words of Isaiah to John also means that he understands Israel to be the host to the nations for salvation. Israel has not simply theological but cosmic significance in God's work in creation.

Responding to the Text

As children, when we listened to the Advent and Christmas texts read in our family gatherings, we would giggle at all the impossible sounding names that either we or others would stumble over in reading the stories of our faith. Why bother with all those names, those remembrances of people past? Naming the names, however, is extremely important for Luke since he is attempting to make a point about the incarnate nature of the gospel, about its express historicity in terms of God's activities among people. Certainly anyone who has looked for housing would agree with the real estate mantra, "Location, location, location!" Luke's list of names and places reminds the listener that where we situate ourselves absolutely determines our perspective. The deliberate care he takes to set the literary stage for Jesus and his ministry bids us also attend carefully to our own setting. Where is God in Jesus Christ active among us? How do we discern the God among us who asks us to seek God's presence in and through the circumstances of our lives?

In proclaiming this passage, the preacher might also give some attention to what John intended by a "baptism of repentance." There is often much confusion about what he is offering, what Jesus' unique baptism signifies, and how our baptism is and is not the same as either John's or Jesus'.

The concluding quote in this passage from Isaiah sets forth several theological issues. First, who are today's voices "crying in the wilderness" for God's sake in

Christ? There are always voices at the margins, a plethora of messages that demand our attention. How are these voices embodied that we might choose which demands our attention? What values are they proposing? This is a significant problem for us: To whom should we listen regarding our salvation and in doing the deeds of salvation? Like John's audiences, we are also left to wonder whether to accept what is being preached to us. Here Bible-interpreting-Bible becomes important as we look for those markers of God among us by which to evaluate any proclamation: calls to repentance, faith, forgiveness, new life, justice, peace, love, compassion, and appropriate sacrifice.

In Isaiah's prophetic words, the metaphoric reconfiguring of everything—including the refashioning of the earth itself—is another venue for preaching the radicality of God's invitation to salvation. How can one preach the notion of turning things upside down or inside out and still see this as a form of invitation to new life in Christ? The repetition of the gospel of hope in the context of the world as we know it makes us ask what could ever possibly be new here. Isaiah's words are a call not only to future realities but to a current and contemporary faith in the God who can change anything, including human hearts that are notorious for their own resistance!

The verse in this passage that might raise the most urgent question is v. 6: "and all flesh shall see the salvation of God." The word that challenges us is the word "all." This word is more important than ever today in the sense that there is a new consciousness about the differences among faith perspectives and their views of God and human community. To whom does this God belong? Some ask this in a proprietary fashion. Some, in fact, find it difficult to imagine the scope of God's historical and cosmic

WE HAVE, IN THE ACTIONS OF JESUS CHRIST, THE RADICAL REMINDER OF A GOD WHO ACTS NOT IN ACCORDANCE WITH OUR EXPECTATIONS BUT OUT OF THE IMPERATIVES OF DIVINE LOVE, THE "COMPASSION OF JESUS CHRIST" TO WHICH PAUL REFERS IN THE EARLIER EPISTLE TEXT FOR THIS DAY.

reach. We often have a hard time thinking of a God who, according to the old idiom, chooses to "act outside the box" or "color outside the lines." This kind of God is neither domesticated nor totally knowable. We have, in the actions of Jesus Christ, the radical reminder of a God who acts not in accordance with our expectations but out of the imperatives of divine love, the "compassion of Jesus Christ" to which Paul refers in the earlier epistle text for this day. When God says "all" in the richness of God's encompassing love, how do we respond when we encounter those who choose to interpret this as only "some of us"?

This Gospel text comes to us with all the shaggy, rough edges of history and with its usual oddness for those who immediately associate "locusts" and "wild animal skins" with John the Baptizer—no matter which Gospel version of his life is read. But this is a prelude portion of the Gospel, something happening way out in the back-forty pastureland. Yet, despite its out-of-the-way sense, Isaiah's prophecy encourages us to make no mistake here: this is for "all flesh," including you and me.

Image for Preaching

The absence of God is a profound topic of concern for those who view the world as exhibiting little, if any, evidence of God's loving care. What kinds of literature can be quoted in a sermon that identify such a concern for listeners? What can one make of letters and articles written from prison, of news reports, of Holocaust documents, of U.N. reports of embattled peoples? Where is God in all of this?

THIRD SUNDAY OF ADVENT

REVISED COMMON	EPISCOPAL (BCP)	ROMAN CATHOLIC
Zeph. 3:14-20	Zeph. 3:14-20	Zeph. 3:14-18a
Isa. 12: 2-6	Psalm 85 or 85:7-13	Isa. 12:2-6
	or Canticle 9	
Phil. 4:4-7	Phil. 4:4-7 (8-9)	Phil. 4:4-7
Luke 3:7-18	Luke 3:7-18	Luke 3:10-18

With the interesting exception of the Gospel, this Sunday's texts continue to add to the crescendo of joy building toward the anticipated arrival of the Savior. Several different communities are addressed in words of prophecy, reassurance, and exhortation. This Sunday's Gospel continues last Sunday's preaching of John the Baptizer. His message is juxtaposed with the messages of rejoicing in the other passages by an emphasis on urgency and on God's impending justice and wrath for the unprepared. In all the readings for this day, the call to change, the reversal of fortunes, and the coming of a new day for the faithful are clearly proclaimed.

IN ALL THE READINGS FOR THIS DAY, THE CALL TO CHANGE, THE REVERSAL OF FORTUNES, AND THE COMING OF A NEW DAY FOR THE FAITHFUL ARE CLEARLY PROCLAIMED.

FIRST READING

ZEPHANIAH 3:14-20 (RCL, BCP); ZEPHANIAH 3:14-18a (RC)

Interpreting the Text

This text is the conclusion of the book of Zephaniah. In its entirety, Zephaniah's words repeat God's judgments on the people and on all nations who stray from the path of faithfulness. Some of Zephaniah's words are also addressed to the remnant of the faithful who continue to remain true to the Lord's commandments.

The appointed verses conclude Zephaniah's prophecies on a triumphant note: God has now restored the fortunes of Jerusalem. Over what should the people rejoice? Two major obstacles have been removed from the people, one consisting of inward relationships and the other of exterior relationships. First, Zephaniah notes that "the Lord has taken away the judgments against you" (v. 15a). In other words, the people's relationship to God has been renewed and the Lord's condemnation has been transformed into a "clean slate." Not only the Lord's relationship has changed with the people, but they also now experience God's hand in releasing them from the threats of their foes: "he had turned away your enemies" (v. 15a). Because of God's presence, the people do not need to fear a threat from any source: "the Lord, is in your midst; you shall fear disaster no more" (v. 15b).

Zephaniah then begins his description of the meaning of God's presence among them. First, they will be strengthened; "do not let your hands grow weak" (v. 16). Power belongs not only to God but is given to the people as well. A renewed sense of the people's power comes about because God's presence is like "a warrior who gives victory" (v. 17). On God's part, there is also joy over the changed relationship as "he will rejoice over you with gladness" (v. 17). God's joy means that God will "renew you in his love [and] he will exalt over you with loud singing as on a day of festival" (v. 17). This reciprocal sharing of joy and love between God and the people gives both parties cause to celebrate.

The work of God on behalf of the restored is now clarified. This God will first "deal with all your oppressors at that time" (v. 19). After dealing with these external threats, God then moves attention to the people and their needs: "I will save the lame and gather the outcast, and I will change their shame into praise" (v. 19). Even those who are helpless and cannot save themselves in any way will be rescued by God and strengthened for a life of praise. Finally, this God does more than "restore your fortunes" (v. 20). And God does this in a public, even cosmic way, "for I will make you renowned and praised among all the peoples of the earth" (v. 20). All of this will be done against the backdrop of God's in-gathering to a place of familiarity and sanctuary: "At that time I will bring you home" (v. 20).

Responding to the Text

If one phrase could be used to describe this text, it is "God's lavishness." This text is remarkable not only for the restoration and blessings given to the people but also for the very happiness and joy of God's own self in doing these works of salvation! It is God's party ("as on a day of a festival," v. 17) and certainly a party to end all parties. All threats are removed, salvation is given as a gift, no one needs to be afraid, what is lost is restored, and even

IF ONE PHRASE COULD BE USED TO DESCRIBE THIS TEXT, IT IS "GOD'S LAVISHNESS."

the most fragile are healed and brought into the chorus of salvation and praise. That God delights in doing these works demonstrates, in Zephaniah's words, a God lovingly and totally involved in creation, in people's lives. This text is a radical demonstration of the fact that God loves, acts, and is involved with creation. Here we find no remote angry God but rather a God who is delighted to send salvation. This text provides a wonderful Advent proclamation of the God who breathes, lives, and moves with God's people.

How often do people feel besieged by life's vicissitudes, wondering who will help them? How many listeners feel judged by God and out of touch with God's expressions of renewal, forgiveness, and restoration? How many who hear this text will consider themselves, or those not able to help themselves, as already redeemed by the God who forgets not even the least able and will "save the lame and gather the outcast" (v. 19)? This text pictures a happy God not only willing and able to accomplish acts of redemption, but delighted to do them!

Perhaps most significant of all, this text asserts that God is in control of the human community. It is not a control that is coercive or dictatorial, but one that gives people, both as individuals and as communities, reassurance that God's power is used in love toward them and intended for blessing and restoration to all, whatever their circumstances.

RESPONSIVE READING
ISAIAH 12:2-6 (RCL, RC = Canticle 9, BCP alt.)

God has provided joyful salvation, compared to a well from which one happily draws water in a land with few water resources. Some regional listeners will be able to identify with issues of water conservation and drought. Drinking of the waters of salvation prompts the individual to "Sing praises to the Lord . . . Shout aloud and sing for joy" (vv. 5, 6). Salvation is not a matter of remaining silent!

PSALM 85 or 85:7-13 (BCP)

The community asks God to restore them (vv. 1-7) and elaborates on the features of that restoration (vv. 8-13). God comes speaking "peace to his people" (v. 8). This salvation is also lyrically compared to two people kissing each other. It is a salvation, then, marked by the intimacy of God and God's people: "Steadfast love and faithfulness will meet; righteousness and peace will kiss each other" (v. 10). The intimacy will only enhance the lot of the faithful, for "The Lord will give what is good, and our land will yield its increase" (v. 12).

PHILIPPIANS 4:4-7 (RCL, RC);
PHILIPPIANS 4:4-7 (8-9) (BCP)

Interpreting the Text

Paul's final words to the Philippians in this chapter enjoin the people to "Rejoice in the Lord always" (v. 4). Why should they do this? Paul sees a function of this rejoicing expressed in "your gentleness" (v. 5) as a sign of God's proximity. Rejoicing also means freedom from worry because of a God who is ever ready to listen to the fears and anxieties of people: "Let your requests be made known to God" (v. 6). Finally, however people might express God's presence in their lives, it is God who gives the gift of that presence through the "peace of God" (v. 7), which is, finally, not totally understandable to people.

Verses 8-9 add even more ways that people express God's presence in terms of their choice of thoughts: "whatever is true . . . honorable . . . just . . . pure . . . pleasing . . . commendable . . . excellent . . . worthy of praise" (v. 8). It is pondering and pursuing these things that Paul understands as additional rationale for living within the sphere of the "God of peace" (v. 9).

Responding to the Text

This brief text is rich in Advent themes and proclamation possibilities. Two themes that Paul addresses in differing ways are rejoicing and peace. Both are gifts prompted by God in the believer, but they entail a choice of attitudes of thought and action as well. So Paul encourages people to "keep on doing the things that you have learned and received" (v. 9).

Perhaps one of the most eye-catching admonitions of Paul is that which says "Do not worry about anything" (v. 6). Of all things, it is our anxieties that might blur our relationship with God: in fact, our anxieties may become our gods, more powerful and more determinative of who we are and what we do than the God of Jesus Christ, who calls us to leave these anxieties with the Lord. In a world torn by many anxiety-causing actions and realities, only the grace and poise of the Savior can keep us steadied in the peace of God—truly one of the promised gifts of the one who is coming to us.

> OF ALL THINGS, IT IS OUR ANXIETIES THAT MIGHT BLUR OUR RELATIONSHIP WITH GOD: IN FACT, OUR ANXIETIES MAY BECOME OUR GODS, MORE POWERFUL AND MORE DETERMINATIVE OF WHO WE ARE AND WHAT WE DO THAN THE GOD OF JESUS CHRIST.

Further, the litany of the attributes of one found to be at peace in God (v. 8) would make an excellent Advent sermon structure. The preacher might ask how each of these ways of thinking and acting keeps us in the company of the God of peace. Some of these are particularly significant for today.

What does it mean to think and do those things that can be characterized as "just" in a world of radical injustice and global examples of growing divisions between rich and poor? What does it mean to be "honorable" in a culture where expediency so easily trumps being honorable? And what is it to think and do that which is considered "pure" in an information society where trafficking in impurity results in the daily spiritual and physical jeopardy of both adults and children?

This peace of God is not so much that of emotional peace (although it can certainly be manifested in that manner), but a deep spiritual reality that has its own anchor for the believer regardless of life's situations. In a poignant hymn text, describing the changed lives of the disciples after Jesus called them for their ordinary lives to suffer and die for the sake of the Gospel, this peace is expressed in this way:

> The peace of God, it is no peace,
> But strife closed in the sod.
> Yet, let us pray for but one thing . . .
> The marv'lous peace of God.[3]

The Gospel
LUKE 3:7-18 (RCL, BCP);
LUKE 3:10-18 (RC)

Interpreting the Text

John the Baptizer is prominent in all Gospel accounts, and it is helpful to compare these texts in order to discover Luke's distinctive emphases. The RCL and BCP lections can be considered in three sections.

First, vv. 7-9 contain John's basic message of salvation. John gives a fiery denunciation of all who would escape from God's judgment. John uses the image of snakes fleeing from fire. The people may indeed be standing before him listening to his words, but their spiritual state is like those creatures who attempt elusive methods to escape the inevitable, "the wrath to come" (v. 7). John anticipates their excuses prior to anyone voicing them: they cannot use their spiritual ancestry— "Abraham as our ancestor"—as grounds to assert their salvation apart from their own actions and attitudes. John's call to repentance is directed to all the people in the crowds, regardless of biological or spiritual affiliation. God is not calling their ancestors and by association them: God is calling them directly to repent. By use of a vivid metaphor of God's far-ranging call and search for the repentant and faithful, John notes that God can make anyone Abraham's descendants, even "these stones" (v. 8). John's listeners are given no way to evade their accountability and responsibility for their relationship with God.

This basic message of the call to repentance is summed up in v. 9. Judgment is imminent, much more so than one might think. John uses the metaphor of the good and bad trees. Those which do not bear good fruit are destroyed. His listeners cannot escape asking, "Do *I* bear good fruit?"

Second, John's message has obviously created interest, anxiety, curiosity, and concern in the crowd, and in the next section of this text, three different groups of listeners want to know "What then should we do?" (v. 10). These three groups represent the general public, the tax collectors, and the soldiers, all having lifestyles and tasks somewhat different from the others. How does John's message apply to their respective situations? In the first instance, John urges them to share their material possessions, clothing, and food (v. 11). Then the tax collectors, qualified by Luke with the word "even" in v. 12, are admonished to keep honest in their dealings between Jews and Romans: "Collect no more than the amount prescribed for you" (v. 13). Finally, soldiers are told to pay attention in two ways regarding their income. "Do not extort money from anyone by threats or false accusation, and be satisfied with your wages" (v. 14).

John points out to everyone that their response to baptism is to take accurate note of the societal interrelationships in which they live and not to take unfair advantage of those they are called to serve. In other words, the call to repentance is accompanied by a willingness to radically rethink different power relationships from those generally holding sway.

The final section of this appointed text, vv. 15-18, portrays a shift in emphasis between John and the crowd. Now the crowd wishes to know about the source and authority for the baptizing that John is doing. "The people . . . were questioning . . . whether he might be the Messiah" (v. 15). John is quick to point out three reasons why he is not. First, his status cannot be compared with that of the Messiah: "I am not worthy to untie the thong of his sandals" (v. 16). Second, John's baptizing differs from the one the Messiah will bring, which is of "the Holy Spirit and fire" (v. 16). (John does not claim the coming of the Holy Spirit in his form of baptizing.) Third, one of the functions of the Messiah will be that of judgment as he separates the wheat and the chaff. This final function is one the listeners would quickly comprehend as such agricultural "separating" is a typical scriptural metaphor for judgment.

Responding to the Text

The beginning of this text is vivid and harsh. Who can imagine a contemporary preacher addressing a congregation in such blunt terms? Yet John urges his listeners to pay attention to his description of their spiritual peril and blindness. What is the proclaimer to learn from John's approach to the people about Advent's urgency? In a wonderfully descriptive organ variation by Max Reger on the old Advent hymn theme "Sleepers Awake!" the pedal part sounds like the urgent rushing and trampling of hurrying feet. John's own message has the same quality: "Listen up, folks! What do you think is going on here?"

John's initial address to the crowds is not heard in quite the same way by us today. In a postresurrection world, we already have been gifted with the presence and power of Christ and the Holy Spirit. We know (or think we do) what the faith walk is about. Yet John's words, challenging the spiritual excuses of the crowd, stand today before us in the same way. What spiritual excuses do we have that need to be addressed during this Advent? Perhaps we have taken for granted the gift of the gospel or do not stop to consider the fact that our lives have little in the way of identifiable good fruit, given our spiritual complacency. Perhaps our spiritual lineage has left us with an arrogant attitude toward those of other faith perspectives, a dangerous prospect in today's complicated and pluralistic world. John asks in effect, "Who do you think you are spiritually?" What might our answers be?

As John proclaims the baptism of repentance, the crowds anxiously ask how they are to respond. Here John details what a life of repentance looks like in specific terms. He answers the different professions and types of people who ask about a life of repentance. The call to repentance is not general but contextual. What exactly does *this* group of believers need to hear? The Advent call to repentance and change must, of necessity, be contoured to the corporate life of any particular faith community. Proclaiming the wise use of power and money to the rich is a different topic from that which can be preached to a poverty-stricken congregation. John's description of social and economic categories as they are lived out in different circumstances indicates that all have responsibilities to the neighbor, regardless of class and income bracket. No one is exempt from service to the neighbor.

JOHN'S DESCRIPTION OF SOCIAL AND ECONOMIC CATEGORIES AS THEY ARE LIVED OUT IN DIFFERENT CIRCUMSTANCES INDICATES THAT ALL HAVE RESPONSIBILITIES TO THE NEIGHBOR, REGARDLESS OF CLASS AND INCOME BRACKET.

One of the most touching aspects of this Gospel text is that John picks up in true pastoral fashion on the questions and expectations that people have about the source of this baptizing. Is he the Messiah? How will we know the Messiah's approach and the Messiah's deeds and mission? The questions have not changed today. Any pew sitter still asks the same questions and is curious about the answers. What images might the preacher choose to describe the Messiah today? The signs of his presence and the work the Messiah continues to do? In one of John's responses to these questions, there is a clue that points the Advent congregation to the future with hope; that is, John's reassurance that the Messiah brings with him the Holy Spirit. The Spirit is the one who constitutes the life of the church, and this reality can emphasize those faith directions that are spoken of in today's second reading.

Luke 3, unlike the other texts for the day, contains much harsh language and abrupt imagery. Yet it does not capitalize on these for the shock value alone. The good news in this text for Advent is that the approach of the Messiah brings the potential for change; it offers new ways to live life and the promise of spiritual power to do just that. The other texts for this day support the Gospel message by additionally offering the themes of joy, God's forgiveness and involvement with humanity, and the gift of God's peace that enables Gospel values and directions to be lived out in a spirit of praise no matter what the circumstances.

Image for Preaching

What contemporary images and examples demonstrate to the listener the qualities of a life of one who is redeemed? What songs by well-known Christian rock groups could provide examples of lyrics that show this? What actions and activities in a faith community portray this?

FOURTH SUNDAY OF ADVENT

Revised Common	Episcopal (BCP)	Roman Catholic
Mic. 5:2-5a	Mic. 5:2-4	Mic. 5:1-4a
Luke 1:47-55	Psalm 80 or 80:1-7	Ps. 80:2-3, 15-16, 18-19
or Ps. 80:1-7		
Heb. 10:5-10	Heb. 10:5-10	Heb. 10:5-10
Luke 1:39-45 (46-55)	Luke 1:39-49 (50-56)	Luke 1:39-45

This final Sunday in Advent is full of prenatal anticipation. The themes of deliverance, fulfillment, and promise link all the lessons. The human reality of the Savior to come finds voice in these texts with an emphasis on incarnation. The writers of Micah, Hebrews, and the Gospel reading for this day focus on the enfleshment of God. God's salvific work will come through humanity and history, not apart from it. The contours of this gift of salvation also signal vast implications for the entire reordering of human life. The forgotten, the oppressed, the unliberated will find in God's new order an answer to their suffering and the reality of a new life of hope rather than despair.

> THE FORGOTTEN, THE OPPRESSED, THE UNLIBERATED WILL FIND IN GOD'S NEW ORDER AN ANSWER TO THEIR SUFFERING AND THE REALITY OF A NEW LIFE OF HOPE RATHER THAN DESPAIR.

FIRST READING
MICAH 5:2-5a (RCL);
MICAH 5:2-4 (BCP);
MICAH 5:1-4a (RC)

Interpreting the Text

Micah is among the contemporaries of Isaiah in the seventh century B.C.E. As a member of the working class of his days, he was keenly aware of the sufferings and injustices his people experienced. They suffered from their enemies within, such as the self-serving authorities of temple and court, as well as from the tragedies of war. Micah speaks harshly against those who believe true worship of God is possible while community leaders simultaneously oppress the helpless. Micah's poetry is in the genre of oracles, the content of which includes both doom for the sinful and the promise of salvation. Today's text is one example of promise: it names Bethlehem as the provenance of the coming ruler (it is cited in Matt. 2:6).

This text foretells the coming of the deliverer from Bethlehem by means of contrast. What is small geographically and politically ("But you O Bethlehem . . . who are one of the little clans of Judah" v. 2) will host the Savior of all. The signal for God's redemption is described in terms of a woman in labor. As a woman's labor signifies the advent of a birth, so will God's action signify the reestablishment of redemption through active political justice among the people (v. 3).

Micah portrays the character of this new ruler in both pastoral and political terms. The one who brings salvation "shall stand and feed his flock in the strength of the Lord" (v. 4a). Likewise, this shepherd will enable the flock to "live secure" (v. 4b). The greatest gift of this new ruler is that "he shall be the one of peace" (v. 5a). Like the affirmations of Mary in Luke, it is impossible to separate the personal, salvific intentions and works of the Savior from their implications for the social and political order.

Responding to the Text

Christians familiar with Luke's version of the nativity feel an affection for Micah's words about the enormous potential of the diminutive. As Bethlehem is small and unnoticed, so the initially unknown birth of a child allows the listener to come near to the ordinary, the seemingly unimportant, and consider what is about to happen in this singular place of promise. God is involved in the intimacy of humanity's affairs.

> CHRISTIANS FAMILIAR WITH LUKE'S VERSION OF THE NATIVITY FEEL AN AFFECTION FOR MICAH'S WORDS ABOUT THE ENORMOUS POTENTIAL OF THE DIMINUTIVE.

This text also echoes the Lukan passage in using the metaphor of impending birth as a signal for the changes God plans to initiate. Just as the birth of a child signals radical change for those who are witness to it, so too will God's mighty acts bring change. In this passage, the ruler will bring gifts of reestablished identity, security, and peace to the flock.

The label on a garment I recently purchased read "Made in Turkmenistan." Many might ask, Where is that place? What language do the people speak? Who made this garment and what is the person's life like? Do we spare enough time to even question the universal intentions of a coming Savior whose concerns are cosmic in focus? Can our own lives reflect God's concerns? Micah pushes the listener to affirm God's gifts through worship of the one who gave them, but also to be concerned about their own responsibility to affirm these gifts of God within the daily social and political order. Micah does not speak of a disembodied or uninvolved spirituality. Given the fragmentation today caused by people's desire to secure only their own welfare and needs, Micah's universal message impels us to examine those labels we go by and ask if our worship is true and our concerns godly. This could mean all the difference between spiritual arrogance and faithful response to God's concerns for others.

RESPONSIVE READING
LUKE 1:47–55 (RCL)

(See the comments on the Gospel for this Sunday.)

PSALM 80 (BCP);
PSALM 80:1-7 (RCL alt.; BCP alt.);
PSALM 80:2-3, 15-16, 18-19 (RC)

This is a plea of the people for God's ear to their prayers and for restoration. In vv. 1-7 the lament refers to "the bread of tears" to be drunk "in full measure" (v. 5). The people have suffered from lack of meaningful sustenance brought on by their sin, and tears as "food" and "drink" heighten that realization.

The predominant image of this psalm, Israel as the vine and God as the vineyard manager and caretaker, is a major biblical image of the relationship between God and the people. Here the wonderful redemption of the people, "You brought a vine out of Egypt" (v. 8), is matched by its tragic destruction and the people's plea for redemption. "Restore us, O Lord God of hosts . . ." (v. 19).

SECOND READING
HEBREWS 10:5-10

Interpreting the Text

Verses 1-4 could also be read as a helpful context for the listeners. Hebrews in its entirety argues for the continuity and discontinuity that Jesus' life and death signify for those who have understood and worshiped the faithful God of the covenant. Its language reflects some of the Platonic "mirroring" of reality in the relationship of earth to heaven. But the author of Hebrews is clear that this reflection has resulted in a supplanting of one by the other. The Law and the former satisfactory ways of life and worship are given new direction in Christ.

Most of this reading is a paraphrase of Ps. 40:6-8, picking up on a common Old Testament theme: true worship consists of a heart obedient to God's will, not simply ritual actions. The term "abolish" is used to indicate that in Jesus Christ we are released from the past and freed for new and holy living in God. The radicality of this is summed up in our relationship to Jesus: "we have been sanctified through the offering of the body of Jesus once for all" (v. 10). There is nothing otherworldly about Jesus' act. In this Savior we can see clearly what it means to lead a sanctified life here and now.

Responding to the Text

In a stewardship class a student noted that she had heard the Sunday offering described as "dues." This certainly undergirds a view of church membership different from that of faithful discipleship. How often have we heard someone say, "I have paid my dues!" The writer of Hebrews is aware of those who believe they have paid their dues. That notion, however, is challenged by the psalmist (Ps. 40:6-8), who indicates that offerings rendered as "dues" are worthless. The proper point is doing the will of God. Holiness comes through the sole work of Jesus and not any work that we might perform. In fact, it is impossible to do any work of sacrifice that yields a sanctified life unless we understand that it is Jesus Christ's sacrifice that makes this possible.

A few years ago, as I and others were moving into a new office building, I noticed that a crucifix I'd been given had suffered some minor damage in the move. One of the small nails holding one of the hands to the cross had popped out, giving the impression that Jesus was leaving the cross. There was a sense of freedom in this changed attitude of the sculpted piece. Hebrews' author, too, signifies such freedom in noting that Jesus' offering contains for us an unimaginable freedom of life—release from the burden of life as sacrifice and participation in the life-giving possibilities of Jesus' life and death.

This passage provides the template for this Advent season. Poised to stand soon before the manger and the child, we are encouraged to look beyond the immense joy of Christmas to consider the implications of this birth. There is ahead a cross and an offering yet to come, which gives Advent Christians a sense of double vision as they approach Christmas.

THE GOSPEL

LUKE 1:39-45 (46-55) (RCL);
LUKE 1:39-49 (50-56) (BCP);
LUKE 1:39-45 (RC)

Interpreting the Text

This part of Luke's Gospel almost literally sings to us from the pages! It comes from a chapter that is somewhat like a major historical set of birth announcements. The principal figures in this passage are women and their unborn children.

In vv. 39-45, Mary visits Elizabeth. Both women are pregnant. Their babies will have much to do with each another in the future. This section of Luke has traditionally been titled "The Visitation." Elizabeth's response to Mary is significant. The first response is nonverbal and physical: the child she carries moves at the sound of Mary's voice. Luke's intention is to signal that even the unborn John recognizes the significance of the baby Mary carries.

Elizabeth responds to Mary through the initiative of the Holy Spirit. Here again her response has been caught up in the liturgical traditions of the church through its adoption into the rosary: "Blessed are you among women and blessed is the fruit of your womb" (v. 42). Elizabeth expresses the great honor that has come to her through Mary's visit, "mother of my Lord" (v. 43), and tells Mary two things: first, that her own baby recognizes the coming Savior and, second, that Mary is blessed for her faith and belief that God had visited her in this manner.

Mary's response, vv. 46-55, has traditionally and liturgically been termed "the Magnificat," a Latin title meaning "magnify" or "exalt." Mary's words are not particular to her alone, for Luke uses the joyous song of Hannah at Samuel's birth to frame similar expressions (see 1 Sam. 2:1-10). This textual replica at many points signifies how Luke understands the coming Savior within the overall framework of Israel's redemption history and its prophecies.

Mary's words are, at some level, hardly typical of a mother's hopes for her son. The first section of this song (vv. 46-49) is Mary's own thanksgiving for being chosen for such an honor. She is mindful of her humble setting in life but also aware that her work as mother has future import: "Surely, from now on all generations will call me blessed" (v. 48).

The next section, vv. 50-55, describes the various actions and intentions of God in sending the Savior. A set of three reversals of the order of life are noted in vv. 51-52. First, God's strength will destroy those who have pride only in their own strength (v. 51); second, those who rule will be removed from rule and replaced by "the lowly" (v. 52); and finally (the converse), the hungry will be fed and the rich, whom we conclude are stuffed, will be sent away empty (v. 52).

The song ends with an affirmation of the God who helps and makes promises not only to the ancestors but to all who are to come "forever" (v. 55). Mary then stays with Elizabeth and returns home close to the time of her delivery.

Responding to the Text

This text functions at two levels. First, it offers a cozy, happy look at two women who are expecting their babies—a common domestic picture. In another way, however, the women's responses to each other and to God are radical and even unnerving. Their expectations hardly seem in sync with those of ordinary mothers.

Mary's song occupies much of the text. Its interpretations have varied over the centuries. It is a song of liberation and God's promises. It is a song of radical reversals. It is a song that demonstrates Mary's strengths and depicts her as a strong model of female faith and courage. It is a song for the coming revolution that will usher in God's reign.

In American culture today, where obesity is a health problem for a significant portion of the population, where the destruction of the global poor is termed "collateral damage," where giving to charities and volunteering one's time have rapidly diminished, it is more and more difficult to sing Mary's song with any integrity. In fact, there seems to be reluctance to challenge people to reassess their attitudes and actions that can only be described as self-serving. Recently in a homiletics class, some students challenged a student preacher who had avoided some of the tough issues posed by the biblical passage that served as his text. His response was, "I don't want to offend anyone who comes to church to hear the gospel." Indeed, a characteristic of much preaching today offers grace without cost, insight without personal involvement.

Mary's song could possibly be read as the basis for a service of confession for our sending the hungry away empty, lowering the lowly even further politically and socially, and enhancing the lot of the proud, while despising the power of God who is the defender of the poor and lowly. Mary's song could also be preached in conjunction with what the author of Hebrews is saying about corporate worship and the role of Jesus Christ's offering of himself as the model for living out God's standard of life.

ALL OF THE READINGS FOR THIS DAY HOLD UP IMAGES THAT SYMBOLIZE THE SPIRITUAL ILLNESSES OF THE PEOPLE OF GOD, ILLNESSES THAT SERVE AS BARRIERS TO FAITHFUL LIVING.

All of the readings for this day hold up images that symbolize the spiritual illnesses of the people of God, illnesses that serve as barriers to faithful living. The image of the destruction of the vine, Hebrews' portrayal of worship gone wrong, the psalmist's invocation of tears as a sign of the people's departure from God, Mary's song of God's action toward the unrepentant—all of these make this Advent Sunday a time to reflect, repent, and change, both individually and corporately.

Image for Preaching

Taking Mary's song as a model, what kinds of songs of liberation can we identify in our own settings? What kinds of songs of liberation can we find in other cultures? What are the elements in a song of liberation? Who sings them and for whom are they intended?

THE SEASON
OF CHRISTMAS

SUSAN K. HEDAHL

Christmas is one of the six major festivals of the church (the others are Epiphany, Easter, Ascension, Pentecost, and Holy Trinity). These festivals constitute the core of the Christian faith because they all are christologically centered.

The contemporary celebration of Christmas has its roots in ancient pagan rites associated with the winter solstice. Since the timing of the solstice varies slightly from year to year, ancient calendars also shifted in several ways, thereby affecting the dates of Christmas and Epiphany.

Actual evidence for the celebration of Jesus' birth does not appear until the fourth century. It is possible that Christians settled on December 25 late in the fourth century based on Emperor Aurelian's decision in 274 C.E. that a sun festival be held on that date.

At the heart of the Christmas celebration is the glorious reality of the God who takes on human flesh. Interpretations of this incarnated God, however, were many, and the celebration of these festivals was deeply linked with the unfolding christological debates and controversies of the day. The celebration of Christmas and Epiphany was used by Christian theologians, clergy, and other church leaders to emphasize the incarnation as a means of fighting Arianism. Despite the differences in emphases on the Nativity in Eastern and Western Christianity, affected both by calendar decisions and theology, Christmas remains a major festival for both traditions.

Fascinating materials and reflections about Christmas come from early sermons. These preachers were concerned about the various theological controversies assailing parishioners, about the competition of the pagan feasts at the approach of the winter solstice, and also about affirming the time of year as one of fasting and the giving of alms.

Customs associated with the celebration of Christmas are heavily influenced by the faith communities to which they are tied, including regional location, ethnic affiliation, and climate. Because of the radical commercialization of Christmas, in some parts of the world the celebration has lost its moorings in the Christian faith and is observed merely as time of gift-giving and change toward the light. Christmas proclamation is a challenge when contemporary practices run directly counter to the themes and realities that the biblical texts describe.

Selected Reading

Augustine. *The Works of St. Augustine: A Translation for the 21st Century*. Ed. John E. Roetelle, trans. Edmund Hill. Part III: Homilies, 6. Hyde Park, N.Y.: New City Press, 1993.

Bond, L. Susan. *Trouble with Jesus: Women, Christology, and Preaching*. St. Louis: Chalice Press, 1999.

Craddock, Fred B. *Luke*. Interpretation. Louisville: Westminster John Knox, 1990.

Keck, Leander E. *Luke, John*. The New Interpreter's Bible 9. Nashville: Abingdon, 1995.

Luther, Martin. *Sermons*. Luther's Works, American Edition 51. Ed. Jaroslav Pelikan and Helmut T. Lehmann. Philadelphia: Fortress Press, 1959.

Mays, James Luther. *Psalms*. Interpretation. Louisville: Westminster John Knox 1994.

Newsome, Carol A., and Sharon H. Ringe, eds. *The Women's Bible Commentary*. Louisville: Westminster John Knox, 1992.

Schmidt, Leigh Eric. *Consumer Rites: The Buying and Selling of American Holidays*. Princeton, N. J.: Princeton University Press, 1995.

Sermons / St. Leo the Great. The Fathers of the Church 93. Trans. Jane Patricia Freeland and Agnes Josephine Conway. Washington, D.C.: Catholic University of America, 1995.

THE NATIVITY OF OUR LORD / CHRISTMAS EVE

DECEMBER 24, 2003

REVISED COMMON	EPISCOPAL (BCP)	ROMAN CATHOLIC
Isa. 9:2-7	Isa. 9:2-4, 6-7	Isa. 9:1-6
Psalm 96	Psalm 96 or 96:1-4, 11-12	Ps. 96:1-3, 11-13
Titus 2:11-14	Titus 2:11-14	Titus 2:11-14
Luke 2:1-14 (15-20)	Luke 2:1-14 (15-20)	Luke 2:1-14

These readings all point to the arrival of a Savior, the consummation of the Advent season, and the revealing of a new reality. This Savior is described as Lord, king, child, heir of the throne of David, the Messiah. Arrival of this Savior brings a mix of responses: joy, thankfulness, praise, and fear. The Savior's arrival also points to the future, for his work is to bring salvation, justice, and freedom for all.

Each of these texts, in its own manner, notes that this Savior impacts humanity on both the spiritual and historical planes. For those who await the Messiah, salvation is total, not partial.

FIRST READING

ISAIAH 9:2-7 (RCL);
ISAIAH 9:2-4, 6-7 (BCP);
ISAIAH 9:1-6 (RC)

Interpreting the Text

The backdrop of this passage is Isaiah's concerns about the presence of the Assyrian Empire and its effects on the people of Israel. The promise of a shift from darkness and gloom to light (vv. 1, 2) symbolizes this. Some of this text is familiar from its use in Handel's *Messiah,* especially descriptions of the deliverer who is known as Father, God, Counselor, Prince of

> THE PASSAGE RADIATES A JOY AND CONFIDENCE IN THE COMING RULER WHO WILL BRING RELEASE FROM CAPTIVES, TRIUMPH IN BATTLE, AND PEACE AND JUSTICE.

Peace, and child (v. 6). This passage is an oracle and was probably used as a text for the coronation of a king. It has a majesty and breadth of thought and intention that describes both the qualities of the king as well as the mission and work of the ruler. The passage radiates a joy and confidence in the coming ruler who will bring release from captivity, triumph in battle, and peace and justice.

It is possible that the person for whom these words were intended was King Hezekiah. But, like others before him, his inability to lead the people out of their oppression from the Assyrians transformed this passage into a song of hope for the coming Messiah who could accomplish the people's release. What earthly kings could not do, this lyrical passage asserts the Messiah is able to do.

Responding to the Text

The beginning of this text, which speaks of the movement from gloom and darkness to light, is read at a time of year when the actual darkness of the landscape clouds the thoughts and feelings of many. For some the fact of light deprivation is severe and has even acquired the medical diagnosis "Seasonal Affective Disorder." It is characterized by a mood of bleakness and depression, even despair, as the human body responds to the loss of light. Even those not experiencing a loss of daytime light to this extent might glean some spiritual insights into the prophetic, spiritual, and historical words the prophet speaks of in this passage.

It is perhaps somewhat more difficult to imagine what this life in the darkness might mean, politically and religiously in a corporate sense, for Americans listening to this text. We have yet to experience the presence on our own soil of an occupying power that affects our lives to the extent that it did Israel's. Yet one need only quote passages from the diaries and autobiographies of contemporary political hostages, many of whom were kept in literal darkness and blindfolded for days at a time, to have a somewhat similar experience. This text is graphic in its portrayal of violence (vv. 4, 5), thus effectively highlighting hope for the liberating work of the coming deliverer.

RESPONSIVE READING
PSALM 96 (RCL, BCP);
PSALM 96:1–4, 11–12 (BCP alt.);
PSALM 96:1–3, 11–13 (RC)

Psalm 96 belongs to the category of enthronement psalms. Praise of God is directed to God's work as creator (v. 3), God's existence and identity as the only real and true God (vv. 4, 5), and God as judge and ruler over all (vv. 3, 7, 10). This psalm is typified by its joyousness. Humanity is encouraged to respond by singing praises (vv. 1, 2); by witnessing to God's cosmic works (vv. 6, 7, 8). And humanity does so by joining all creation, which in its own way, responds similarly (vv. 11, 12).

For many who read this psalm in North America during Christmas, a time of winter cold and stillness, the activities of the entire creation worshiping God offers a sense of hope, activity, and joy in the coming of the Redeemer, the Lord of life!

Second Reading
TITUS 2:11-14

Interpreting the Text

Who was Titus? This small book (only three chapters) refers to a co-worker of Paul's and is written much like the exhortatory materials in 1 Timothy. The first part of chapter 2 examines the different ways various groups of people should lead their lives. These sections, directed toward older and younger women, younger men and slaves, focus on types of desirable behavior but also what their purposes are: "So that the word of God may not be discredited" (v. 5); "any opponent will be put to shame, having nothing evil to say of us" (v. 6); and "they [slaves] may be an ornament to the doctrine of God our Savior" (v. 9).

This is followed by today's passage. The wording of this lyrical text suggests that this may be an excerpt from a liturgy of the early church. Its sentiments express the aims of godly living because "we wait for the blessed hope and the manifestation of the glory of our great God and Savior, Jesus Christ" (v. 13). Like the previous section, it is concerned that the godly life reflect itself in the wider world. Here the writer notes that living the holy life means we are evidence that God will "redeem us from all iniquity and purify for himself a people of his own who are zealous for good deeds" (v. 14).

One of the unusual things about this text appears in v.13 where Jesus is identified with God: "the manifestation of the glory of our great God and Savior, Jesus Christ." This identification gives support to the hymnic, liturgical sense of the passage and affirms Jesus as the manifestation not only of present realities but of greater realities to come.

Responding to the Text

Titus 2, including the verses for today, offers exhortation and advice on living the godly life. In some ways the information sounds strange, the values out of keeping with contemporary culture, community, and family structures. Certainly in preaching this text, within the context of the entire chapter and book, it is important to keep in mind that, indeed, Christian faith and life are counter-cultural to some extent. What the writer is urging us to consider is not always easy. In fact, the words of the text almost sound anti-Christmas! These words certainly challenge the listener to decide what type of daily living befits the arrival of the Savior.

Important in preaching this text is also the "beyond Christmas" sense it offers us. The manger is not the stopping place. We are pulled to look beyond this first coming of Jesus to his second coming with a spirit of anticipation and preparedness.

THE GOSPEL
LUKE 2:1-14 (15-20) (RCL, BCP);
LUKE 2:1-14 (RC)

Interpreting the Text

Luke 2:1-20 is divided into two parts. Verses 1-7 address the historical background of Jesus' birth. Verse 1 immediately shows that the Jews were dominated by a foreign power, in this case the Roman Emperor Augustus. There is uncertainty over a census decreed by Augustus, and it is possible, as Acts 17:7 indicates, that the Quirinius mentioned in the next verses was actually the one responsible for the census. He ruled a territory called Syria whose boundaries extend beyond today's Syria to include what are now the areas of Galilee and Judea in present-day Israel. While "all the world" (v. 1) sounds a bit far-ranging and pompous even to contemporary ears, it probably meant that the census was intended for the entire Roman Empire. In any event, such a census and the consequences it entailed for taxation, identification, and control of the populace by outside rulers was never well received. According to Luke, it meant that Mary and Joseph had to journey to their home territory for state purposes.

Joseph's place of origin and destination are included in v. 4. Nazareth at the time was an obscure village with no claim to fame of any sort. Joseph's destination, Bethlehem, however, is key for two reasons. First, Bethlehem (meaning "house of bread") was known as the place of origin of King David (1 Sam. 16:1; 17:12). Second, Luke asserts that Jesus was from the house of David (vv. 1:27; 3:23-38).

Verse 5 tells only what Joseph did and who was with him—his pregnant wife. The Gospel writer does not comment on any of Joseph's words, motives, or actions other than that he obediently made the journey with his spouse to his place of origin. What could he have been thinking as a husband and a soon-to-be father?

The birth is described in the last two verses of this section. It happens while they are away from home in Bethlehem. Two things are significant here: the child is a son, and the birth took place in a barn or animal shelter of some sort because the numbers of people in the area, possibly due to the census-taking, left them with no normal lodging. It is also possible that the place of the birth was not as much of a farmyard setting as is implied, since many homes of the peasant populace were divided into two sections, one for humans and the other for the livestock they kept. Despite the fact that having a son was considered a special blessing of God (see Luke 2:23; Exod. 13:2; Num. 3:12-13; 18:15-16), the child's birth occurs in humble surroundings and his first bed is in an animal's feed box!

The second section focuses on two groups, shepherds and angels. The shepherds were watching their flocks, "living in the fields" (v. 8), with nighttime especially dangerous, due to the potential predators of their livestock. That Luke identifies the shepherds as the foremost message bearers of the Savior is significant in terms of the emphases on the marginalized in his Gospel. Shepherds are not the groomed, well-coifed rich

> THAT LUKE IDENTIFIES THE SHEPHERDS AS THE FOREMOST MESSAGE BEARERS OF THE SAVIOR IS SIGNIFICANT IN TERMS OF THE EMPHASES ON THE MARGINALIZED IN HIS GOSPEL.

and privileged of that era. So in naming them as the messengers of the good news, Luke is describing God's concerns with the forgotten, those of humble occupation and status.

The next three verses focus on the appearance and announcement of a single angel. Although angels are often identified by name in both Testaments, this one is not. The angel's appearance brings "the glory of the Lord" to the landscape, and what was once usual nighttime pasturing becomes illuminated with the overwhelming brilliance of God (see Isa. 6:5-6). The angel's appearance is a reassuring one, and it parallels the announcement of the angel to Zechariah in Luke 1:11-13.

After the angel bids them not to be afraid, the reason for the visit is explained: "To you is born this day in the city of David a Savior, who is the Messiah, the Lord" (v. 11). This single verse contains a great deal of information alluding to the nature and future work of the child. First, the place of the birth links the child to the house of David. Second, although the word "Savior" is little used in the Gospels, it was typically used as one of their titles of the Roman emperors and as such was adopted by the Jews and understood in both political and religious senses (Isa. 43: 3, 11). Third, "the Messiah," a Hebrew word (Greek: "the Christ"), designated a kingly ruler (Acts 2:36; 10: 38).

The angel notes that the sign of this is to be found in "a child wrapped in bands of cloth and lying in a manger" (v. 12). Following this announcement, the sole angel is joined by "a multitude of the heavenly host" (the Greek defines this more definitively as an "army" of angels!). In their corporate witness, described in v. 14, they connect God's purposes with the affairs of humanity.

The shepherds obey the angelic instructions and go "with haste" (v. 16) and find the family group in Bethlehem as it was described to them. It is possible to assume from the remainder of the text that the new parents were unaware of the meaning of the birth themselves, since the shepherds told what they had heard and the response in v. 18 is noted as "all who heard it were amazed at what the shepherds told them."

Mary valued the words of the shepherds, although the contents of what she "pondered" is not elaborated on here. But it is further commented on by the evangelist when others respond to the child at Jesus' presentation in the temple and again later in his childhood years (see Isa. 8:18; Luke 3:3-35, 51).

Responding to the Text

It is the Christmas Eve tradition in our family to have someone read this birth narrative from Luke. Through the years as each child eventually was chosen to read this passage, it was always accompanied with much giggling over the inability to pronounce some of the strange names at the beginning. This encounter with the textually unfamiliar is symbolic of our own sense of hearing this story: it comes from unknown places with odd characters, some not of this daily world, bringing news that we still continue to wrestle with and question. Savior of what? Of whom? Why?

Answers to these questions come by looking again at the first bearers and recipients of the good news that Luke so lovingly sketches. The humble, the ordinary, the sometimes ridiculed, the everyday person are all designated as those who recognize and worship the Savior. It is they whom the Savior blesses with the gift of God's presence.

Image for Preaching

Do we have room in our hearts for those for whom the Savior came? Luke claims this ongoing thematic in this Gospel and thereby manages to underscore the incarnate Savior who yet acts in the world's communities of those who are endangered, abused, impoverished, and threatened. The God in Jesus the child asks of us if we might respond with open hearts and lives in like manner. A hymn text by a contemporary composer describes this Christmas challenge well:

> LUKE MANAGES TO UNDERSCORE THE INCARNATE SAVIOR WHO YET ACTS IN THE WORLD'S COMMUNITIES OF THOSE WHO ARE ENDANGERED, ABUSED, IMPOVERISHED, AND THREATENED.

To Bethlehem two strangers came
   To find a lodging place.
The night was cold, their bodies worn,
   But none would give them space.
      Earth had no room for them that night.
      Earth had no space to spare.

They walk again on city streets
    Where people pass them by.
They hold out empty hands but hear
    This answer to their cry:
        "There is no room for you tonight.
        We have no space to spare."

O Christ, whose parents sought in vain
    A room to give you birth,
In these, the poor, you seek again
    A welcome on the earth.
        Will there be room for you tonight?
        Will we have space to spare?

Lord, open wide all hearts kept closed
    By selfishness and fear
Until no doors are shut to those
    In whom you still draw near.
        Lord, help us welcome you tonight!
        Let love make space to share![4]

Image for Preaching

What rooms can the proclaimer name that have shut the Savior out or welcomed him in?

THE NATIVITY OF OUR LORD / CHRISTMAS DAY

DECEMBER 25, 2003

REVISED COMMON	EPISCOPAL (BCP)	ROMAN CATHOLIC
Isa. 52: 7-10	Isa. 52: 7-10	Isa. 52:7-10
Psalm 98	Psalm 98 or 98:1-6	Ps. 98:1-6
Heb. 1:1-14 (5-12)	Heb. 1:1-12	Heb. 1:1-6
John 1:1-14	John 1:1-14	John 1:1-18 or 1:1-5, 9-14

The texts for this service move us from adoration and consideration of Jesus' earthly birth to a focus on *the meaning* of the birth. Both Isaiah and the psalmist examine the content of the messengers' message. And there are many messengers noted: people who witness to God's goodness and salvation such as John, the elements of the created order, and the angels. All proclaim a unified message: the birth of Jesus extends into the joyful recognition that Christ is God. The cosmos need wait in expectation no longer for the Savior and Lord; he has arrived among us. Both the writers of Hebrews and John definitively link this Jesus with the unity, person, and acts God.

> THE TEXTS FOR THIS SERVICE MOVE US FROM ADORATION AND CONSIDERATION OF JESUS' EARTHLY BIRTH TO A FOCUS ON THE *meaning* OF THE BIRTH.

FIRST READING
ISAIAH 52:7-10

Interpreting the Text

Isaiah 52 emphasizes God's mighty acts in redeeming Jerusalem. Notes of triumph, joy, and confidence sing through these verses. The arrival of God's good news focuses on the image of the messenger's feet. Calling feet "beautiful" is startling, given the condition of most feet! Yet they signify the arrival of "peace," "salvation," and "good news (v. 7). In the following verse, people are admonished to "Listen!" to the contents of the message that announces one thing: the return of the Lord to Zion (v. 8). The return of the Lord comes not to a scene of prosperity and contentment but rather to "you ruins of Jerusalem" (v. 9), showing by such contrast the eagerness and joy that greet the Lord's return. God's power is expressed in a typical biblical expression denoting God's power in v. 10: "The Lord has bared his holy arm." The writer further notes that this vision of God's return is not simply for the benefit of the bereft people of Jerusalem, but a revelation of the one God whose power will be seen "before the eyes of all the nations." Salvation comes to not just a few, but is witnessed by all right to "the ends of the earth."

Responding to the Text

How often in life do we find ourselves waiting for news of something that will change life for the better? The phone rings, an e-mail note flashes up on the computer screen, a knock sounds at the door, and we eagerly jump to respond to see what is in store for us. With this liturgy's emphasis on the messengers of God's salvation and the unity of God, Isaiah's words extend to all across the ages who move with hope and urgency to announce redemption to those who so eagerly long for it. Isaiah's words for today's hearers are no different than they were to those in exile long ago. These words tell us to pay attention (despite worldly evidence to the contrary) that God is our God and we are among the redeemed! The redemption we are given is named and complete. None will be able to challenge or destroy our relationship with the God who claims us completely. Preaching on this text, we invite others to listen not simply to words but to presence, to the full import of God among us in Jesus Christ. We can listen to our God with hearts of adoration, thoughtfulness, and attentiveness. The quietness and calm of this final gift from God invites us to the silence of listening with joy and expectation that herein we meet our God and our Savior!

RESPONSIVE READING
PSALM 98 (RCL, BCP);
PSALM 98:1-6 (RC, BCP alt.)

Psalm 98 has one primary focus: joy! In the first three verses, all are invited to sing "a new song" because God has brought "vindication" and "victory." Verses 4-6 are directed to humanity, who are to sing praises with voice and with instruments. Verses 7-9 shift the focus slightly and also show how the entire creation metaphorically responds to God's victory: "sea," "floods," and "hills" all participate in praising God! The marvelous legacy of our Christmas hymns echo this psalm in many ways.

SECOND READING

HEBREWS 1:1-4 (5-12) (RCL); HEBREWS 1:1-12 (BCP); HEBREWS 1:1-6 (RC)

Interpreting the Text

The book of Hebrews comes from a somewhat later time in the development of the Christian community than other New Testament books—possibly toward the end of the first century C.E. Although the conclusion of the book is in epistolary form, the rest of the book and the style of writing point more to a written sermon. The opening chapter functions as a reminder to the listeners (possibly disheartened Christians) that God's address to humanity comes over time "in many and various ways by the prophets" (v. 1). But now God's mode of communicating has shifted from several sources of guidance and information for the believer to one source only, because God has "spoken to us by a Son" (v. 2).

A thumbnail sketch of Christ's person, attributes, and status are described in the rest of the chapter. The status of this Son is described in vv. 2-3: the Son has been "appointed heir of all things," and God created "the worlds" through this Son. Furthermore, if the listener wishes to know how the Son and Father relate to one another, Christ is described as "the reflection of God's glory and the exact imprint of God's very being." The Son's activities are those of one who speaks "his powerful word" and thereby "sustains all things."

The writer of Hebrews uses the evidence of Scripture to buttress his arguments. In describing the Son's status, he places him higher than the angels and devotes vv. 5-7 to showing how God's birthing of Jesus is distinctly different from the creation of the angels, who are mere messengers of God, "his servants of flame" (v. 7). Verses 8-9 quote Ps. 45:6-7 as a way of reinforcing the argument that Christ is God, and that God has anointed Christ "with the oil of gladness beyond your companions" (v. 9). Verses 10-12 also affirm the eternal substance and reign of Christ, coexistent with God, through a quotation from Ps. 102:25-27.

The writer of Hebrews demonstrates impressive rhetorical agility in making his case for Christ's relationship to God by quoting a number of sources. The honored title "Son" is used in vv. 2, 5, and 8 a total of four times—the primary and only title used in chapter 1 to emphasize both Christ's status and the believer's relationship to him who is the "heir of all things" (v. 2).

Responding to the Text

Today we often hear about "identity theft." By acquiring someone's credit cards or the ability to access someone's bank accounts or computer files, a thief can take on a personality and life that really belong to someone else. The author of Hebrews gives us some sense of the identity questions the readers of this sermon might have had. Clearly one of them was, "What identity are we to ascribe to this Jesus Christ who promised to come to us again?"

Whoever the intended audience might have been, the author senses that Christ's real identity is in danger of being misinterpreted or compromised to the detriment of the temporal and spiritual lives of those who make up the community. On the basis of the author's arguments, we can assume that the people being addressed were hearing from a number of sources that Jesus was an angel or perhaps something neither fully human nor divine. Perhaps some of the listeners had concluded that Jesus was not the Christ but simply a mere human being. The author affirms that Jesus is the Son of God. These doubts and concerns are no different today from what they were in the earliest days following Jesus' resurrection. People still question Jesus' identity, still struggle with the meaning of his presence and existence.

> THE AUTHOR OF HEBREWS GIVES US SOME SENSE OF THE IDENTITY QUESTIONS THE READERS OF THIS SERMON MIGHT HAVE HAD. CLEARLY ONE OF THEM WAS, "WHAT IDENTITY ARE WE TO ASCRIBE TO THIS JESUS CHRIST WHO PROMISED TO COME TO US AGAIN?"

A few years ago, my twin nephews presented me with a "gag gift" at Christmas. It was a plastic statue of a Jesus with moveable parts, manufactured in China. What made the gift so interesting was the description that someone had taken time to write on the back of the packaging. The words were a collage of fragments from the Lord's Prayer, quotes from the Bible and from obscure Gospels that never made it into the canon, and speculation about who Jesus was. It was a message from another part of the world that demonstrated how this Jesus Christ continues to preoccupy many people even today about his identity. Hebrews 1 is a trumpet fanfare celebrating the vast love of God in historical and eternal terms, unmistakably the God who, for the love of us all, begot the Child Jesus and made us all heirs with him!

THE GOSPEL
JOHN 1:1–14 (RCL, BCP); JOHN 1:1–18 or 1:1–5, 9–14 (RC)

Interpreting the Text

To a much greater degree than with the Synoptic Gospels, the formidable philosophical and religious thinking of the Greeks serves as a background to the content of John's Gospel. John 1 is designated as a prologue to the entire

Gospel, and its syntactical and grammatical structures are echoed in 1 John 1:1-4, which was written prior to this text. The style of the writing offers the possibility that portions of this prologue could have been part of a song or liturgical text.

The reading from John 1 echoes both Old Testament reflections on wisdom as well as the Greek concept of *logos*. *Logos* has multiple meanings, depending on how one understands its historical tributaries and usages. To translate it as "word" can obscure its dynamic sense as John and his listeners would have understood it. Some of its meanings and connotations, which find resonance in both the Old and New Testaments, are: God's instrument of creation; a means of self-expression; the expressive sense of God's wisdom; and a designation—as here—for the preexistent Christ. The author appears to combine the rich and complicated concept of "logos" with the wisdom literature of Israel, thus giving his readers new perspectives on the identity of Jesus.

The prologue falls into four natural divisions. Verses 1-5 cast the Word of God into an eternal context. John plays on the "light" in contrast to the world's "darkness." The second section, vv. 6-8, focuses on the witness of John the Baptizer. It seems likely that the evangelist was speaking to those who were either confused or had doubts about the differences between John and Jesus. He therefore makes clear the differences in v. 8 by noting that John the Baptizer is "not the light" but one who has testified to it.

The third section, vv. 9-13, somewhat depressingly asserts that the appearance of the "true light" went almost unrecognized by the world. Worse yet, those who should have recognized him refused him: "His own people did not accept him" (v. 11). John does note the few who did recognize the Christ, and it is those who were adopted by God "to become children of God" (v. 12). He carefully distinguishes between the usual manners of birth, indicating that those who did recognize the Christ were born/reborn "of God" (v. 13).

Finally, vv. 14-18 describe how salvation is accomplished in Jesus Christ. Using the words of John the Baptizer's witness, this "logos" became part of humanity and gives to all "grace upon grace" (v. 16). Two more Johannine contrasts are set up in the last two verses. The source of the Law is Moses, but "grace and truth came through Jesus Christ" (v. 17). The final verse reorients the human Jesus, a child of God, to his divine origins. Only Jesus Christ has seen God, "who is close to the Father's heart" (v. 18).

Responding to the Text

John's prologue definitely takes preacher and listeners to the highest roads of christological thought and writing. Even in English translation, the use of contrasts, the phrasing of the passage, the familiar pairings of light/dark, acceptance/rejection, human history/God's eternity, Old and New Testament allusions,

John/Jesus sweep all into the grand scope of John's opening chapter. History and faith can be written no larger than the canvas on which John has chosen.

Just as with the Hebrews lection, John also takes up the issue of Jesus' identity. Perhaps the most poignant parts of the entire passage, linked in their own manner, are found first in v. 10 where John asserts that "the world did not know him," and in the final verse where Jesus is described as one "who is close to the Father's heart" (v. 18). How is it that we often do not recognize God in our lives, in the faces of others, in the world around us?

Certainly as Christians we assert that we recognize God in Jesus Christ through the proclamation of God's word, the reception of the sacraments, and the community of

> WE TURN OUR OWN RECOGNITION OF THE CHRIST INTO A CONSTANT INVITATION TO THE WORLD AROUND US ALSO TO RECOGNIZE THIS LIGHT OF THE WORLD.

the faithful. Yet this raises an even more significant issue today as we must ask ourselves how we turn our own recognition of the Christ into a constant invitation to the world around us also to recognize this light of the world.

Image for Preaching

The cosmic sweep of the prologue in John's Gospel pushes listeners to think of the cosmic Christ and therefore of all the ways this Christ is viewed by humanity in many times and places.

In a course on feminist christologies, students discussed a book that thoroughly engages Jesus Christ as the black Christ for African Americans. Womanist theologian Kelly Brown Douglas says of the incarnate and present Christ: "My grandmother's Christ was one whom she could talk to about the daily struggles of being poor, Black, and female. So, it is in this regard that I continue to learn from my grandmother's faith. Her faith in Christ's empowering presence suggests, at the very least, a womanist Christ. But most importantly, it is in the face of my grandmother, as she struggles to sustain herself and her family, that I can truly see Christ."[5]

FIRST SUNDAY AFTER
CHRISTMAS / HOLY FAMILY

DECEMBER 28, 2003

REVISED COMMON	EPISCOPAL (BCP)	ROMAN CATHOLIC
1 Sam. 2:18-20, 26	Isa. 61:10—62:3	1 Sam. 1:20-22, 24-28
Psalm 148	Psalm 147 or 147:13-21	Ps. 84:2-3, 5-6, 9-10
Col. 3:12-17	Gal. 3:23-25, 4:4-7	1 John 3:1-2, 21-24
Luke 2:41-52	John 1:1-18	Luke 2:41-52

Texts for today present a variety of views on who and what constitute the household of God's faithful people. All people are called to a new life in grace through the birth of Jesus. There is a warmth and intimacy about these lections, which invite listeners to see that holiness consists of living out the patterns of a faithful life, regardless of age and family configurations. In these readings for Holy Family Sunday, listeners hear of Jesus' response to the call of God as a child. The texts take seriously the early roots of faith in children and their witness to the adults around them.

FIRST READING
1 SAMUEL 2:18-20, 26 (RCL);
1 SAMUEL 1:20-22, 24-28 (RC)

Interpreting the Text

Eli was the chief priest of Shiloh. Family matters frame this text by contrasting the destructive actions of Eli's sons (the "brat pack" of Israel) with Samuel, whose parents had dedicated him to God. The text begins by describing Samuel's dress, which was a very simple "linen ephod," a sign of a youth who bears the status of a priest-in-training (v. 18). Typical of any loving mother visiting a child who lives away from home, Hannah takes a "little robe" to him each year when they visit the temple to fulfill their yearly religious obligations (v. 19). Sensitive to the parents' willingness to offer their only child to the service of the temple, Eli blesses the couple and predicts more children for them both as comfort for the "loss" of Samuel and as God's reward for their faithfulness (v. 21). The appointed text describes the appearance of "a man of God" (v. 26) who describes Eli's ancestral lineage and blessing, all of which come to nothing because of the behavior of his sons.

Responding to the Text

There is great tenderness and spiritual commitment among the adults over the welfare of the child Samuel. His parents have been courageous enough to commit him to a formal religious life for training, even as a child, despite the loss to themselves of his companionship and presence. Eli also values the child and blesses the parents, knowing their sense of loss and their obedience in giving up the daily presence of their only child. Although most children are not literally separated from their parents today for religious reasons, the passage certainly looks at a typical human issue, that is, allowing children to chart their own lives at some point. The text raises the question for all listeners of what devotion to God means and the sometimes long path of discernment that such devotion entails.

ISAIAH 61:10—62:3 (BCP)

The prophet's words use a number of images to express the joy the exiles will experience at the return of their Lord and God's gifts of salvation and righteousness. The prophet uses the first person pronoun to express the magnitude of this joy by saying that "my whole being shall exult in my God" (v. 10). Two more images are used to describe the effects of God's salvation. One is an image of clothing, "garments of salvation," similar to the luxurious wardrobe of a bride and bridegroom, which the prophet calls "robe of righteousness" (v. 10). The other is an organic metaphor, comparing God's righteousness to a garden (v. 11). Verses in chapter 62 represent the prophet as irrepressible in his joy over God: "For Zion's sake I will not keep silent" (v. 1). In the final verse of this reading, Jerusalem as a city encircled by its ramparts and walls is described as symbolic of the redeemed who corporately will be a "crown of beauty in the hand of the Lord" (v. 3).

RESPONSIVE READING
PSALM 148 (RCL)

This rapturous call to praise God might best be expressed if it is read antiphonally by the congregation. In the first part of the psalm, vv. 1-10, the call to praise is addressed to the elements of creation: the heavenly bodies, the creatures and contents of the earth that come from God, "for he commanded and they were created" (v. 5). For those who hear this psalm in northern climates at this time of year, it is good to affirm that God made "fire and hail, snow and frost, stormy wind fulfilling his command!" (v. 8). The second part, vv. 11-14, invites the human inhabitants of earth to also join this joy. Everyone, regardless of gender, age, or status is called forth to "Praise the Lord!"

PSALM 147 or 147:13-21 (BCP)

This psalm may be considered in three general sections. The first, vv. 1-6, notes the nature of a God who defends and heals all those who cannot help themselves: "gathers the outcasts," "heals the brokenhearted," "lifts the downtrodden" (vv. 2, 3, 6). The middle section focuses on God's beneficence to all creation. The final section, vv. 12-20, describes the benefits God gives to Israel through the creation and through "his command," his word," and his "statues and ordinances" (vv. 13, 18, 19, 20).

PSALM 84:2-3, 5-6, 9-10 (RC)

This psalm is "one for the road," as it probably was used to mark one of the yearly trips to a religious festival in Jerusalem. Many might recognize this psalm for its setting by Johannes Brahms in the anthem "How Lovely Is Thy Dwelling Place," part of his *Ein Deutsches Requiem*. The scope of God's enormous love is clearly expressed in this psalm, especially for those of little note in creation, such as the sparrow, the swallow, and the minor servant who is a doorkeeper. The tone of this psalm is enhanced by the repeated use of the word "happy" to describe those who are secure in the knowledge that they are safe in God's keeping.

Second Reading
COLOSSIANS 3:12-17 (RCL)

Interpreting the Text

This reading features several specific calls to action that each believer must attend to in living in Christ. People are to "clothe yourselves," imagery reminiscent of baptismal imagery, with the fruit of the Spirit (v. 12). They are to "bear with one another" and "forgive each other" (v. 13). The bid to "clothe yourselves" is repeated by noting the most necessary garment of all, which is love, and which unites those words and deeds mentioned previously. As in the Gospels and other Pauline writings, love is *always* the plumb line of everything else that determines the Christian life.

> AS IN THE GOSPELS AND OTHER PAULINE WRITINGS, LOVE IS ALWAYS THE PLUMB LINE OF EVERYTHING ELSE THAT DETERMINES THE CHRISTIAN LIFE.

Believers are also urged to let Christ be the primary one to "rule in your hearts" and, as a consequence, to be thankful (v. 15). The final two verses have to do with both allowing "the word of Christ" to affect one's life but also to let one's words and deeds be done in Christ's name. In other words, Christ and the believer's life and actions are related in a continuous, antiphonal response to life.

Responding to the Text

The clothing imagery used in this text, as well as references to it earlier in chapter 3, are reminiscent of the fashion dictate that says that in colder seasons of the year it is wiser to wear "layered" clothing, that is, dress with a number of garments rather than just one warm sweater or coat. Such layering is healthier and prevents the wearer from being subjected to the elements. Paul's advice to the Colossians is similar to this seasonal maxim. He also notes the layers of word and deed that must characterize the true Christian life and also that final outer garment that pulls it all together—love!

In working with Paul's admonitions, the proclaimer can utilize the imagery Paul himself uses and combine it with a metaphorical look at today's fashion realities. How does the spiritual clothing of today's Christian look? What garments might we wear that do not befit our relationship with Christ? What do we do when our spiritual garments become threadbare and worn? How does the baptismal imagery of new clothing fit with this passage as we consider the beautiful, often handmade white dresses the baptized wear?

Every verse of this text is its own homily! And the preacher could, indeed, choose to focus on only one verse for a worthwhile expression of Paul's invitation to live the Christian life. While Paul's list of imperatives is lengthy, the wonderful and delicate interplay of community around these words and deeds of the Christian life invites the listener to a new life in the name of Jesus Christ.

GALATIANS 3:23-25; 4:4-7 (BCP)

These verses use a number of images that attempt to convey the difference between life before and after the coming of Christ. The contemporary existential question is always how today's listeners experience the "law" in their own lives.

Verses 23-25 are part of a much longer explication of law and faith. In v. 23 Paul describes experience of God's law for the sinner, prior to Christ's coming, as one who is "imprisoned" and "guarded." There is a slight shift in v. 24 in which the law is also called "our disciplinarian." The explanation of the Greek word is useful for assisting the listener to appreciate the extent of what Paul means; "disciplinarian" in Paul's time referred not to a teacher of children, but usually to the household slave designated to protect and guard them. In other words, the law left all people in subjection.

In chapter 4 the birth of Christ and the change in status it signifies for sinners under the law are described. Paul notes that while we are still "children," the birth of Christ no longer leaves us as slave children or children lacking freedom, but children of God, ones who "receive adoption" and who also then become "heirs."

1 JOHN 3:1-2, 21-24 (RC)

This passage builds on a number of different dynamics of the parent-child relationship as John uses it to explain the God-human relationship in Christ. The relationship between God and humanity is based on God's love, which is the initiator of our title "children of God." John warns about the nature of being the child of such a parent, since being of God may run counter to the perceptions of the everyday world as to the nature of God. One should not be surprised that others fail to understand the Christian life, since they are unfamiliar with (or might have rejected) God from whom such life is derived.

This status of "child" is not a demeaning one. According to John it is simply the state of things as they are now. Only final revelation will reveal the ultimate status of maturity in Christ which lies ahead for the believer. We are left with a mystery as to what that will be like.

The final section describes the active relationship between a trusting Christian and God. We are invited to have "boldness," since we are confident in our relationship with this God of love. Obedience to God's commandments is linked to the invitation to ask of God what we will. Furthermore, such obedience means we also "abide" in God. This mutuality of abiding presences is seconded and secured by God's Spirit, who governs our obedience. The image of Christ as the loving and obedient child, the keeper of God's commandments, is mirrored in our own lives through the power of the Spirit.

THE GOSPEL

LUKE 2:41-52 (RCL, RC)

Interpreting the Text

This is the second of two descriptions of Jesus in the precincts of the temple, both unique to Luke: first his presentation and now as an older child—possibly after his bar mitzvah (meaning "son of the commandment"). These reflect Luke's priorities of reiterating Jesus' continuity in word and deed with his Judaic heritage and writing his Gospel with the templates of Old Testament stories. Moreover, they both depict Jesus in accord with the settings, rituals, festivals, and expectations of a faithful Jewish child maturing within his faith community.

This story appears to be based on the Old Testament model of Samuel's life, his spiritual growth and call to faith and action. In the same fashion, his mother, Hannah's, response to the gift of her pregnancy with Samuel is similar to Mary's response (see 1 Sam. 2:1-10). Mary's song to God uses much of the same phraseology found in Hannah's song of praise. Like Samuel, Jesus was found as a child in the temple as one interested in and faithful to the call of God.

After the Passover the parents go home and Jesus goes to the temple. Given the size of caravans, it is not strange that Jesus' absence went unnoticed for what Luke calls "a day's journey." Eventually, after three days, the parents locate their child, alive and well, and doing what they had not expected: "sitting among the teachers, listening to them and asking those questions" (v. 46).

One of the startling aspects of this story is the contradiction set up between Jesus' presence in the temple and the distress this causes his parents. Jesus' response to his earthly parents is played off against his perception of God when he asks them, "Did you not know that I must be in my Father's house?" (v. 49). Jesus' insistence on the fact that he is in the right place at the right time, doing what God intended him to do, is a theme reinforced in other parts of Luke's Gospel in terms of emphasizing Jesus' mission (see Luke 4:43; 9:22; 13:33).

Jesus' question does not override the real human ties he has with parents, including Mary's question, "Look, your father and I have been searching for you in great anxiety" (v. 48). The return to Nazareth found Jesus "obedient" to his parents, and Luke echoes Mary's thinking about her son in v. 51b as it relates back to the same observation in 2:19.

Responding to the Text

Almost all parents have had that panic-stricken moment in a supermarket, a store, or a parking lot when they realize their child has suddenly disappeared. Our culture lives with milk cartons bearing missing children's descriptions. Teachers and law enforcement personnel spend considerable time educating both children and parents in how to remain safe in an often unsafe world. When a child goes missing, everything that is beautifully characteristic of children focuses our fears for the child's well-being: naiveté, innocence, defenselessness, and curiosity. All of these are good and yet can be the reasons for the child's disappearance. We can all identify with the panic that Mary and Joseph must have experienced when they realized Jesus was missing. Where would a twelve-year-old boy go in a city like Jerusalem, and no doubt a city exactly like the cities of the world today?

What a mixture of relief and upset typifies the response of Mary to Jesus when they do find him! Until this point in the Gospel, Jesus has been a passive agent, but in this story he becomes the young person taking the lead in his own life, acting on his own agency. With this episode in Luke's Gospel, we all experience the first signal that something is different about this child. His response to his parents in the form of two questions shows that he has a space apart from them, a relationship to God that Luke tells us they did not understand.

While this biblical text is about the boy Jesus, it raises for all listeners the question of what it means to mature in faith and be about God's business regardless of age. What *is* God's business that each of us engages in it—or flees from it—in our daily lives? Jesus offers an excellent model for responding to the call of God by "sitting among the teachers, listening to them and asking them questions" (v. 46). This model is not one of instant understanding but of allowing oneself proximity to other faithful seekers of God, of discernment and education through listening and speaking. Jesus' model of seeking God is one of going to those sources that will nourish his faith life.

> WHILE THIS BIBLICAL TEXT IS ABOUT THE BOY JESUS, IT RAISES FOR ALL LISTENERS THE QUESTION OF WHAT IT MEANS TO MATURE IN FAITH AND BE ABOUT GOD'S BUSINESS, REGARDLESS OF AGE.

Jesus' presence among the teachers and elders of his faith also offers homiletical possibilities for describing the potential riches of sharing faith cross-generationally. It shows that whatever the age of the God-hungry seekers, conversation and learning together can only enhance mutual growth in faith. Learning about God is not an educational one-way street in any faith community.

This portrayal of Jesus seeking knowledge of God and God's wisdom is a call to all believers to respect the variety of ways in which God acts in each person's life, even though individual struggles and responses to be faithful may seem unclear or unusual to others. In an even uncomfortable way, this story signals the fact that each person's most basic allegiance is not to family or friends, but to God. We have in this jarring story of the boy Jesus evidence of God's presence and call and one person's response to that. And we have characters in the story, including his parents, who must ask, What does this person's allegiance to God mean for us?

JOHN 1:1-18 (BCP)

[See the comments on the Gospel for The Nativity of Our Lord (Christmas Day), December 28, 2003.]

Image for Preaching

The concept and process of discernment are featured in today's passages. What does it mean to discern God's will in one's life? How does that look in daily attitudes and action? What relationship do parents and children have in this matter of discernment, and how can the generations speak to each other about what they see as important and developing in their own lives?

THE NAME OF JESUS /
HOLY NAME /
MARY, MOTHER OF GOD

NEW YEAR'S DAY
JANUARY 1, 2004

REVISED COMMON	EPISCOPAL (BCP)	ROMAN CATHOLIC
Num. 6:22-27	Exod. 34:1-8	Num. 6:22-27
Psalm 8	Psalm 8	Ps. 67:2-3, 5, 6-8
Gal. 4:4-7	Rom. 1:1-7	Gal. 4:4-7
or Phil. 2:5-11		
Luke 2:15-21	Luke 2:15-21	Luke 2:16-21

The texts for this day speak to the question, "What's in a name?" God's name is presented in various ways in these passages, ranging through the historical, liturgical, and theological. It is a name that blesses and by blessing makes claims on those over whom it is pronounced, as the examples of priestly blessings on the people of Israel in Exodus and Numbers show. The psalms for today demonstrate how God's name is expressed in the exuberant thankfulness of believers. From historical and theological perspectives, the name of Jesus is initiated in the ordinary way of parents circumcising and naming a boy child, but is given deeper meaning by Paul in showing how Jesus Christ is the name in which salvation is offered to all the created order.

> THROUGHOUT THIS BLESSING THERE IS A SENSE OF GOD'S VAST LARGESSE. NO ARENA OF HUMAN ENDEAVOR IS EXEMPT FROM GOD'S BLESSING AND PEACE. THIS GOD BLESSES WITH LOVE AND BOUNTY.

FIRST READING
NUMBERS 6:22-27 (RCL, RC)

Interpreting the Text

The literary structure of this priestly benediction uses repetition and parallelism. Three times the Lord (YHWH) is called on to bless, to cause his face to shine on the people, and to lift up his countenance. In each instance, the reason for this invocation is slightly different and is intended to ask God to keep the people, be gracious to them, and to give them peace. The second and third sections use language that sounds somewhat odd to contemporary ears. In the second clause, God's face "shining" has a history in both biblical testaments, indicating God's protection of the people. Some will be familiar also with the significance of human faces shining (e.g., Moses, the martyred Stephen) as a sign of those who converse with God. In the last clause, God's "lifting up his countenance" indicates that God gazes favorably and with kindly intentions on those who receive God's attention. Throughout this blessing there is a sense of God's vast largesse. No arena of human endeavor is exempt from God's blessing and peace. This God blesses with love and bounty.

Responding to the Text

This priestly blessing intersects the turn into the new year, a time when resolutions are made and blessings past and those anticipated occupy our attention. What will the new year bring? Some face it with confidence while others feel foreboding. This benediction reminds us of the incredible scope of God's blessings. Good health, employment, adequate income, the love and support of family and friends, life itself, are all instances of God's blessings. Other blessings may not be so obvious but just as important, such as new insights, assuming new responsibilities, leaving a destructive situation, the end of a loved one's suffering, a suddenly closed career door with the consequent opening of new possibilities. Whether obvious or hidden, God's blessings are unceasing and all encompassing, and this blessing can be received joyfully by any hearer or by a community of faith pondering God's actions among them.

The wording of this blessing has also been refashioned by a generation of feminist interpreters to further widen our images and understandings of God and can be read in this way:

> The Lord bless you and keep you;
> The Lord's face shine on you, and be gracious to you;
> The Lord's countenance rest on you and give you peace. Amen.[6]

EXODUS 34:1-8 (BCP)

This text charts the slow restoration of Israel to the presence of God after their lapse into idol worship. The original tablets of command that Moses smashed on being confronted with the people's sin (32:19) now are restored by God's command to Moses to reappear on top of Mount Sinai for further instructions. The first revelation Moses experiences is the revelation of God's name (YHWH). The import of the name is then proclaimed by God in vv. 6-7.

Moses' mountaintop experience of God is not one of the ecstatic order. Exodus does not emphasize the visual expressions of the revelation, only the auditory. There is work to be done, information to be conveyed. God's power is expressed first in naming the name of God to Moses and then in explaining to him what God's nature denotes for the people of Israel. God loves, is merciful and gracious, forgiving—and also holds the people accountable for their deeds. Once Moses hears the details, his final request of God is to take back the people of Israel, and so the covenant is renewed.

What is God up to? This passage demonstrates that God's intentions for humanity are straightforward, loving, and clear. There is no impenetrable mystery concerning God's will and covenant with Israel. All are called, held accountable, and made aware of the God who blesses and preserves. Certainly this text presents a clear and loving mandate for faith communities for the new year!

RESPONSIVE READING
PSALM 8 (RCL, BCP)

Periodically, news and media reports will invite the populace outside on a given night to see yearly meteor showers in a number of constellations. There is a joy and awe at seeing the heavens fill with "shooting stars" and blazing beauty. This psalm reflects that human awe and radiates God's praise from beginning to end. Its scope is all of the created order, the heavens and the earth. Verses 4-8 take up the relationship of this all-powerful God to humanity. The psalmist marvels that human beings have primacy of rank over all other creatures, in fact, are even called to act as stewards of other beings (v. 6). The psalm is an expression of joy. It is also a reminder that the ascendancy of humanity has its negative side as well. Human stewardship is sometimes imperfect, even destructive; and as the New Testament proclaims in eschatological terms, it has yet to achieve its true fulfillment and completion (Heb. 2:6-8; Rom. 8:19-21).

PSALM 67:2-3, 5, 6-8

This psalm, in part, reflects the Aaronite benediction in Num. 6:24-26. The people's plea for a blessing rests partially on the realization that such blessing will be a witness to other nations of the power and goodness of God. Further, the God who blesses Israel is also the one who is able to "judge the peoples with equity and guide the nations about earth" (v. 4).

SECOND READING

GALATIANS 4:4-7 (RCL, RC)

Interpreting the Text

Paul is intent on signifying humanity's shift in relationship to God because of the birth of Jesus. He does so by noting two commissionings or sendings of God. First, God's plan is not calendar-dependent but "appropriate," or what Paul calls "the fullness of time" (v. 4), and in this fullness Jesus is sent. This Jesus experiences our humanity fully in his manner of birth and his necessary human subjection to the law. He does so for one purpose: that we might be adopted as God's children.

Second, in order that we might recognize our new status, God sends Jesus' Spirit, so that with loving familiarity we can call God our parent, a Father, as Paul describes God. Our ability to do this designates us as heirs of God. (See other comments on this reading in the alternate second reading for the First Sunday after Christmas.)

Responding to the Text

What does it mean to read these verses at the juncture of the new year? Paul refers in these verses to the passage of time and what that means in God's sight and for humanity. Driven as we are generally by a calendar and tight schedules, it is easy to lose track of alternative time frames. The fullness of time to which Paul refers has nothing to do with a calendar but with an individual or corporate sense of agreement that something needs to happen. God's decision to send the Christ is contra-calendar and pro-humanity. God acts both in and apart from our familiar time referents to create the gift of salvation. As such, pondering the new year gives us opportunity to consider where God's sense of timing may be quite different from ours and to be alert to that.

Electronic forms of calendar-keeping are now common. These personal desk organizers are of great help to their owners but also frame time in such a way that such realities as the opportune moment, the hour of decision, the appropriate time are simply not possible to factor in, for they are human and personal. In the human and the personal, God meets use in Christ with new life, new recognitions, and new opportunities, not asking *what* time it is but *whose* time it is.

PHILIPPIANS 2:5-11 (RCL alt.)

Interpreting the Text

This magnificent passage is considered by some to be a pre-Pauline liturgical text. The progress of this text is almost visual, moving from the depths of humiliation where Jesus willingly is found to be "taking the form of a slave" (v. 7) to his exaltation as "Lord." Paul is concerned that the Philippians focus on the model and center of their faith as a means of understanding how they are to treat one another. They should actually think like Christ Jesus so that "the same mind be in you." These verses cluster in two major ways: Jesus' life as a human and his humiliating death (vv. 6-8), and his exaltation (vv. 9-11).

The key to this second set of verses is the focus on "name." God is the one who gives Jesus his name, one superior to all others. It is also the name that elicits worship throughout the entire creation. In these verses there is a progression from a name given, to the "name of Jesus," and finally to the full expression of the name, "Jesus Christ." This last verse with its "Lord" (translated as "master") is a significant title. It is not only a title of honor in and of itself but is echoed throughout this epistle also as a means of describing Paul's relationship with Jesus, in that Paul defines himself as "slave" to him.

Responding to the Text

Today the humiliation that Paul finds in Jesus' life and uses as a model for human behavior is little understood or valued. In proclaiming this text, the preacher will need adequate time to sort out the tragic issues related to the history of slavery (both biblical and those found in many societies even yet today) and the positive meaning Paul ascribes to slavery by using the term as characteristic of his relationship with Jesus Christ. Additionally, the historical and contemporary problems related to the subservient roles often carried out by women in church and society means homiletical diligence will avoid reinforcing negative stereotypes and, instead, emphasize those realities of freedom-in-relationship that Paul is attempting to describe.

ROMANS 1:1-7 (BCP)

As with other passages for this day, this opening salutation from Paul to the Romans is concerned about names and naming. It also expresses the characteristics of Jesus and of Paul and what constitutes their relationship to each another. First, Jesus Christ was promised according to the prophets, descended from the line of David, and made God's Son through the power of God in resurrecting him from the dead. What is expressed about Paul, because of Jesus, is also important. Paul has been called as an apostle, is a recipient of God's grace, and has been given a mission to the Gentiles.

Finally, Paul addresses those specifically at Rome as people "called to be saints." "Saints" are historically thought to be those who lived lives of significant and high-profile sacrifice. The word is sometimes now used in cartoons or sarcastically to refer to those who are supposedly perfect. The word has little to do with perfection and much more to do with those who attempt to lead holy lives in Jesus Christ. In the church in which I grew up in Minnesota,[7] carved oak panels of biblical and historical names, great witnesses to the faith, encircle the circumference of the worship space. Two panels that complete the circle are blank. We were always told that *our* names were inscribed on one of these panels as a saint of God! Paul's introduction charts a clear historical and contemporary description for the saints as to the one whom they call God's Son and in whose name they are to live.

THE GOSPEL

LUKE 2:15-21 (RCL, BCP);
LUKE 2:16-21 (RC)

Interpreting the Text

This portion of the birth narrative follows the departure of the angels and the responsibility of seeking the Savior given to the shepherds. Again, this text, which has figured strongly in recent services, is framed within the context of the celebration of the Name of Jesus. There are two important elements: the role of the shepherds and the naming of Jesus at his circumcision. First, the role of the shepherds in these verses moves from their witness to God's action as they have heard it from the angels to a focus on their role of testifying to the identity of Jesus to others. On arriving at Bethlehem they tell others what they have been told. Whom did they tell besides the parents? We do not know, but obviously what they shared created a good deal of consternation and excitement. This text is one more of those great biblical narratives that can be called "Say! Did you hear about . . .!"

OF ALL THOSE WHO HEARD THE SHEPHERDS' STORY, LUKE'S DESCRIPTION OF MARY SEEMS TO INDICATE SHE WAS NOT COMPLETELY SURPRISED. THERE IS A SERENITY AND THOUGHTFULNESS THAT HAS HER TREASURING AND PONDERING THE SHEPHERDS' WORDS.

Of all those who heard the shepherds' story, Luke's description of Mary seems to indicate she was not completely surprised. There is a serenity and thoughtfulness that has her treasuring and pondering the shepherds' words.

Finally, the last verse describes the circumcision and naming of Jesus, "the name given by the angel." This verse confirms the earlier statement made in Luke 1:31

when the angel tells Mary what she will name the child. The name Jesus is a variant of the name Joshua, which means "salvation of God." Here his naming confirms and extends the meaning of the other names already described in Luke and in chapter 2, such as Savior, Messiah, the Lord. Jesus is a little baby with his mission already set toward the future through the witness of the angels in the presence of humanity.

Responding to the Text

Perhaps some of the more hilarious and interesting conversations to be had are those about how someone came to be named. Many children eventually ask, "Why was I given the name I have?" Names are chosen because they belong to other members of the family or are a means of honoring a friend. Some favor biblical names while others like more contemporary names. One couple said they closed their eyes and let their finger stop randomly at a name in a baby's list of names because they could not agree otherwise on what to call their child! People can be named after relatives, seasons of the year, flowers, heroes, animals, figures in mythology, or ethnically derived names.

The name of Jesus came from other than human sources. Mary was told what to name her child, and his name became the name above all others, describing his person and his work. His name is part of our liturgy, our biblical texts, our confessions of faith, and our prayers. We are washed and fed at Christ's table in that name. His name is invoked not simply in remembrance, but as the central means of honoring his very presence among us. At meals this invitation is often prayed, "Come Lord Jesus, be our guest!"

In Jesus' name people affirm all the major spiritual events of their existence ranging from baptism to burial. The mention of Jesus' name is power, and that power can change everything: exorcise the demoniac, heal, and redeem. The name of Jesus is irresistible. During the transition from pagan to Christian beliefs in the Roman Empire, it is said that the Emperor Marcus Aurelius

> THE MENTION OF JESUS' NAME IS POWER, AND THAT POWER CAN CHANGE EVERYTHING: EXORCISE THE DEMONIAC, HEAL, AND REDEEM.

acknowledged in his dying hour, "You have conquered, O pale Galilean!" As we stand poised at the beginning of a new year, in whose name do we contemplate the future?

Image for Preaching

The proclaimer may wish to look at those key names that are central to the life of the faith community historically and now. What are those names? Why are they important? What impact do they have? What does it mean to have a name that is "ordinary"? How does the name of Jesus relate to our name? How is the name of Jesus understood in a given faith community?

Notes

1. William Butler Yeats, "The Second Coming," in *Michael Robartes and the Dancer* (Churchtown, Dundrum: Cuala Press, 1920), 28.

2. C. U. Wolf, "Fuller," *The Interpreter's Dictionary of the Bible* (Nashville: Abingdon, 1962), 2:330.

3. William A. Percy, "They Cast Their Nets," *Lutheran Book of Worship* (Minneapolis: Augsburg; Philadelphia: Board of Publication, Lutheran Church in America, 1978), no. 449.

4. Herman Stuempfle, "To Bethlehem Two Strangers Came," from *Redeeming the Time: A Cycle of Song for the Christian Year* (Chicago: GIA Publications, 1997), no. 5.

5. Kelly Brown Douglas, *The Black Christ* (New York: Orbis, 2001), 116–17.

6. Paraphrase by author.

7. Vinje Lutheran Church, Willmar, Minnesota.

THE SEASON
OF EPIPHANY

JOHN S. MCCLURE

At the end of her book of poems, *Kneeling in Bethlehem*, on the birth of Jesus, Ann Weems includes this poem, "It Is Not Over":

> It is not over,
>   this birthing.
> There are always newer skies
>   into which
>   God can throw stars.
> When we begin to think
>   that we can predict the Advent of God,
>   that we can box the Christ
>   in a stable in Bethlehem,
>   that's just the time
>   that God will be born
>   in a place we can't imagine and won't believe.
> Those who wait for God
>   watch with their hearts and not their eyes,
>   listening
>   always listening
>   for angel words.[1]

The lectionary texts from Epiphany to the Transfiguration shout emphatically, "It is not over!" As the Magi approach the stable, bringing their gifts of thanksgiving and expectation, we are beckoned to follow them on a breathtaking spiritual journey that is only just beginning. As Jesus is baptized by John, the pathway veers into strange waters of spiritual adoption. At Cana we find ourselves attending an eschatological celebration of the abundance of God's mercy in Christ. In the temple, we are shocked and thrilled to hear Jesus identify his presence with God's great Jubilee. By the seashore we marvel and wonder at Jesus' prowess as a catcher of fish and people. At the Transfiguration, we struggle up a mountain to pray, only to be confronted with a terrifying holy presence.

During Epiphany, the church celebrates the manifestation or "showing forth" of Jesus *as Savior*. The pathway from the manger, through baptism, to Transfiguration is filled with marvelous moments in which Jesus' saving power is put on display for those who have eyes to see and ears to hear.

THE PATHWAY FROM THE MANGER, THROUGH BAPTISM, TO TRANSFIGURATION IS FILLED WITH MARVELOUS MOMENTS IN WHICH JESUS' SAVING POWER IS PUT ON DISPLAY FOR THOSE WHO HAVE EYES TO SEE AND EARS TO HEAR.

It is likely that the feast of Epiphany came into being as the result of a controversy over when, exactly, God revealed the identity of Jesus as Savior. Was it at the moment of Jesus' birth, as Luke and Matthew contend? Was it at the moment of Jesus' baptism, as early Gnostic Christians believed? Should we see Jesus' revelation of himself as Savior in his first great sign at Cana as testified in John 2:1-11? The separation of the celebration of Christ's birth to December 25 in the West was a way of accentuating that the saving work of Jesus Christ begins at the incarnation. The season of Epiphany as a whole, however, continues to emphasize all of the original saving manifestations of Jesus Christ, including his incarnation, baptism, and early signs. Epiphany is not only about God's action; it is also about the human reception of God's grace in Jesus Christ and the beginnings of our lives as faithful witnesses to Jesus Christ as the Light of the World.

THE EPIPHANY OF OUR LORD

JANUARY 4/6, 2004

REVISED COMMON	EPISCOPAL (BCP)	ROMAN CATHOLIC
Isa. 60:1-6	Isa. 60: 1-6, 9	Isa. 60:1-6
Ps. 72:1-7, 10-14	Psalm 72	Ps. 72:1-2, 7-8,
	or 72:1-2, 10-17	10-11, 12-13
Eph. 3:1-12	Eph. 3:1-12	Eph. 3:2-3a, 5-6
Matt. 2:1-12	Matt. 2:1-12	Matt. 2:1-12

Epiphany is a time of gathering at the light of Christ that has appeared amid the desperate circumstances of this world. Because this light is in our midst, empowering us, we can now "arise" and "shine." The people of God are extensions of this light and find their strength for mission by gathering to celebrate its presence and power. The texts for Epiphany make it clear that this gathering around God's light in Christ is not without danger. It is, in many ways, a subversive gathering, recognized by those in power to be a serious threat to the status quo.

FIRST READING
ISAIAH 60:1-6 (RCL, RC); ISAIAH 60:1-6, 9 (BCP)

Interpreting the Text

Chapters 60-62 form the core witness of Third Isaiah (Isaiah 56-66). Chapter 60 bursts forth with an exclamation of renewed energy and hope, "Arise, shine; for your light has come." The prophet offers the discouraged, resettling community of Jerusalem a powerful word expressing God's unfailing resolve on their behalf. The circumstances into which these words are spoken are rather grim. Inspired by Second Isaiah's prophecy of hope and deliverance, some have returned home from exile and are met by those who have survived the destruction of their homeland. Together, they are now experiencing the grating discrepancy between the poetic visions of their prophets and the hard realities of rebuilding an economically secure, politically safe, and socially just society. Chapters 56 through 59 set forth in stark relief the shortcomings and outright failures of this fledgling community. The two core issues that need to be resolved include welcoming strangers (chapter 56), and economic and social justice (chapter 58).

The tone and style of chapter 60 turns the corner toward hope for the future. The chapter as a whole is a powerful assertion of the reversal of Israel's fortunes for the better. The prophet picks up the older theme of Zion and paints a picture of restored glory. In sharp contrast to exile and submission to foreign powers, now "the wealth of the nations shall come to you" (v. 5). The glory of Yahweh is on the rise, and this will lead to a massive ingathering of lost sons and daughters, nations and kings, and the bounty of the earth.

Although Isaiah 60 is almost overwhelmingly theocentric, so that it would appear that God's agency is all that is required to restore Israel's glory, note that in vv. 17-18 the rebuilt city of Jerusalem will have walls that are called "Salvation," gates that are called "Praise," an "overseer" called "Peace," and a "taskmaster" called "Righteousness." The way out of the despair identified in v. 2 is to build a city that respects God's glory in every aspect. The new city anticipated by the prophet will be a city in which the issues of welcoming the stranger and justice, urged in chapters 56 and 58, will be attended to with great care and with some expediency.

Responding to the Text

In the context of Epiphany, the preacher will do well to pay attention to the verses in which the prophet instructs us what to do when God's salvation is near: "Arise, shine" (v. 1). "Lift up your eyes and look around!" (v. 4). "See and be radiant!" "Thrill and rejoice" (v. 5). Praise, the "gate" to the new city of God, is the only way to enter into an awareness of God's manifestations of glory. Preachers must be careful not to become either triumphalist or moralistic, singing forth praise choruses, on the one hand, or, on the other hand, shaking fingers and exhorting listeners to "pay attention to the glory of God all round you." The homiletic goal here is one of *encouragement in the midst of distress.* Strive to help your community, nation, or individuals in the congregation to rise up from beds of mourning, despair, and capitulation, to lift weary eyes in order to shift their vision past the overwhelming odds of injustice and structural evil in the world. Show those who are listening how they are already those who reflect the glory of God, who are "radiant" in God's eyes, and, therefore, can be agents of hope and reconciliation, building a new city of righteousness.

Another important theme for Epiphany is the theme of *gathering at the light that God has brought forth into the world through Zion.* It is clear that Matthew had in mind this image of representatives of nations near and far bringing "gold and frankincense" to Zion when he told the story of the Magi. If we remember that "Salvation" is what buttresses the walls of God's great city of hope, then it is easy to see why Matthew would recall Isaiah 60. The meaning of salvation is the same for Matthew as it was for the prophet. Salvation is the fulfillment of peace and righteousness on earth. This salvation is ultimately what attracts and gathers in people who are lost, in exile, or simply distracted by their own wealth and prosperity.

Isaiah 60 is one of the great liturgical utterances of Israel's prophets. This suggests another theme for preaching. Although Epiphany is a special celebration of the gathering of people far and wide to God's saving presence, *every* time the church worships, Christians gather to the glory of God.

> SALVATION IS THE FULFILLMENT OF PEACE AND RIGHTEOUSNESS ON EARTH. THIS SALVATION IS ULTIMATELY WHAT ATTRACTS AND GATHERS IN PEOPLE WHO ARE LOST, IN EXILE, OR SIMPLY DISTRACTED BY THEIR OWN WEALTH AND PROSPERITY.

Every Sunday and on many weekdays and nights, in spite of the weather, what's on television, Little League games, stressful jobs, overwhelming pain, grief, or sadness, those who believe that God's love and power are available to help them live and rebuild their lives walk through church doors and take seats between walls that have proved safe and supportive over the years. They know that the doors and walls of churches come and go, indeed, that bricks and mortar everywhere will not last. But they also know that God has resolved in God's deepest heart to act for their salvation. Because of this promise, and in order to see this salvation once again, the faithful arise and lift their eyes and look around, and in God's good time, they see God's glory and become radiant with rejoicing. Every act of worship, therefore, bears witness to God's Epiphany. Worship is a time of arising, gathering, and attending to God's promised and anticipated glory.

RESPONSIVE READING
PSALM 72:1-7, 10-14 (RCL); PSALM 72 or 72:1-2, 10-17 (BCP); PSALM 72:1-2, 7-8, 10-13 (RC)

A coronation psalm, Psalm 72 prays for a king who will rule in a way that redeems the people from violence, poverty, and oppression. Verse 7 in particular reminds us of Isaiah 60, in which the true "overseer" of the people is called "Peace," and the people's "taskmaster" is called "Righteousness." According to the psalmist, righteousness will flourish and peace will abound when a king who is given these qualities by God rules the people. This psalm tells the people what to expect of those who govern them. These expectations establish a set of bedrock assumptions regarding God's true design for our leaders. These assumptions become embedded deep within our consciousness *because they are spoken and prayed in the assembly.* In spite of the fact that we often feel powerless to affect political and social structures, this coronation psalm encourages the imagination of justice, peace, and righteous governance. By virtue of their constant repetition in worship, imagination is joined to prayer. By extension, we learn to expect these things, believe that they are possible, and work for their establishment.

SECOND READING
EPHESIANS 3:1-12 (RCL, BCP);
EPHESIANS 3:2-3a, 5-6 (RC)

Interpreting the Text

In preparation for preaching on these passages from Ephesians 3, it is important to remember Eph. 1:9-10. The larger context for chapter 3 is the cosmic plan to "gather up all things" in Christ, "things in heaven and things on earth." The "mystery" to which the writer of Ephesians refers is a great cosmic gathering of all things to God in and through Jesus Christ. In particular, Ephesians 3 tells of Paul's unique apostolic "commission" (*oikonomia,* vv. 2, 9) as a part of this greater scheme: the commission to gather together into one body both Jews and Gentiles. This is Paul's unique commission, but it is simply one aspect of the cosmic gathering together of all things in Christ.

At the heart of these verses is a message of empowerment for all of those who wish to follow in Paul's footsteps by discovering and pursuing their own unique commissions as a part of this great gathering. We are empowered because we have many helpers for our tasks. One helper is Paul himself, and the "few words" that he has written are "a reading of which will enable you to perceive my understanding of the mystery of Christ" (vv. 3b-4). Another helper is the Spirit who reveals the mystery to apostles and prophets (v. 5). We also have the help of the church itself as a community of diverse witness (v. 10). Most significantly, we are empowered by Christ, "in whom we have access to God in boldness and confidence through faith in him" (v. 12). Discerning the meaning of God's mystery for our time, therefore, is not magic. It is a matter of faith in Christ, prayer for the

Spirit's help, and an intentional reading of the words of Scripture within the context of the church.

No matter what our witness to this great mystery might be, our audience is not merely those people who fall within our influence. The audience for Christian witness is ultimately "the rulers and authorities in heavenly places" (v. 10). In the larger context of Ephesians, proclamation of the gospel is always a proclamation to the powers themselves. Our Christian witness is a part of a cosmic battle against the "spiritual forces of evil in the heavenly places" (6:12) that are hostile to God.

Responding to the Text

As the Magi gather to Bethlehem, and as the writer of Ephesians imagines a great gathering together of all things in Christ, we as Epiphany preachers can ask ourselves, as the apostle Paul did, "What is our commission or assignment as a part of this great ingathering?" In asking this question, avoid nagging folks to "get going." It is easy in the pulpit to turn the commission that grows naturally and joyfully out of our identity as baptized Christians into a kind of clock-punching, time-card watching, programmatic burden for those still willing to listen to us. Instead of this, the homiletic goal is to show that the gathering together of all things in Christ is itself a singular enlistment into what is nothing short of a cosmic Peace Corps. Those enlisted are all working together *for* peace

> THE GATHERING TOGETHER OF ALL THINGS IN CHRIST IS ITSELF A SINGULAR ENLISTMENT INTO WHAT IS NOTHING SHORT OF A COSMIC PEACE CORPS.

and justice and *against* the "spiritual forces of evil" in this world. This is an exciting, unifying mission that is meant to gather all people to the love of God manifest in Jesus Christ.

Just as Paul's commission was inclusive, our commission can cross boundaries of race, nationality, and confession. Like a tree with many branches, this wonderful and mysterious commission has many diverse aspects. Discovering and enacting one's own, unique commission within this larger enlisted force is not something that we do in isolation under a heavy weight of guilt or with an attitude of works-righteousness. Instead, we work with one another in the church, reading and studying the words of Scripture and supporting one another in diverse forms of witness. Most of all, we live into our commission empowered by joy and hope because we are a part of God's great mystery initiated in the incarnation and baptism of Jesus Christ.

THE GOSPEL
MATTHEW 2:1-12 (RCL, BCP, RC)

Interpreting the Text

In Matthew 2 Jesus moves from being the divinely conceived Emmanuel to the politically endangered child-ruler of Israel. At this early stage Matthew's narrative begins to establish the larger context of violence and rivalry for power that will ultimately lead to Jesus' crucifixion. This chapter also begins to set forth one of Matthew's subtexts, in which Jesus' life is paralleled to the life of Moses, who, due to circumstances beyond his control, found himself exiled in Egypt. So it is that the child Jesus escapes into Egypt when Herod out of jealousy orders the murder of all children in proximity to Bethlehem who were two years and under.

One of Matthew's goals in this portion of chapter 2 is to establish the fact that there are different degrees of receptivity to Jesus as Messiah. Preachers should be aware of the potential to promote a message of anti-Judaism in response to the way that Matthew structures his narrative at this point. On one extreme is Herod, who is openly hostile to the Messiah, fearful for his lineage in response to the child whose Davidic genealogy Matthew so clearly established in chapter 1. In a second group are the chief priests and scribes, whom Matthew associates with Herod as unwitting collaborators. In relation to the larger narrative, Matthew wants to paint a picture of Jewish leaders who are beginning to recognize the threat to their own authority and way of life that is represented by a birth that is attracting Gentile worshipers into the holy city. The possibilities for the disruption of the religious and political status quo would have been evident. Herod and (by guilt of association) the chief priests and scribes stand in narrative contrast to the passionate Magi, astrologers from Persia, who represent Gentiles from far and near who seek after the truth. Whereas King Herod and *"all* Jerusalem" are "frightened" (v. 3) and seek in various ways to ignore or undermine the messianic mission, the Magi journey through this entire scene with bold determination and dignity. Their one mission is to pay homage to the Christ child. As we will see, this association of the scribes and Pharisees with violent political forces will need to be handled very carefully by preachers in order to avoid furthering dangerous stereotypes of Jews in the church today.

Matthew's Christology takes another leap forward in this chapter. In chapter 1, Jesus was genealogically connected to the David monarchy. Here he is also, as a child, made into a narrative figure of the humble and gentle Davidic king. Jesus is called "the child" eight times in chapter 2, and his own life is placed within the context of Israel's other children, who will suffer terrible violence at the hands of Herod. In v. 6, Matthew indicates, in the legitimating words of Mic. 5:2, that this child is also the shepherd of Israel, who like David rises from humble origins under the star of God's favor and providential care. The presence of the star possibly indicates to the reader that this child is a David-type who will be a shepherd for God's people.

Matthew's Gospel was written around 85–90 C.E., probably to a primarily Jewish-Christian congregation. The many parallels that Matthew draws between Jesus and Moses and David would not be lost on this audience. Each comparison, however, highlights both similarities and differences. In this instance, the primary difference lies in the identity and mission of Matthew's church. This church has begun to incorporate Gentiles into its midst. For this reason, it is important that this new shepherd of Israel is gathering to himself Gentiles from afar as well as Jews. Hospitality to strangers, which is at the very heart of the Law, is finding a new, creative impetus through Jesus, and Matthew's narrative indicates that this hospitality emanates from the manger in Bethlehem.

Responding to the Text

Parker Palmer, in his book *The Courage to Teach: Exploring the Inner Landscape of a Teacher's Life* identifies what he calls a "sequence of fears" that exerts great control in all of our lives. This sequence begins in a "fear of diversity." Once diversity is embraced, a second fear emerges, "the fear of conflict." At the heart of this fear is a third layer of fear, the "fear of losing identity." Deeper still, Palmer identifies one final fear: "the fear that a live encounter with otherness will challenge or even compel us to change our lives." He concludes, "Otherness always invites transformation."[2] This multi-layered fear of the encounter with the other is, in large part, what "frightens" Herod and all of Jerusalem with him. The wise men who have come to pay homage to the Christ child represent other cultures, other faiths, other philosophical systems, and other ways of seeking God's presence and power. The Epiphany of Christ is in many ways a gathering to the glory of God, the same glory found throughout the Hebrew scripture. This glory is once again being extended not only to insiders, but also to many others.

The appearance of strangers in our midst naturally generates some fear, but it can also present an opportunity for us to overcome our fears of genuine encounter with others who are seeking after God, and to consider the transformation in our own lives that can come from such encounters. One homiletic strategy might be to find a way for your hearers to experience something of the fear of diversity, conflict, loss of identity, and change that the presence of these wise men represented to the status quo on that day long ago . . . the same kind of fear that the presence of people of other faiths creates in our own lives. As you do this, avoid stereotyping the Pharisees and scribes. Their fears were quite natural and not tied necessarily to any evil motive or plot—as was the case for Herod. It is the same kind of fear that Christians, Jews, and those of other faiths experience for each other—fear that need not escalate into conflict or violence, but could, perhaps, lead to life-changing encounters. What are parallels in our own time? What does this mean for our understanding of our own identity and mission as Christians? How can we extend the hospitality of the manger to those of all faiths? How can we make it clear to Jews

HOW CAN WE EXTEND THE HOSPITALITY OF THE MANGER TO THOSE OF ALL FAITHS?

today who, in a post-Holocaust world, may feel threatened by the presence of Christians, that they need not fear; indeed, that Christ can be seen in many ways as a living presence of the universal, welcoming *shalom* at the heart of *torah*, and not a threatening supersession of it?

Another strategy for preaching is to bring the congregation into a sustained dialogue with these wise men from the East. How is it that in an age so burdened with political chaos and the deceptive secrecy of Herod these wise men are able to cultivate an almost naïve, single-minded determination to seek God's truth? There is something refreshing about the determination of these wise men that makes them important role models for us as Epiphany Christians. Søren Kierkegaard entitled one of his books *Purity of Heart Is to Will One Thing*.[3] This certainly rings true of these Magi.

Another question that we might ask of these wise men is, "How can you be so receptive to God's signs that lead you in your journey?" Although most of us are not carefully attuned to stars and dreams, what can we learn from these wise men about looking at the world and into our own inner lives in search of signs that will lead us to Christ? Another part of our dialogue with the Magi concerns their emotional receptivity to Christ. What kinds of religious feelings and sensibilities have they cultivated in their lives that help them to release themselves so that they can be "overwhelmed with joy" (v. 10) in the presence of Christ? How can we learn to rise above our feelings of fearfulness, inadequacy, anxiety, or boredom, and permit the presence of Christ to overwhelm us with joy?

Another question: What can we learn about thankful worship from these strangers in our midst? How is it that their response to Christ leads them not just to fumble through a few habitual phrases of obeisance, but to kneel down and "open their treasure chests" (v. 11) and offer Christ the very finest gifts that they could bring? What do they see in that manger that prompts all of this mysterious activity that seems to take place in a different reality altogether than that of Herod? What makes them willing to cross borders, set aside their own religious, cultural, and philosophical presuppositions, even for a moment, and acknowledge this child as the one worthy of worship?

Finally, remember once again the terrible context of idolatry and violence in which this wonderful act of worship takes place. Madeleine Sweeney Miller in her poem "How Far to Bethlehem?" includes these verses:

> "How far is it to Bethlehem Town?"
>
> "Just over Jerusalem hills adown,
> Past lovely Rachel's white-domed tomb—
> Sweet shrine of motherhood's young doom."[4]

The journey of the Magi through Jerusalem is a long and winding pilgrimage under the shadow of death itself. Epiphany, therefore, begins to sound the sobering note that Christmas has begun a journey toward Lent and Good Friday. The power that attracts the Magi to Christ is the power of love. In Matthew's Gospel we can already see that God in Jesus Christ is not planning to enter into armed combat with the forces of evil in the world. God acts on God's own terms, and those terms are defined by love. In spite of the violence of Herod and others who would like to set the terms by which we live according to standards that are hostile to God, the God of love creates life—a child, whose mission and purpose is to gather all people to the love of God. The Christ child has come to help reestablish the very terms of our engagement with one another as human beings.

THE BAPTISM OF OUR LORD / FIRST SUNDAY AFTER THE EPIPHANY

JANUARY 11, 2004
FIRST SUNDAY IN ORDINARY TIME

REVISED COMMON	EPISCOPAL (BCP)	ROMAN CATHOLIC
Isa. 43:1-7	Isa. 42:1-9	Isa. 40:1-5, 9-11
Psalm 29	Ps. 89:1-29	Ps. 104:1b-2, 3-4, 24-25,
	or 89:20-29	27-28, 29b-30
Acts 8:14-17	Acts 10:34-38	Titus 2:11-14; 3:4-7
Luke 3:15-17, 21-22	Luke 3:15-16, 21-22	Luke 3:15-16, 21-22

This Sunday presents an opportunity to point to Jesus Christ as a harbinger of hope—not only in the first century but in our lives today. Just as the voice from heaven confirms that Jesus is God's beloved, we can hear the same message. At the same time, we celebrate our own baptisms; that we too have gone into the waters of God's redemptive grace and are now living a radically new identity. This identity unfolds in many ways during the season following the Epiphany, ways that are often mysterious, sometimes challenging, and always life-transforming.

FIRST READING
ISAIAH 43:1-7 (RCL);
ISAIAH 42:1-9 (BCP);
ISAIAH 40:1-5, 9-11 (RC)

Interpreting the Text

In Isa. 39:5-7, the prophet foretells Judah's exile in Babylon. Between chapters 39 and 40, an interlude of 150 years takes place. During this interval Israel is indeed led into a terrible captivity in Babylon. Worst of all, the city of Jerusalem was destroyed, along with the temple. The resounding note of comfort sounded in 40:1-11 answers the lamentations of God's people (Lam. 1:1-2, 9, 17, 21).

Although chapters 42-43 begin to sound the note of God's deliverance, it must be remembered that the Babylonian exile is interpreted by the prophet as God's judgment. Deliverance, therefore, is deliverance from sin, as well as a deliverance from undeserved suffering. Because its witness of justice had failed, Israel lost favor in God's eyes. There was some question about whether God's special covenant with Israel remained steadfast. In chapters 40, 42, and 43, Second Isaiah announces that God has decided to reestablish this covenant relationship. Israel is the "servant" who will bring forth justice to the nations (42: 1), a "covenant to the people, a light to the nations" (42:6). God has decided to go so far as to let go of God's favor for nations, notably Ethiopia, Egypt, and Seba, "in exchange for" Israel (43:3).

Isaiah 43 addresses people who are fearful, dispersed, feeling anonymous, and in danger of being overwhelmed by their circumstances. YHWH speaks to them as a loving creator and adoptive parent who calms their fears, calls them by name, gathers them from the east and west, and offers them power, strength, and courage to endure the floodwaters and fires around them. Whenever there is some question about whether or not God is faithful to God's people who find themselves in the direst of circumstances, these words of the prophet can be applied like a healing ointment. Here God chooses us and adopts us in the same way that we are adopted and called by name at our baptisms. At the same time that water and fire of our baptism tests our faith and refines our hope, baptism grafts us to a God who walks with us in this difficult process.

WHENEVER THERE IS SOME QUESTION ABOUT WHETHER OR NOT GOD IS FAITHFUL TO GOD'S PEOPLE WHO FIND THEMSELVES IN THE DIREST OF CIRCUMSTANCES, THESE WORDS OF THE PROPHET CAN BE APPLIED LIKE A HEALING OINTMENT.

Isaiah 43 is a prophecy of deliverance, but ultimately this deliverance is for God's glory (v. 7). When God has decided to embrace Judah, the glory of Judah becomes the glory of YHWH. Judah's deliverance shines a glorious light onto God, who becomes a hope for all people everywhere who are lost, exiled, scattered, or overwhelmed.

Responding to the Text

Equilibrium must be disrupted in order for change to occur. These texts are a testimony to this hard fact of human existence. Judgment precedes deliverance. Baptismal identity can only be had by journeying through the sometimes chaotic waters of repentance and regeneration. These same chaotic waters rage all around us in a post-everything generation. Preachers can point this out by raising certain questions. As our children claim entitlement to cell phones, personal computers, nicer cars, and bigger houses, do we yet feel the disequilibrium of living in a foreign land? What will it take for those of us in North America to wake up to the hard reality that, as we sink further and further into consumerism and militarism, we may well be becoming the late modern equivalent of Babylon? If September 11, 2001, was not enough to expose the chaotic waters roaring beneath us, what will it take? Nuclear or environmental disaster on a global scale? Clearly something in the 150-year interlude between chapters 39 and 40 caused a great many in Judah to cry out to God for change, for themselves as individuals and for their entire community. What will it take for us to come to a similar point of openness and readiness for real and lasting change?

Even as these questions are raised, the opening words of chapter 43 loom on the horizon as a deeply desired destination: "But now!" "Do not fear, for I have redeemed you; I have called you by name, you are mine." Perhaps we have been so busy naming this or that as God's "blessing" in our lives, or naming the world after our own likeness (Microsoft, Enron, Napster) that we have been unable to hear our own names called by God. The first step in transformation is to quit naming and renaming the world and to let ourselves be named by the God of love and justice. This is an experience of ourselves as "precious" in God's sight, "honored" and "loved" (v. 4). The reorientation that will solve all of our disorientations is this one: a radical reframing of our lives as held, sustained, and loved by God. God's alternative to Babylon begins with this naming, this adoption, the decisive word of belonging and support from God.

RESPONSIVE READING
PSALM 29 (RCL);
PSALM 89:1-29 or 89:20-29 (BCP);
PSALM 104:1b-2, 3-4, 24-25, 27-30 (RC)

Psalms 29, 89, and 104 are psalms of adoration. The words of the poet push and strain against the limitations of language. How can the glory of God be expressed? God is worthy of praise and worship (29:1-2). God is the creator who makes and sustains all things (89:11-13). God is a heavenly ruler and administrator, a righteous and just magistrate who works to strengthen the people and to bless them with peace (89: 5, 7, 10; 29:10-11). The people of Israel are especially joyful because God has made a covenant with Israel and has sustained this covenant through the servant David (89:19-29). Perhaps most striking for this Sunday, the Baptism of our Lord, is the accent on God's voice in Psalm 29. Verses 3-9 extol the power, majesty, and glory of God's sometimes creative, sometimes destructive, and sometimes redemptive voice. This voice, of course, will be heard again at the baptism of Jesus.

SECOND READING
ACTS 8:14-17 (RCL);
ACTS 10:34-38 (BCP);
TITUS 2:11-14; 3:4-7 (RC)

Interpreting the Text

The gospel of Jesus is spreading far and wide. Philip has taken the good news into Samaria, a people with a long and disputatious history with the Jews. The message of universal salvation in Acts 10:34-38 is at the heart of Luke's writing. God is impartial (v. 34) and accepts everyone from every nation who fears God and does what is right (v. 35). Luke makes it clear that, after John's baptism of Jesus, the message that has gone out is that Jesus is Lord of *all* (v. 36). Jesus both *is* this message and *has spoken* this message *(logos)*. This is now the message and mission of the church in Acts.

> LUKE MAKES IT CLEAR THAT, AFTER JOHN'S BAPTISM OF JESUS, THE MESSAGE THAT HAS GONE OUT IS THAT JESUS IS LORD OF *all*. JESUS BOTH IS THIS MESSAGE AND *has spoken* THIS MESSAGE.

It is the power of the Holy Spirit that makes this entire mission to the Gentiles a possibility. This power is so wondrous that it has attracted the attention of a famous magician in Samaria named Simon. Simon has observed that, by the laying on of hands, the apostles are able to bring about tremendous change in the lives of their followers.

Tucked within this story of Simon's confrontation with Peter and John is the lectionary passage for this Sunday. Acts 8:14-17 gives voice to an early tradition in which water baptism and the conferral of the Spirit by the laying on of hands were two separate acts. By the time of the writing of the book of Acts, these two actions had been put together (2:38; 19:5-6). It is clear that the standard practice that emerged in the early church is one in which baptism was a unified action of both repentance and spiritual adoption. Evidently, this early tradition did not ultimately hold sway and therefore should not be used to legitimate ideas of a second baptism or blessing.

What is highlighted theologically in this passage is the fact that baptism is a form of spiritual adoption. The writer of Titus also emphasizes this fact. In 3:5 he says that baptism is "the water of rebirth and renewal by the Holy Spirit." Without this power it is simply not possible to attain to the virtues of a holy life.

Responding to the Text

George Macdonald once said that "faith opens all the windows to God's wind."[5] For many in the church over the centuries there has been a nagging sense that there is something more to baptism than repentance and acceptance of Jesus Christ, as important as those things might be. Without separating spiritual adoption from baptism, making it into a separate ritual or an exotic second blessing, it is possible for preachers to ponder with their congregations the meaning of this "something more" of baptism. First, the Spirit brings a sense of deep belonging to God. As we have already seen in Isa. 43:1, spiritual adoption breaks through our anonymity with God, providing us with the experience of having been "called by name." Second, the Holy Spirit at baptism is power. This is what Simon the Magician found so attractive that he was willing to pay for it. The power conferred by the Holy Spirit, however, is not the power to lord it over others. Rather, it is the power to bear witness to the good news that Jesus Christ is Lord of all (10:36). The Holy Spirit, therefore, is the universalizing power of the gospel. Finally, the Holy Spirit is an agent of regeneration and renewal in the Christian life. This is what the Samaritans were experiencing, and this is what the letter to Titus emphasizes so strongly. It is the power of God alone that can create new life in and through us.

THE GOSPEL
LUKE 3:15-17, 21-22 (RCL);
LUKE 3:15-16, 21-22 (BCP, RC)

Interpreting the Text

Luke does not dwell on the baptism of Jesus but moves quickly to the revelation of God's confirming voice that immediately follows. In fact, his Gospel leaves us with some questions about who, indeed, baptized Jesus, since John is already in prison (v. 20). Luke clearly wants our focus to be shifted off of John and his baptism and onto Jesus and the revelation of his identity to the world. This revelation is underscored by Luke in three ways. First, "the heavens were opened." This is a frightful occurrence, because not only are the heavens the abode of God, but within the tiered cosmology of that time, the heavens also protected the earth from the waters of chaos. An opening in the heavens indicates both extreme vulnerability and the possibility of theophany. Second, the Holy Spirit descends upon Jesus. The Spirit appears to those gathered as a dove. For Luke the entire ministry of Jesus is attended and empowered by this Spirit. Third, a voice from heaven, reminiscent of the thundering voice of God in Psalm 29, announces, "You are my Son, the Beloved, with you I am well pleased" (v. 22). What, for us, is spiritual adoption at our baptism is, for Jesus, the affirmation of a sonship already claimed for him by Luke at the annunciation. For Jesus, therefore, baptism is not adoption, but divine affirmation. All three of these revelations work together to make Jesus a very significant target for the temptations by the devil that follow immediately in chapter 4.

The context of the wilderness and its parallels to the exile in Isaiah 40-43 should not be taken for granted. Not only does John's proclamation of Jesus take place in the wilderness, Jesus' baptism in Luke takes place beyond the boundaries of narrative location. We are not told where the baptism takes place. Already, Jesus is joining John in that wilderness place between worlds, a place where repentance is required, chaff will be burned away, and a new reign of God will begin. In this place, prayer is more than a pious plea for help. It is the actual touchstone of divine revelation itself (v. 21). Time and time again, in Luke's Gospel, the prayers of Jesus are pivotal to the meaning and direction of

his ministry (3:21; 6:12; 9:18-22; 9:28-29; 11:1; 22:32, 41; 23:34, 46). In the wilderness, in the nameless, placeless times of life, it is prayer that opens our lives to heavenly affirmation and direction.

Responding to the Text

Just as Luke and John the Baptist strive to take the camera lens and shift it onto Jesus, preachers can adopt the same strategy. Although it is good to rejoice at our own spiritual adoption in baptism, there is finally the requisite need to turn our eyes and behold with fear, wonder, and gratitude the divine confirmation of Jesus at *his* baptism. This is what the people who were "filled with expectation" and "questioning in their hearts" (v. 15) were longing to see and hear. They do not need another teacher. They do not need another prophet of doom. They are desperate for salvation. They are standing in the need of the prayers of one who will bring God's attention and favor upon them, who will bring the year of God's Jubilee. For Luke, the postbaptismal revelation of God announces once again that Jesus is the long-awaited messenger who will save God's people from their sins.

Our preaching and our liturgies should, therefore, in the last analysis strive to emphasize Christology and soteriology. This is the one whom God has sent into the wilderness of our lives to save us. The doorway to heaven has been cracked open, and we are beholding God's salvation and glory. The meaning of this salvation should be clear from our reading in Acts 3: God has decided to cross all boundaries and to embrace all people. God's love and justice are for all, for the whole world. In this sense, Jesus' baptism is a cosmic affirmation for a truly cosmic Christ.

SECOND SUNDAY AFTER THE EPIPHANY

JANUARY 18, 2004
SECOND SUNDAY IN ORDINARY TIME

REVISED COMMON	EPISCOPAL (BCP)	ROMAN CATHOLIC
Isa. 62:1-5	Isa. 62:1-5	Isa. 62:1-5
Ps. 36:5-10	Psalm 96 or 96:1-10	Ps. 96:1-2a, 2b-3, 7-8, 9-10
1 Cor. 12:1-11	1 Cor. 12:1-11	1 Cor. 12:4-11
John 2:1-11	John 2:1-11	John 2:1-11

The texts for this Sunday invite us to consider what happens when the wine runs out. In the midst of human suffering (Isa. 62:1-5), questions regarding the nature and mission of the church (1 Cor. 12:1-11), and the depletion of our resources for joy and celebration (John 2:1-11), God is faithful to provide a new way. In each instance, it is God's creative, renewing, and restoring mercy that brings new life and hope.

FIRST READING
ISAIAH 62:1-5 (RCL, BCP, RC)

Interpreting the Text

Israel has endured suffering during the time of a profound silence from God. In these five verses, Israel is compared to an abused and abandoned woman who experiences herself as forsaken by an unanswering God. This plight reminds us of the opening verses of Psalm 22:

> My God, my God, why have you forsaken me?
> > Why are you so far from helping me,
> from the words of my groaning?
> O my God, I cry by day, but you do not answer;
> > and by night, but find no rest.

In this case, it is the kings and nations that have abused Israel, stripping her of her name and leaving her desolate.

The prophet, however, indicates that God has decided to break the silence and to intervene on Israel's behalf. Israel will be given a new name, a new opportunity for renewal, growth, and productivity. Her old names, "forsaken" and "desolate," will be exchanged for new names, "my delight is in her" and "married" (v. 4). The Hebrew word for "married" comes from the same word for fertility, *be'ulah,* and is the root of our expression "Beulah land." The great builder has decided to marry Israel, to reestablish a covenant of love and care with her and to restore her to glory (v. 5). This image of God and Israel as bridegroom and bride should not be sentimentalized. After the almost naïve optimism of chapters 60 and 61, these verses assert that YHWH is now beginning to act for Israel's vindication. This marriage is not just a new "falling in love." Rather, this marriage is a social and political act, the assertion of God's power for justice. God has heard the cries of the abused and suffering Israel and will now intervene to restore her honor in the face of her abusers.

Responding to the Text

There are many people all around us whose lives are torn apart by violence, abuse, neglect, and abandonment, for whom God's voice has seemed silent for years. We are not speaking here of the pervasive and largely unnoticed silence of God that exists in a culture of luxury and ease, as important as that may be to recognize. Here we are talking about the more radical silence of God experienced by those who have been victims of violence against their own personhood, bodies, and/or nation. Johannes Baptist Metz, in his final lecture at Münster, argued that European and American Christians have much to learn from Israel's suffering:

THIRD ISAIAH, BY REFERRING TO THE SILENCE OF GOD, REMINDS US THAT WE, AS CHRISTIANS, CANNOT JOIN FORCES WITH AN AFFLUENT SOCIETY THAT TRIES TO AVOID, DENY, OR OVERLOOK THE INNOCENT SUFFERING THROUGHOUT HISTORY AND ALL AROUND US.

> Christian God-talk has lost its sensitivity to suffering. From the beginning Christian theology attempted to keep its distance from the troubling question of justice for innocent sufferers by transforming it into a question of the redemption of sinners. . . . Christianity transformed itself from a morality of suffering into a morality of sin; a Christianity sensitive to suffering became a Christianity sensitive to sin. Primary attention was given not to the suffering of creation but to its guilt.[6]

Third Isaiah, by referring to the silence of God, reminds us that we, as Christians, cannot join forces with an affluent society that tries to avoid, deny, or overlook the innocent suffering throughout history and all around us. Both God's silence and our silence can become a matter of complicity with evil.

Once we have identified the web of violence and innocent suffering that stretches from the domestic abuse in our midst to oppression and genocide around the world, one homiletic strategy is to begin to identify ourselves as the missing helper in these verses, one who takes God's part as a "builder," who "marries" the forsaken and desolate in order to provide for new names, new opportunities for fruitfulness and life. Our congregations can be invited to see themselves as God's representatives, no longer silent, but those who call the forsaken by new names, whose mission is one of vindication and salvation for those who suffer.

RESPONSIVE READING
PSALM 36:5-10 (RCL)

The controlling theme of Ps. 36:5-10 is God's steadfast love *(hesed)*. Verses 5-6 offer a vision of the *extent* of God's *hesed,* and of the other qualities of God's providence that accompany it: faithfulness, righteousness, judgment, and salvation. Verses 7-9 articulate the *benefits* of God's *hesed*. Not only does it provide refuge, it establishes abundance of food and drink and wellsprings of light and life. The references are clearly liturgical as well as social and economic. Finally, the psalmist prays for the *continuance* of God's *hesed* (v. 10). The redundancy of the idea of "continuing" that which is "steadfast" only serves to accentuate the plea of the psalmist for God's favor within the covenant.

PSALM 96 or 96:1-10 (BCP);
PSALM 96:1-3, 7-10 (RC)

Psalm 96 is a psalm of proclamation. We are told to "sing," "declare," "ascribe," and "say" that the Lord is great and greatly to be praised (vv. 2, 3, 7-8, 10). This psalm encourages us to use everything that we have to express God's glory in our midst. This is also a psalm that invites us to consider new ways of praising, proclaiming, and worshiping God. We are encouraged to sing "a new song" (v. 1), to "bring an offering," and to "worship the Lord in holy splendor" (vv. 8-9). At the heart of all of our proclamation and worship is praise, and the praise of God is new every day.

SECOND READING

1 CORINTHIANS 12:1-11 (RCL, BCP);
1 CORINTHIANS 12:4-11 (RC)

Interpreting the Text

First Corinthians, which is actually the second letter Paul wrote to this church (see 1 Cor. 5:9), was written in large part to address news of conflict within the church. This news had reached Paul's ears through messengers sent by Chloe (1:11). In chapter 12 Paul is addressing a division that has arisen because some have asserted that there is, or should be, a hierarchy of spiritual gifts. Paul begins to address this problem by arguing that the Holy Spirit, and the power and gifts given by that Spirit, are not things to be trifled with (v. 3). He reminds the Corinthian congregation that they are no longer pagans who can be enticed and led astray by idols. They are now those who confess that "Jesus is Lord," a confession that brings them squarely within the domain of God's singular and unifying Spirit. In vv. 4-6, Paul uses proto-trinitarian language, referring to the "same Spirit," the "same Lord," and the "same God" to show the Corinthian church members that the unity-in-diversity that they are to express in their common life should mirror the unity of God's own self-expression.

In all cases, the "saming" dynamics move toward God and God's Spirit, while the "othering" dynamics move toward the needs of the world. The Greek words for "another" (*hetero* and *allo*) are mixed together in vv. 8-10 to show a constant process of gifting "others," accomplished by the "same" Spirit.

to another . . . the utterance of knowledge	according to the same Spirit
to another faith	by the same Spirit
to another gifts of healing	by the one Spirit
to another the working of miracles	
to another prophecy	
to another the discernment of spirits	
to another various kinds of tongues	
to another the interpretation of tongues	activated by one and the same Spirit

It is the Spirit who "allots" these gifts as the Spirit chooses (v. 11). Just as the Spirit is always seeking "another" way to heal, redeem, and unify the church, so the Spirit also controls the process whereby these gifts are chosen and distributed. Church members need not worry about ordering or arranging this process.

Postmodernity brings with it a sense of exhaustion. How can we prop up a weary and increasingly irrelevant church? How can seminaries create the kinds of leaders that will be needed for the next generation? What can we do when the old gifts for preaching, worship leadership, Sunday school teaching, and social witness don't seem to fit the way the world is heading? One way to respond would be to follow the members of the church at Corinth and seek to create a tighter system whereby gifts for ministry can be discerned, trained, and ordered. Within an airtight system, with a clear hierarchy of gifts, those having certain gifts would be chosen and placed accordingly. Perhaps the best scientific procedures for church management should be used to guide us in this generation.

Without denying the need for structure in the church, 1 Corinthians 12 warns us against attempts to too tightly control, bind, or constrict the "gifting" work of the Holy Spirit in the church. Preachers therefore can encourage the church to pay attention to the "othering" work of the Holy Spirit, those creative ways through which the Spirit is seeking to meet the needs of this generation. In this process it will be necessary to draw attention to the

> WITHOUT DENYING THE NEED FOR STRUCTURE IN THE CHURCH, 1 CORINTHIANS 12 WARNS US AGAINST ATTEMPTS TO TOO TIGHTLY CONTROL, BIND, OR CONSTRICT THE "GIFTING" WORK OF THE HOLY SPIRIT IN THE CHURCH.

"same Spirit" who gives these gifts. This will help the church avoid creating a new hierarchy whereby someone with the newer and more electrifying gifts is placed in a position of more importance than someone whose gift is more traditional or less conspicuous. The gift of crafting "seeker services," for instance, cannot be more highly valued than the gift of hospital visitation. Preachers therefore can accentuate two things: the reality that the Holy Spirit is still choosing to allot "another" set of gifts to churches in need of renewal and hope, and the fact that every gift, no matter how seemingly small, is a gift from the same Spirit, and is, therefore, of equal value to God.

THE GOSPEL
JOHN 2:1-11 (RCL, BCP, RC)

Interpreting the Text

The wedding at Cana is one of the most mysterious and ambiguous stories in the entire Bible. The notation "on the third day" (v. 1) is patently unclear.

The nature and purpose of Jesus' conversation with his mother in v. 4 is vague at best. Jesus' refusal to act, followed by his striking performance of a miracle, makes him appear somewhat indecisive or unaware of what is happening. It is hard to imagine what need there might be for somewhere between 120–180 gallons of wine. The steward's elliptical reference to "having kept the good wine until now" (v. 10) invites multiple interpretations. It is hard to see how saving a wedding party, even by means of a miracle, can be interpreted as having "revealed his [Jesus'] glory" (v. 11), something that in John's Gospel is almost entirely reserved for Jesus' passion and resurrection. Alongside of this is the fact that, in light of Isaiah 62, the entire metaphor of the wedding itself is shot through with eschatological significance as an image of the surplus and joy that will accompany the final redemption of God's people. Is this story meant to indicate that Jesus is a fulfillment of this prophecy? But then he is not the bridegroom at Cana; he is a guest. What are we to make of this odd "paradigm shift"? Clearly, this story invites confusion and baffles us—which is, in part, its "point." Jesus is a disruptive, unpredictable, and subversive presence, wherever he goes.

In the midst of this confusion, it is important not to forget Mary's role in this story. The Roman Catholic lectionary used to include v. 12, in which Jesus' mother is included with his brothers and disciples in his mission to Capernaum. This helps us to see her persistence in this story as a picture of healthy discipleship. She trusts that Jesus will act, even though he has sternly reminded her that she must honor his freedom and timing. By telling the servants to do whatever he tells them to do, she indicates that she has not lost her fundamental belief that Jesus will respond to this crisis so that the celebration might proceed.

In the final analysis, this story, as John tells us, is meant to be a sign. Within the ethos of mystery and through his single-minded sense of mission and divine timing, Jesus is revealing to his disciples and to all those who will believe that his life is a direct manifestation of God's glory. Albeit naïvely, the steward correctly identifies that Jesus is the "good wine" that has been saved until last. The wedding at Cana is a sign that the good wine is abundant and that the celebration of the Word made flesh has begun.

> THE WEDDING AT CANA IS A SIGN THAT THE GOOD WINE IS ABUNDANT AND THAT THE CELEBRATION OF THE WORD MADE FLESH HAS BEGUN.

Responding to the Text

The mystery and ambiguity of this story set the tone for preaching. Somehow the preacher must capture the feeling that Jesus simply does not fit in neatly as an invited guest in the ordinary routines and rituals of our lives. Bernard of Clairvaux once said that "God . . . has sent to earth a sackful of his mercy, as it were; a sack that in the passion must be rent, so that the price of our redemption may pour out of it. Only a little sack it is, but it is full."[7] The strangeness and abundance of God's glory manifest in Jesus Christ will not be easily contained in the old wineskins of our habits or expectations. In John's Gospel, Jesus is the Word made flesh, and the flesh can barely contain the word that it embodies. We can only approach this Jesus with awe and wonder, and with complete openness to what he can and will do in our lives.

Within the context of Jesus' strangeness and abundance as the Word made flesh, we may venture to trust deeply, as Mary did, that Jesus will act to meet the desperate scarcity that haunts each of our lives and the world in which we live. We can be bold, as she was, to bring that scarcity before Jesus. We can also trust Jesus' freedom and sense of timing, reigning in our own impatience and reminding others to be sure to do what he asks once he decides to act.

Ultimately, however, we cannot reduce this story to the framework of our own needs. Something huge is being pointed to in this story, in between its lines, in and through the ambiguity and mystery that keeps it from reducing to one or two easily preachable "points." This story acts as a symbol, which as Paul Tillich tells us "points beyond itself" and "participates in that to which it points." This is why "glory" is revealed by Jesus' actions in this story, not because he met a human need, as important as that is, but because this is the Word of God made flesh to dwell among us, in all of its richness, strangeness, and abundance.

THIRD SUNDAY
AFTER THE EPIPHANY

January 25, 2004
Third Sunday in Ordinary Time

Revised Common	Episcopal (BCP)	Roman Catholic
Neh. 8:1-3, 5-6, 8-10	Neh. 8:2-10	Neh. 8:2-4a, 5-6, 8-10
Psalm 19	Psalm 113	Ps. 19:8, 9, 10, 15
1 Cor. 12:12-31a	1 Cor. 12:12-27	1 Cor. 12:12-30
		or 12:12-14, 27
Luke 4:14-21	Luke 4:14-21	Luke 1:1-4; 4:14-21

This Sunday the community of faith moves into the foreground as a redemptive agent. The Nehemiah text makes it clear that when the community of faith is experiencing times of trouble, the people of God must take initiative. The texts from 1 Corinthians 12 support this idea, encouraging the community to find new ways to value its members, especially those who are considered to be of lesser value. At the center of this community resides the greatest gift: love. This love is made possible because God's Jubilee has begun in Jesus Christ and is finding its way into the world in and through the mission of the church.

First Reading
NEHEMIAH 8:1-3, 5-6, 8-10 (RCL);
NEHEMIAH 8:2-10 (BCP);
NEHEMIAH 8:2-4a, 5-6, 8-10 (RC)

Interpreting the Text

We move now to a very different point in history, following the conquest of Babylon by King Cyrus of Persia in 539 B.C.E. Ezra-Nehemiah is the only biblical document we have that provides some insight into the formation of the new nation, now reduced to a small province of the Persian Empire called Judah (Judea). What is at stake for the people of God is far more than the reestablishment of a viable economy and society. This was the center of Nehemiah's efforts as ruler. What is really at stake is the restoration of the people's sacred identity as God's covenant community. This, in particular, was the task of Ezra. Ezra, in chapter 8, emerges as a kind of new Moses who will help to focus energy and imagination on this specific religious concern. Two key differences, however, mark Ezra's leadership. Both of these are readily seen in 8:1-10.

First, there is now a dramatic shift away from the singular leader toward the community itself as those who are responsible to redefine religious identity. Notice that it is the "people" (vv. 1, 5, 6, 7, 8, 9) rather than the leaders who "gathered together into the square before the Water Gate" and "told the scribe Ezra to bring the book of the Law of Moses, which the Lord had given to Israel" (v. 1). The community is now taking the initiative, insisting that the leaders in their midst help them to find their way.

Second, it is now the written text of the Law *(torah)* that has become the primary source for the inspiration and guidance of the people of God. We are told that "the ears of all the people were attentive to the book of the law" (v. 3). It is this book that Ezra interprets from a pulpit-like wooden platform (v. 4) and to which his assistants give "sense" so that all may understand (vv. 5, 7, 8). Another striking indication that the locus of authority is shifting from the mouth of their leaders to a more participatory form of text-based interpretation and discernment is the participation of women in this official religious gathering *(qahal).*

These verses in chapter 8 are the climax of Ezra-Nehemiah. After the walls of Jerusalem were restored, it was fitting that the people gather for a public hearing of their ancestral stories, poems, and teachings. What better occasion for this than the holy day of Sukkot. This provided an occasion for an extended festival of recommitment and hope. The stories of Israel's past relationship with God, of ancient blessings, broken and restored relationship, difficult passages through waters and wildernesses, read from early morning until midday reduced the people to lamentation and tears. It is not

> THIS IS AN ABSOLUTELY PIVOTAL TEXT FOR ANY COMMUNITY OF FAITH THAT, HAVING EXPERIENCED BROKENNESS, DECIDES TO GO IN SEARCH OF ITS OWN HEALING.

clear whether this was Ezra's intention, but having experienced through this deep act of remembrance their own guilt, sin, and separation from God as well as their own relationship with God, Ezra exerts his leadership by reminding them that this is a holy day: a festival of celebration and joy. The reading and interpretation of God's word is, ultimately, meant to bring about healing and renewal (v. 9-10).

Responding to the Text

This is an absolutely pivotal text for any community of faith that, having experienced brokenness, decides to go in search of its own healing. Time and time again, communities that have been destroyed by natural disasters, social or political upheaval, internal dysfunction, or the sinfulness of their leadership must find their way toward healing. The first step in this process is to gather together and to call forth a leader who will faithfully read and interpret their sacred texts and traditions. This work of interpretation can be expanded through the designation of many assistants who will see to it that the plain sense of these texts and traditions are heard and understood by all.

The second thing that needs to happen is that the community must grieve what it has lost. Hearing God's Law, *torah,* reminds the community of how far it is from God's vision for it. So much has been lost. How can it ever be recovered?

The final movement is to begin to experience the redeeming presence of the holy in the midst of the community. The holiness of God is no longer bound to sacerdotal people or set-apart places. It is a gift available for whatever community embraces torah and is able to follow torah in the living of life everyday. This is something that can be celebrated, and that can bring joy and hope in the midst of despair. It is also the cornerstone of a new identity and of new forms of community.

RESPONSIVE READING

PSALM 19 (RCL);
PSALM 19:8-10, 15 (RC);
PSALM 113 (BCP)

─────────────────────

Psalm 19 begins by celebrating the wonders of God in nature. Although vv. 1-6 stand well enough alone as a hymn to God's creation of heaven and earth, these verses serve the purpose of setting up the presentation of the perfection, value, and desirability of the "law of the Lord" in vv. 7-10. Not only is the glory of God revealed in the natural world, but God's glory is also poured out richly in *torah.* Notice that vv. 7-10 reads like a litany:

Leader:	The law of the LORD is perfect,
Congregation:	reviving the soul;
Leader:	the decrees of the LORD are sure,
Congregation:	making wise the simple;
Leader:	the precepts of the LORD are right,
Congregation:	rejoicing the heart;
Leader:	the commandment of the LORD is clear,
Congregation:	enlightening the eyes;

Leader:	the fear of the LORD is pure,	
Congregation:	enduring forever;	
Leader:	the ordinances of the Lord are true and righteous altogether.	
All:	More to be desired are they than gold, even much fine gold; sweeter also than honey, and drippings of the honeycomb.	

This is the stuff of powerful and moving liturgy, centering the congregation on *torah,* which adds a new aspect of glory to the God who created heaven and earth.

Keeping *torah,* however, must be a matter of the heart as well as the lips. The psalmist, therefore, pleads for a final grace, that those who pray the psalm might be cleared "from hidden faults" (v. 12). Only in this way will the sacrifice of praise and the meditations of the heart expressed in the psalm become "acceptable" (v. 14).

Psalm 113 strikes a similar note of praise for the God of creation. This psalm, from the cycle of psalms called the Hallel (Psalms 113–118), was a part of the Passover celebration and would have called to mind Israel's experience of suffering and redemption during the Exodus. The psalmist extends God's goodness not only to the creation and to those who approach God with a deep desire to keep the law, but to all of those who are needy, poor, or experiencing barrenness (vv. 7-9).

SECOND READING

1 CORINTHIANS 12:12-31a (RCL);
1 CORINTHIANS 12:12-17 (BCP);
1 CORINTHIANS 12:12-30
or 12:12-14, 27 (RC)

Interpreting the Text

This is one of the most remarkable texts in the New Testament for its subtle subversion of status quo expectations for social and institutional relationships. The "body" was frequently used by orators as a metaphor for social and political institutions. The normal usage of this metaphor was in support of hierarchical social arrangements designed to subordinate less important members of society to those with more status and ability. Paul subverts this idea and presses the metaphor toward a new vision of community in which lesser members of a community are seen to be of significant value.

We should be clear that Paul does not abandon hierarchy. As v. 31 reminds us, Paul does believe that some parts of the body have "greater gifts" than others. Paul has no problem in retaining this aspect of the metaphor. What Paul calls into question, however, is the equation of this giftedness with an increased *value* in God's eyes. The dissension within the Corinthian church stemmed, in part, from a devaluation of those whose gifts were less pronounced, more modest, or even hidden from sight altogether.

Paul's argument begins, as it did in vv. 1-11, with the ground-leveling oneness of the Holy Spirit (vv. 12-13). From there, he argues for the diversity of the body of Christ. In order to make this argument, he emphasizes how ludicrous or even grotesque it would be if the body were simply a "single member" (v. 19). From this visual picture of diversity, Paul moves on to argue for the profound interdependence of the members of the body (v. 21). Based on this interdependence, Paul asserts finally that the "weaker" and less significant parts of the body are, in fact, "indispensable" (v. 22) and worthy of honor and respect (vv. 23-24). This, he concludes, should help the Corinthian congregation to overcome the dissension in their midst. Since they are profoundly interdependent, they should be able to show the same care for one another (v. 25), the kind of care that is expressed in mutual suffering and rejoicing in the living of life (v. 26).

It is on this platform of diversity, interdependence, and mutual respect and care that Paul begins to build his argument toward *love* as the greatest gift that each member of the church can have in chapter 13. Verses 27-31a begin this buildup, highlighting the diverse gifts in the church and the fact that some of these gifts can, indeed, be striven for in prayer and action. The hierarchy that has been submerged by Paul's argument for interdependence and

IT IS ON THIS PLATFORM OF DIVERSITY, INTERDE-
PENDENCE, AND MUTUAL RESPECT AND CARE THAT
PAUL BEGINS TO BUILD HIS ARGUMENT TOWARD LOVE
AS THE GREATEST GIFT THAT EACH MEMBER OF THE
CHURCH CAN HAVE.

mutual value among the gifts reemerges at this point. It is crucial to remember, however, that "greater" (v. 31) does not, in this context, mean more valuable, honorable, or respectable, or in any way set apart and distinct from the rest of the body.

Responding to the Text

Similar to preaching one of Jesus' parables of reversal (the Good Samaritan, for instance), the preacher is confronted with the difficult task of taking this all too familiar text and bringing out the truly subversive qualities that it communicated in its own context. What metaphors today do we apply to human institutions that can harbor a similar destructive vision for communal life that needs correcting? Perhaps one metaphor is the "network." Everyone today knows what it means when we are told to "network." It certainly doesn't mean "honoring" the "inferior members" of a social institution. The most valuable members of our "network" are those who have the most important gifts and functions—our doctors, lawyers, brokers, chief administrators, and so on. Whatever analogy is chosen, the preacher can rely on its usual usage to accentuate the ways that certain "members" surface as more honorable, respectable, indispensable, and independent. Are these same dynamics at work in the church? If so, where do we get these ideas about our social life? Where do these metaphors come from and why is it that we feel compelled to use them to support not only a hierarchy of function, but also a parallel hierarchy of value in the church and in our places of work?

The preacher can move on to press the metaphor from the perspective of our unity in the one Spirit of Christ, in the same way that Paul presses the metaphor of "body." The goal here is to show that, in Christ, a hierarchy of giftedness does not necessarily mean a hierarchy of value.

It is important to note that Paul does not call for "equal" respect and honor for "inferior members" (v. 24). Knowing that the tendency will be to "go with the flow" and to assume the prevailing interpretations of social life, Paul stresses that "greater

> A HIERARCHY OF GIFTEDNESS DOES NOT NECESSARILY MEAN A HIERARCHY OF VALUE.

honor" and "greater respect" (v. 23) will be accorded to these members so that there might be no opportunity for dissension to arise (v. 25). Since the tendency will be to adopt the status quo version of social relationships, Paul invites us to insist that, within the church, great care should be taken to subvert the status quo in the way that we live our corporate life. The best way to create this counterbalance is to raise up the lesser members of the body of Christ for more recognition and support.

Finally, it is crucial to emphasize the theological context in which the lesser members of the community are revalued. This context is the unifying, baptismal grace imparted by the "one" Spirit, in which "Jews and Greeks, slaves and free" (v. 13) and "male and female"(Gal. 3:28) are given ultimate value by God. This nullifies race, class, and gender as significant designations for establishing any hierarchy of role or value in the church. If we do not point this out, Paul's separation of a hierarchy of gifts from one of value, no matter how revolutionary, could be used subtly to undermine the pursuit of these gifts by those who are typically society's "lesser members." In other words, we might be accused of saying, in essence: "You have inferior gifts (as a woman, person of another nationality, etc.)—but that's OK—you're still valued by God. You do not need to pursue further gifts." We need, therefore, to go one step further, and to point out that, within Paul's writings, *all* are ultimately invited to "strive for the greater gifts" (v. 31).

THE GOSPEL

LUKE 4:14-21 (RCL, BCP); LUKE 1:1-4; 4:14-21 (RC)

Interpreting the Text

This is not the first time that Jesus has visited the house of God. Luke 2: 41-51 gives us the impression that Jesus may have made regular visits. Indeed, 4:16 says that it "was his custom" to go up to the synagogue on the Sabbath day, where it is likely that he took his turn reading from the scroll, providing an interpretation, and debating with those present.

This picture of Jesus unrolling the scroll and standing up "to read" (v. 16) provides a marvelous parallel to Ezra's reading of *torah* at the Water Gate. In many respects, the synagogue represented the institutionalization of the kind of participatory, scripture-centered worship that began after the Babylonian exile. The idea that Israel's leaders would emerge from among the people as interpreters and doers of the written word is an important thing to remember when we observe Jesus' ministry of proclamation in the synagogue.

If for Ezra the accent fell upon remembrance and weeping as a prelude to celebration, for Jesus, the accent clearly falls on the present moment as an eschatological fulfillment of past hopes. The words that Jesus reads, which combine the Septuagint versions of Isa. 61:1-2a with Isa. 58:6, indicate that God is present and active *now*, anointing the prophet "to bring good news to the poor," "to proclaim release to the captives and recovery of sight to the blind," and "to let the oppressed go free and to proclaim the year of the Lord's favor" (vv. 18-19). Instead of interpreting this as past event, centering in the life and ministry of the prophet, Jesus' first word to his hearers is the word "today." God's salvation is in their midst *now*. "Today, this scripture has been fulfilled in your hearing (v. 21). The future, long-awaited reign of God has finally arrived.

Note how Luke frames this new reign of God. By using Isaiah 61 as his text, Jesus indicates that he has come to inaugurate the Jubilee year. According to Leviticus 25, a Jubilee year was to occur every fifty years. During this year, the land would lie fallow, debts would be canceled, servants would be offered their freedom, and land would be restored to its original owners. Just as Paul shows that the Spirit subverts the way that we understand our social relationships (1 Corinthians 12), the idea of Jubilee is nothing short of a revolution in the way that economic relationships are to be conceived. In particular, the idea of Jubilee undermines the ability of a few to accumulate wealth at the expense of others. Jubilee mandates that every fifty years the entire economic system must begin all over again from scratch. This is not a comfortable idea for the status quo. Evidently, as we read onward in Luke's Gospel, what is good news for the poor, the captives, the blind, and the oppressed will receive a mixed reception. So it is that the way to Good Friday begins with the reading, proclamation, and faithful living out of God's Word as something not to be postponed until tomorrow, but as something requiring our most urgent response *today*.

Responding to the Text

Several years ago, John R. Colt, the author of *Becoming a Millionaire within a Year with No Effort,* coauthored with Angus MacFarlane a book entitled *Jesus of Nazareth, CEO.*[8] In this book, Colt and MacFarlane reimagine Jesus of Nazareth as the founder of a huge, global organization and examine his approach to leadership and management. The book focuses primarily on Jesus' leadership style, his charisma, the way that he held audiences spellbound, his confidence and capacity for accomplishment, his ability to make things happen, his clarity about his beliefs, his motivational skills, and his gifts as an organizer.

By using the image of Jubilee to define Jesus' ministry, Luke encourages us as preachers to control our desire to reduce Jesus' life and ministry to any set of convenient meditations on Jesus' style of leadership, no matter how practical and inspirational those meditations might be. While some of these traits may be true as broad descriptions of Jesus' leadership style, it is clear, without a doubt, that the *content* of Jesus' message would hardly lend itself to goals like "becoming a millionaire within a year with no effort." This is nowhere made more clear than in this inaugural one-sentence motivational speech by Jesus in the synagogue, in which he claims that he has come to fulfill a prophecy and become the leader of a complete economic reorganization plan, what we might call "the Jubilee plan." According to the Jubilee

> BY USING THE IMAGE OF JUBILEE TO DEFINE JESUS' MINISTRY, LUKE ENCOURAGES US AS PREACHERS TO CONTROL OUR DESIRE TO REDUCE JESUS' LIFE AND MINISTRY TO ANY SET OF CONVENIENT MEDITATIONS ON JESUS' STYLE OF LEADERSHIP, NO MATTER HOW PRACTICAL AND INSPIRATIONAL THOSE MEDITATIONS MIGHT BE.

plan, many of the goals of productivity and capital gain have to be checked at the door. The Jubilee plan requires that the land be permitted to rest, that we live in support of the environment so that it might support us. The Jubilee plan mandates that the wealthy forgive debts that are owed in order to provide a fresh start for those for whom the burden of debt has become debilitating. It requires that the system of exchange that has become a prison-house of debt, envy, and greed loosen its grip on the lives of each one of us so that we might be freed up to discover relationships that are not defined and motivated primarily by the need for monetary gain or success. The Jubilee plan encourages the limitation of growth, earning, accumulation, and speculation. At the same time, as Maria Harris points out, Jubilee encourages us to take the limits off of literacy, education, and the provision of basic economic needs such as life, liberty, health care, housing, and food.[9] Finally, the Jubilee plan means justice, that we "sort out what belongs to whom and return it."[10] The economic and social plan for which Jesus is the CEO cannot be contained within any political, economic, or social system or ideology.

Although this may sound like bad news to some—and indeed it did to many to whom Jesus proclaimed it on that day in the synagogue—it is, in fact, unflinching good news for a world that is seeking a way toward a sustainable and livable future for all. More and more, Jubilee is looking less like an impractical ideal and more like good common sense, a practical pathway toward repairing the fabric of human relationship on local, national, and global scales. Jesus, "CEO," is indeed presenting a workable answer, rooted in ancient laws and traditions, to problems that often feel overwhelming. Perhaps it is time to listen and to respond like some did that day, "amazed at the gracious words that came from his mouth" (4:22).

FOURTH SUNDAY
AFTER THE EPIPHANY

FEBRUARY 1, 2004
FOURTH SUNDAY IN ORDINARY TIME

REVISED COMMON	EPISCOPAL (BCP)	ROMAN CATHOLIC
Jer. 1:4-10	Jer. 1:4-10	Jer 1:4-5, 17-19
Ps. 71:1-6	Ps. 71:1-17	Ps. 71:1-2, 3-4,
	or 71:1-6, 15-17	5-6, 15, 17
1 Cor. 13:1-13	1 Cor. 14:12b-20	1 Cor. 12:31—13:13
		or 13:4-13
Luke 4:21-30	Luke 4:21-32	Luke 4:21-30

Jeremiah, Paul, and Jesus present challenging messages that bring them into conflict with the powers that be. In the texts from Jeremiah and Luke for this Sunday, we begin to see that being a bearer of God's word can be a difficult, fearful,
and sometimes threatening prospect. In the midst of this, the church is challenged
to set its sights on God's unique vision for the world, given in Jesus Christ. There
can be no wavering. And when there is squabbling or the kinds of internal church
conflict that might sap energy from this calling, the church must remember its mission and enforce a single-minded ethic of love (1 Corinthians 13-14).

FIRST READING
JEREMIAH 1:4-10 (RCL, BCP);
JEREMIAH 1:4-5, 17-19 (RC)

Interpreting the Text

The prophet Jeremiah wrote during turbulent times of political and social
transition. During his lifetime, Jeremiah experienced the dissolution of the Assyrian Empire, which destabilized the Southern Kingdom, Judah, so badly that no
less than four kings came and went during his watch. The nation was so badly
destabilized that Judah was a hotbed of political and social anxiety, frustration, cor-
ruption, and intrigue. Because of this, Jeremiah became exceedingly unpopular.
No one, least of all this procession of struggling kings, wanted to hear Jeremiah's
prophecies of judgment. Jeremiah's voice, however, became a touchstone that

communicated to those who would listen that God was still sovereign over the lives and history of God's people, no matter how chaotic or confused life seemed to be.

In Jer. 1:4-10, the prophet recounts his calling to be God's chosen spokesperson. The words of this text make it clear that this calling is entirely the work of God. The only words that Jeremiah speaks are words of hesitation that call to mind Moses' complaint that he was "slow of speech and slow of tongue" in Exod. 4:10. Unlike Moses, Jeremiah's complaint is that he is too young: "I am only a boy" (v. 6). This hesitation further accentuates that it is the power of God that will give the words of the prophet authority and power, not the oratorical skill or experience of the prophet himself. God's reply to Jeremiah in v. 7 emphasizes that Jeremiah's prophetic journey and his words will likewise be completely up to God.

As usual, the prophet has the need to be fearful. Anticipating the Gospel for this Sunday, in which the words of Jesus in the synagogue are rejected by those in his own hometown, the words of Jeremiah will also be rejected by many. Verse 8, therefore, speaks words of comfort: "Do not be afraid of them, for I am with you to deliver you, says the LORD." Then, as if to connect this word of comfort with Jeremiah's commissioning by God, Jeremiah presents a powerful vision of God touching his mouth (v. 9). Here the intimacy of touch is conjoined with the fearful commissioning to be God's mouthpiece in a dangerous situation. The message that Jeremiah is to bring is a divinely appointed word of judgment and hope. In the face of abuses of power and authority, Jeremiah will "pluck up" and "pull down," "destroy" and "overthrow." Where there is repentance and turning to God, Jeremiah will "build" and "plant" (v. 10).

Responding to the Text

When preaching on these words of Jeremiah, it is important to avoid a simple identification between the *person* Jeremiah and ordinary people, such as the members of a congregation. To assume that all people are known by God in this intimate way, consecrated to God's service while in the womb, is unfounded. This is also true of everyone who is called to preach. This is not necessarily the best ordination sermon text. It is unwise to assume that all preachers have had their mouths touched by God and have been appointed by God over nations and kingdoms.

> IT IS UNWISE TO ASSUME THAT ALL PREACHERS HAVE HAD THEIR MOUTHS TOUCHED BY GOD AND HAVE BEEN APPOINTED BY GOD OVER NATIONS AND KINGDOMS.

Although we cannot identify easily with the person of Jeremiah, we can identify with his *calling*. The mission of every Christian is to be a bearer of God's word in a world that does not always want to hear that word. This is a fearful and sometimes life-threatening prospect, but it cannot be avoided. This mission is uncompromising in its resistance to injustice and violence, and unrelenting in its service to freedom from idolatry and peace.

Perhaps the most profound message in this text is the picture that it paints of a sovereign God, who in the midst of tremendous social chaos and flux, acts to provide a stable reference point for all who will listen. At no other point in the history of God's people were they more in need of an awareness of God's sovereign presence. This is also true today. In a time when every system of thought is up for grabs, when people are pulled to and fro between Wall Street, pop culture, the Internet, and individual searches for meaning, success, and fulfillment, it is not difficult for us to identify with the anxiety and flux experienced by the people of Judah. Where do we look for answers? Do we ask the political scientists? The economists? Do the physicists and nuclear scientists have an answer? Do we just muddle our way through?

These verses in Jeremiah remind us that God is present in such circumstances, not as a vague amorphous mood or feeling, but as one who wants to speak to us through messengers. God's presence is heard wherever Jeremiah's hatred of idolatry, concern for abuses in worship, lamentations on behalf of the poor and destitute, and oracles of consolation and hope are faithfully lived and proclaimed.

RESPONSIVE READING
PSALM 71:1–6 (RCL);
PSALM 71:1–17 or 71:1–6, 15–17 (BCP);
PSALM 71:1–6, 15, 17 (RC)

Life is beset with snares and dangers. No one knows this better than the elderly, for whom death is an ever-present companion. Theologian and reformer John Calvin once said:

Innumerable are the evils that beset human life: innumerable, too, the deaths that threaten it. We need not go beyond ourselves; since our body is the receptacle of a thousand diseases. . . . Embark upon a ship, you are one step away from death. Mount a horse, if one foot slips, your life is imperiled. Go through the city streets, you are subject to as many dangers as there are tiles on the roofs. If there is a weapon in your hand or a friend's, harm awaits. All the fierce animals you see are armed for your destruction. But if you try to shut yourself up in a walled garden, seemingly delightful, there a serpent sometimes lies hidden. . . . Amid these tribulations must not man be most miserable, since, but half alive in life, he weakly draws his anxious and languid breath, as if he had a sword perpetually hanging over his neck?[11]

The psalmist knows what it is like to be but "half alive in life," to have a "sword perpetually hanging over his neck." Psalm 71 is written by one who, like Calvin, is aware that life is at best precarious and insecure.

The psalmist does not lie around moping and fretting. Instead, he cries out to God for help in the midst of distress. The psalmist knows that God can be trusted for deliverance from all of the enemies that lie waiting. When we join in repeating these words in worship, we too are crying out in confidence that God is "the rock of refuge," a "strong fortress" (v. 3). As with many other psalms of lament, the context for lamentation is trust in God that is rooted in the memory of what God has already done for us personally and for all of God's people in every generation.

Second Reading
1 CORINTHIANS 13:1-13 (RCL);
1 CORINTHIANS 12:31—13:13
or 13:4-13 (RC);
1 CORINTHIANS 14:12b–20 (BCP)

Interpreting the Text

By now it should be clear that Paul considers the church to be a charismatic fellowship. It is therefore incorrect to use chapters 13-14 to denigrate speaking in tongues. Paul makes it clear that he himself speaks in tongues and finds it to be a valuable aspect of this own spiritual life (vv. 14, 17). He also tells us that it is the Spirit who gives to us the many gifts, including tongues, that exist in the church, as we saw in chapter 12.

In chapters 13 and 14, however, Paul makes it clear that the entire charismatic life and energy of the church must be under the governance of an ethic of love in which building up the body of Christ is the fundamental commitment. According to Paul, it is love that is a "still more excellent way" (12:31). Love is not one of the gifts per se. Rather, it is the "way" in which all of these gifts come to their proper fulfillment.

In order to make this argument for love as the ruling ethic for church life, Paul begins by emphasizing that it is love that gives *substance* to all of the spiritual gifts in the church. Without love, these gifts simply amount to nothing. They have no real, lasting substance (vv. 1-3).

Paul moves on to define eight essential characteristics of love (vv. 4-7). These characteristics are precisely the opposite of the character traits that are bringing division into the Corinthian congregation: envy, pride, rudeness, irritability, resent-fulness, and so on. Paul is saying that love is the best way to overcome the divisiveness that is plaguing their church. Before the Corinthian Chris-

> PAUL IS SAYING THAT LOVE IS THE BEST WAY TO OVERCOME THE DIVISIVENESS THAT IS PLAGUING THEIR CHURCH.

tians speak or act, Paul would have them ask: "Am I doing this with love in my heart?" If not, it is probably time to reconsider. Love is not just a feeling, there-fore, but an orientation of one's life toward others in thought and in deed.

In the final section of chapter 13, Paul emphasizes that love is the only reality in the church that will endure into eternity. All of the other gifts, including prophecy, are for helping the church during the in-between times. They exist to build up the church and to support its ministry, but they will no longer be needed at the time of the eschaton. In the larger scheme of things, these gifts for ministry and life together are all for our "childhood" as Christians. But when we become adults, in the age to come, when we will see "face to face," they will no longer be needed (vv. 11-12).

Since all of the gifts are for the "building up" of the body of Christ, these gifts must be ruled by the same principle of love when they are expressed in worship. In 14:12a-20, Paul asserts that praying in tongues is unedifying in worship unless accompanied by interpretation (vv. 13-15). Most notably, outsiders, visitors to worship, will have difficulty knowing what is going on unless there is some attempt to interpret things for them. Again, Paul is not denying the validity of speaking in tongues; he is simply concerned that speaking in tongues is not help-ful for the building up of others into Christ's body during public worship.

Responding to the Text

We should be humbled to discover that all of our gifts, no matter how helpful, meaningful, and necessary, are ultimately passing away. They are only a part of our "childhood" in Christ during the present age. It should give us pause to consider this, and to put our good gifts on behalf of the gospel in their proper per-spective. What, then, will endure? Is there any way that it can be said that our prophecies, ministries of healing, teaching, work as missionaries or evangelists, or lay ministries will endure as a part of God's reign? Paul gives us a very simple answer. Inasmuch as they are a part of the *way* of love, they will endure. Inasmuch as our spiritual ministries express the love of God in Jesus Christ and the nondivisive character of that love, they will endure into the age to come.

In her novel *Dead Man Walking,* Sister Helen Prejean tells about going into a chapel to pray with Lloyd LeBlanc, whose son David had been brutally murdered by Patrick Sonnier. It is after Patrick's execution, and Lloyd is still struggling with his painful memories that make it difficult for him to move on with his life.

> The chapel is warm and close and filled with silence and the smell of beeswax. Lloyd and I kneel on the prie-dieux. He takes his rosary out of his pocket. . . . Holding a rosary is a physical, tangible act—you touch and hold the small, smooth beads awhile and then let go. "Do not cling to me," Jesus had said to Mary Magdalene. The great secret: *To hold on, let go. Nothing is solid. Everything moves. Except love—hold on to love. Do what love requires.*[12]

Sister Prejean knows what the apostle Paul knew: that only love endures. All of the rest, no matter how good or helpful or meaningful, passes away like Lloyd's rosary. For that reason, we do what love requires—so that we might partake of that which does not pass away.

Unlike Paul's generation, in which church members were preoccupied with the almost luminous power of their new spiritual gifts, we live in a generation that seems to be more enamored with the various crafts of church leadership. "How to" manuals on church management, preaching, pastoral care, spirituality, Christian education, and worship fill our shelves to overflowing. We are divided among ourselves about which method, model, or system is the best in order to achieve success. Paul's admonition to be governed by love should have the same meaning for us. We can become exciting and magnetic preachers, impressive teachers, dynamic worship leaders, convincing evangelists, long-suffering missionaries, or help one another to follow the five or seven or twelve steps to recover from grief, divorce, or addiction, but if we do all of these things without love in our hearts, we are simply "clanging cymbals." If we desire all of these things to endure as a part of God's reign in the world now and into the future, then love is the only way for us to proceed: preaching as love, teaching as love, worship as love, evangelism as love, mission as love, administration as love, caregiving as love. This will unify us, and it will save all that we do from ultimately perishing.

LUKE 4:21–30 (RCL, BC);
LUKE 4:21–32 (BCP)

Interpreting the Text

More than anything else these verses accentuate the fact that Jesus is God's free and sovereign agent who will operate on his own terms. Although he has proclaimed himself to be the fulfillment of God's promise of Jubilee, Jesus will set about the work of establishing Jubilee in ways that will be controversial at best. Jesus knows that his hearers are expecting some immediate evidence that God's Jubilee is beginning in and through him (v. 23). Jesus, however, lets them know that most likely his work will only touch their lives in a roundabout way. Placing himself in the shoes of Elijah and Elisha, Jesus tells them that the fruits of his ministry will take root more readily among the Gentiles among whom familiarity is not as likely to breed contempt (vv. 24-27). This, of course, appears to them to be presumptuous, if not blasphemous. In their rage, they chase him to the top of a hill with the intention of hurling him off a cliff (v. 29). Jesus, however, passed through the midst of them and went on his way (v. 30). Luke presents us here with a picture of Jesus as absolutely sovereign, on his way to Capernaum under sealed orders to be about God's business, letting the chips fall where they may.

There is a strong foreshadowing in this text of the rejection and threatening of Jesus that is to come in Luke's Gospel. The stage is set for Jesus' crucifixion, as Luke's plot begins to demonstrate how easily the ministry of Jesus can be misunderstood, experienced as threatening to the status quo, and seem to be arrogant or blasphemous when placed within the context of the ordinary religious expectations of the Jewish people. It is important to remember that stoning someone would not have been an unusual response if that person identified himself with prophets such as Elijah or Elisha. Jesus has begun to make claims for himself that will ultimately land him in the Sanhedrin in Jerusalem with his credibility on the line. Jesus would have understood how serious this self-identification was, and its likely consequences. Nonetheless, he sets his face resolutely toward Capernaum, on a road that will ultimately lead him to Jerusalem.

Responding to the Text

Facing persecution, Luke's church would have strongly identified with this Jesus, who resolutely sets his sights on the unique and unexpected calling of God and does not waver. Peter Marshall, in one of his well-known sermons, "John Doe, Disciple," writes these words:

Nothing could stop them.

The Romans made human torches of believers to light the arenas on their
    holidays.

Yet in death, these Christian martyrs made converts to their strange preaching.

Hunted and persecuted,

    throw to the lions,

    tortured and killed,

Still the number of those who made the sign of the cross grew . . .

    and grew.

Rome could not stop Jesus. . . .

In all of history, has there ever been such an extraordinary sequence of events?

Who is this Jesus?

What is the explanation of His power?

Etched against the skyline of every city,

    carried in the forefront of every human endeavor,

      the cross on which He died has become a haunting symbol of a haunting
        Person.

Christ is an end . . . and a beginning.[13]

Jesus is, indeed, a "haunting person" in this passage. It is important that we help our congregations to experience just how wonderful and yet strange Jesus is in this text. This is our deepest identity also, to be resolute in following this Christ, who breaks so dramatically with everything that we have known before and who will finally reveal to us the very depths of God's love for the world. David H. C. Read, the great preacher from New York City, once said that it is important to create a mood or "tone" in our preaching.[14] In this case, we can take our preaching "tone" directly from the text, a tone of strangeness, mystery, of being part of something that cannot be contained within the tiny vessels of organized religion or the social institutions with which we have become so comfortable.

Jesus declares himself to be the fulfillment of prophecy—the harbinger of God's Jubilee! Jesus announces that Jubilee will be for Gentiles! Jesus is about to be hurled off the side of a cliff, but then he turns and walks through the crowd untouched! This is not a Messiah who *fits*. He is a piece of the puzzle who changes the entire puzzle itself. This is someone who operates almost entirely outside the lines. Welcome to a world in which God is free and sovereign: to heal, restore, and to redeem . . . to do whatever God wants to do. Welcome to the world of the good news of Jesus Christ.

FIFTH SUNDAY
AFTER THE EPIPHANY

FEBRUARY 8, 2004
FIFTH SUNDAY IN ORDINARY TIME

REVISED COMMON	EPISCOPAL (BCP)	ROMAN CATHOLIC
Isa. 6:1-8 (9-13)	Judg. 6:11-24a	Isa. 6:1-2a, 3-8
Psalm 138	Psalm 85 or 85:7-13	Ps. 138:1-2a, 2b-3, 4-5, 7-8
1 Cor. 15:1-11	1 Cor. 15:1-11	1 Cor. 15:1-11 or 15:3-8, 11
Luke 5:1-11	Luke 5:1-11	Luke 5:1-11

This Sunday the meaning of Epiphany shifts into the realm of personal and existential transformation. Jeremiah's entire life is undone and then given back to him in a new way. Likewise, Paul teaches that the resurrection is an event in which two distinct spheres of existence, the bodily and the spiritual, come together and are transformed into something new. Finally, Simon the fisherman makes the life-changing mistake of inviting Jesus to get into his boat, an invitation that transforms his life forever.

FIRST READING
ISAIAH 6:1-8 (9-13) (RCL);
ISAIAH 6:1-2a, 3-8 (RC)

Interpreting the Text

This text serves to legitimate the person Isaiah (Isaiah of Jerusalem) and to legitimate also the entire set of writings in the book, which includes the words of Second Isaiah (Isaiah 40-55) and Third Isaiah (Isaiah 56-66). Isaiah of Jerusalem appeared on the scene in the eighth century following the death of the very successful King Uzziah. In this text, Isaiah has entered the sanctuary, presumably on the Sabbath, and there he receives a powerful vision of God within the heavenly court.

Scholars have observed that the structure of Isaiah's experience constitutes one of the earliest and best outlines for worship, an outline that is both rooted in Israel's cultic life and will become a common structure for worship in the synagogue and later in Christian congregations. This structure begins with praise (vv. 1-4), moves on to confession (v. 5), then forgiveness (vv. 6-7), and finally a commissioning to service (v. 8). This "liturgical" interpretation of the passage opens the possibility of using this text in support of teaching about worship from the pulpit.

It is not coincidental that this order of worship accompanies the process of personal transformation in the life of individuals. We often assume that rituals are only used to legitimate the status quo (Fourth of July parades, Memorial Day picnics, etc.). Rituals, however, can also be used in support of human transformation. This transforming pattern is one of orientation, disorientation, reorientation. In this instance, Isaiah's disorientation begins in v. 1 when he sees "the LORD sitting on a throne, high and lofty." Isaiah finds himself attracted further into the vision where seraphs attend to God's holiness, calling to one another in constant doxology, "Holy, holy, holy is the Lord of hosts" (v. 3). At the depth of this process of transformation Isaiah confronts himself and is undone. In the presence of the holy God, he becomes painfully aware of the limitations of his purity, vision, and direction in life. He cries out: "Woe is me! I am lost, for I am a man of unclean lips, and I live among a people of unclean lips."(v. 5a). Isaiah's entire framework for living is suddenly called into question. He is "lost," so that his former orientation in life no longer works. And yet he is not without hope. After all, he is in the presence of God: "yet my eyes have seen the King, the Lord of hosts!" (v. 5b). It is at this point that one of the seraphs touches Isaiah's mouth with a live coal so that he experiences a blotting out of guilt and sin (vv. 6-7). Isaiah does not reorient his life on his own, but God's messengers touch him and begin to renew his spirit and his vision. At this moment he receives his commissioning in a profound dialogue with God in which God asks him if he will "go for us" (v. 8a), to which he responds, "Here am I" (v. 8b). God promises a new vision and a new mission by indicating that God will "send" Isaiah. Isaiah seizes hold of this new framework for his life, claiming this reorientation as his own. This transforming ritual process comes to a close as God defines the precise message that Isaiah is to take to the people on God's behalf (vv. 9-13).

THIS "LITURGICAL" INTERPRETATION OF THE PASSAGE OPENS THE POSSIBILITY OF USING THIS TEXT IN SUPPORT OF TEACHING ABOUT WORSHIP FROM THE PULPIT.

Responding to the Text

In his book *Christian Worship: Glorifying and Enjoying God*, Paul Byers writes: "Christian worship may be distinguished from other kinds of worship in that those who are pulled in are also sent out."[15] Likewise, Greek Orthodox theologian Alexander Schmemann reminds us that our worship is not oriented toward personal salvation but toward "the life of the world."[16] Worship attracts us into the heavenly court where we get what Byers calls the "big picture," seeing the world from God's perspective. This creates a powerful contrast. We begin to see how small, insignificant, and sinful our usual picture of the world is: the rat race, the achievement orientation, the envy, the greed, the daily abuses of power, the many ways that we hide from the image of God within us. And yet God does not abandon us. If we turn from this "small picture" orientation, God is there to give to us a new vision and a new message. God sends us out as new people with something important to do and to say.

JUDGES 6:11–24a (BCP)

The call and sending of Gideon is filled with irony and humor. The picture of the complaining, whining young boy whom the angel addresses as a "mighty warrior" (v. 12) reminds us of the call of Moses in Exodus 3. By the end of this story, it is as if the writer has written in bold print: **Thank goodness God is in charge!** This story, like so many of the call and commissioning stories in the Hebrew Bible, accentuates the sovereignty of God in, through, and in spite of the human foibles of the leaders whom God calls.

RESPONSIVE READING
PSALM 138 (RCL);
PSALM 138:1–5, 7–8 (RC);
PSALM 85 or 85:7–13 (BCP)

In Psalm 138, the postexilic singer voices praise and thanksgiving in unison with the entire community. In response to God's great salvation of the people, the psalmist demonstrates the life of praise-filled prayer that the community is now compelled to lead. God has "answered" the cries of the people (v. 3a). The result is an increase in their "strength of soul" (v. 3b). The result of salvation is a heart brimming over with praise and thanksgiving.

Psalm 85 demonstrates that the postexilic community not only learned to praise God but to continue to petition God for help. The work of rebuilding the community was difficult, and there was still need for God's saving work in their midst. Verse 10 provides a glorious picture of what salvation really looks like. Salvation is the union or "kiss" of four things: "steadfast love," "faithfulness," "righteousness," and "peace." These attributes of salvation are both gifts from God and responses by the people to God's presence and favor. In other words, salvation is not only the result of a personal *metanoia,* or "turning," as it was for Isaiah in the temple, but it is also a social reality experienced by a redeemed community as it attempts to find its way amid the difficulties of life.

Second Reading

1 CORINTHIANS 15:1-11 (rcl, bcp);
1 CORINTHIANS 15:1-11
or 15:3-8, 11 (rc)

Interpreting the Text

In chapter 15, Paul shifts his attention from the behavior of the Corinthians to their beliefs. In this instance, probably because of their keen interest in spiritual matters, the Corinthian congregation seems to be missing the meaning of the resurrection. Without negating their awareness that Christ's Spirit is powerfully active in their midst, Paul reemphasizes that the resurrection is not only a spiritual reality but a bodily reality as well. As Paul goes on to point out in vv. 42-49, the spiritual aspects of resurrection are not unimportant. They are, however, grounded deeply in that which comes *first,* the body, and they do not leave the body behind. As C. S. Lewis once pointed out, the resurrection body "is differently related to space, and probably to time, but by no means cut off from all relation to them."[17] According to Lewis, the risen body of Jesus Christ was an objective, real body, a "New Nature" that is "interlocked at some points with the Old."[18] At the same time, the risen body of Jesus Christ partook of the profound spiritual reality that the Corinthian congregation already knew so well as they discovered their new gifts of proclamation and service.

In vv. 1-11, the lectionary text for this Sunday, Paul begins his argument on behalf of the resurrection of the body by underscoring that this resurrection was at the heart of the apostolic *kerygma* (proclamation) of the church. An apostle was one who had witnessed the risen Christ. Paul presents an outline of this kerygma: "Christ died for our sins," "was buried," "was raised on the third day," and "appeared to Cephas and then to the twelve" (vv. 3b-5). All of this was "in accordance with the scriptures," by which Paul means, at the very least, that it occurred according to the great pattern whereby God takes that which is old, in this case our old nature, and remakes it into something entirely new.

In this case, that which is new is not merely spiritual, inasmuch as that means disembodied, phantasmal, nonspatial, and nonhistorical. It is not the appearance of something so unrecognizably new as to be unrelated to the old. Rather, as C. S. Lewis again reminds us: "A new nature is not merely made, but made out of an old one. We live amid all the anomalies, inconveniences, hopes, and excitement of a house that is being rebuilt. Something is being pulled down and something is going up in its place."[19] Paul includes himself among those who have witnessed the risen Christ and found themselves suddenly in reconstruction as one "untimely born" (v. 8). The very existence of the Corinthian church is testimony to the power of this event in Paul's life and to the way that it motivated his proclamation in their midst. If they opt for a purely spiritual gospel, they will, quite simply, miss the fact that the "good news" (*euangelion*, v. 1) is that God wants to remake the very particular stuff of their embodied lives together. If they choose to escape from all of the "anomalies, inconveniences, hopes, and excitement" of this demolition and reconstruction, then they will have missed both the meaning and the miracle of the risen Christ.

> PAUL INCLUDES HIMSELF AMONG THOSE WHO HAVE WITNESSED THE RISEN CHRIST AND FOUND THEMSELVES SUDDENLY IN RECONSTRUCTION AS ONE "UNTIMELY BORN."

Responding to the Text

This is the first installment in Paul's argument regarding resurrection. The next two Sundays' lectionary texts carry the remainder of his arguments. If all three are to be preached, then the preacher may want to use this Sunday to establish the broader context in our culture for an emphasis on resurrection. I have already quoted from C. S. Lewis's chapter "Miracles of the New Creation" because I have found it to be an indispensable companion when speaking about the resurrection. Although it was written in the 1940s, it remains relevant today. I recommend it highly for use when preaching on these texts.

According to Lewis, and to Paul, resurrection is the "good news" that the church represents in the world. Lewis asserts that contemporary thinkers are willing to accept two options to resurrection quite easily. On the one hand are "Naturalists" who believe in "a one-floor reality: this present Nature is all that there is." On the other hand, spiritualists (like the Corinthians were wanting to be) are "prepared for reality as 'religion' conceives it: a reality with a ground floor (Nature) and then above that one other floor and one only—an eternal, spaceless, timeless, spiritual Something of which we can have no images, if it presents itself to human consciousness at all, does so in a mystical experience which shatters all our categories of thought."[20] In short, "we feel quite sure that the first step beyond the world of our present experience must lead either nowhere at all or else into the blinding abyss of undifferentiated spirituality, the unconditioned, the absolute."[21] What the witnesses to the resurrection testified to, which naturalists and spiritualists are "not prepared for," is "something in between," a "partial contact" between these spheres which does not "obliterate their distinctness."[22] It is this third way that constitutes the "New Nature" testified to by the apostles, a "Nature beyond Nature," in which we can observe the old passing away and the new being "untimely born."

THE GOSPEL
LUKE 5:1-11 (RCL, BCP, RC)

Interpreting the Text

Like Isaiah of Jerusalem, Simon Peter begins with a respectful orientation toward all things religious (in v. 5 he called Jesus "Master"), moves through an intense disorientation that leaves him trembling in fear (v. 8), and arrives at a new orientation of obedience as a disciple of Jesus (v. 11). At the heart of this experience is an "epiphany" or "manifestation" of Jesus' authority and power in his teaching and in the mighty deed of fishing.

Unlike the early calling of the disciples in Matthew and Mark, Luke's portrayal of this calling of Peter, James, and John comes later in his Gospel, following on the heels of several powerful deeds. The fame of Jesus has spread. He is experiencing increasing popularity. When the story begins, this notoriety has presented Jesus with a problem. He needs a place to stand and teach, where all can hear him. He gets into Simon's boat and asks that he be put out a short distance from the shore (v. 3). This gives him a broader perspective so that he can teach the crowd more easily. He also probably knows that his voice will carry better across the water. We do not know what, exactly, inspires him to turn his attention toward Simon. Perhaps it is Simon's generosity in lending him the boat. Perhaps it is his desire to thank him for lending him the boat. At any rate, Jesus invites Simon to let down his nets in the deep water for a catch (v. 4). Simon, like Gideon in Judges 6, does not hesitate to complain. They have already worked all night and have caught nothing (v. 5). And yet Simon has one characteristic that is absolutely essential for every follower of Jesus Christ: obedience in spite of one's own estimation of the situation. His response is a classic formula for discipleship: "Yet if you say so, I will let down the nets" (v. 5).

The event that follows is often sentimentalized in Christian literature. It is easy to miss the frightful excess and chaos of "catching" so many fish that "their nets were beginning to break" (v. 6). According to the narrative, the catch was so large that both of their boats "began to sink" (v. 7). Something strange and mysterious was happening, and Simon (now Simon Peter) is observant enough not to miss it. Like Isaiah who calls out "Woe is me!" he falls down at Jesus' knees saying, "Go away from me, Lord, because I am a sinful man!" (v. 8). Jesus acknowledges that this is fearful for Peter and also for James, John, and others. Looking at Peter he attempts to calm his fears: "Do not be afraid; from now on you will be catching people" (v. 10). This event was powerful enough for these three men, and perhaps many more, to leave everything and follow him (v. 11). No ordinary event! No ordinary prophet! No ordinary mission: to "catch people!"

Responding to the Text

"Breaking Nets and Sinking Boats!" This is what God is up to in Jesus Christ. This story makes it clear that a calculated and measured approach to a "religion of Jesus" will not be possible. In line with the entire season of Epiphany, this story shouts at us that Jesus will not be measured and weighed according to our usual tables for meting out religious life. He has come to bring a sometimes fearful and chaotic plentitude into our lives: to catch more people into the reign of God than can fit into our usual containers for them.

William James, in his classic book *Varieties of Religious Experience,* asserts that there are two different kinds of religious people. In the initial category is the "first born" person, of whom he says "from the outset, their religion is one of union with the divine."[23] Although being "first born" may have been Jesus' experience, it was certainly not the experience of most people in Luke's Gospel. They tend to fall under James's second category, the "twice born." Peter is certainly in this group, for whom, according to James "there lurks a falsity in its very being," and for whom "renunciation and despair of it are our first step in the direction of truth."[24] Both Isaiah of Jerusalem, who cried, "I am a man of unclean lips!" and Peter, who lamented, "I am a sinful man" would resonate with Søren Kierkegaard's despairing self, Rudolph Bultmann's inauthentic existence, and Paul Tillich's ontological anxiety. In the face of the holy, they experience despair at the self's inadequate resources to sustain itself. The epiphany of Jesus in this story, therefore, reveals to Peter a transcendent, self-revealing redemptive power which is the answer to the "falsity" that plagues his life.

> THE EPIPHANY OF JESUS IN THIS STORY, THEREFORE, REVEALS TO PETER A TRANSCENDENT, SELF-REVEALING REDEMPTIVE POWER WHICH IS THE ANSWER TO THE "FALSITY" THAT PLAGUES HIS LIFE.

In spite of the revelation of God in Jesus Christ at the heart of this text, Peter, James, and John could simply have said no. Many were already rejecting Jesus and his message. Their fear of him could have led them to turn tail and run. After all this would require of them their very lives, that they "leave everything and follow." Perhaps it would be better to resist, to sleep on it, to wake up the next morning, repair their nets, and reestablish their routines as fishermen.

Surrounded by the crowd, however, these would-be disciples realize that God is doing something new and "astonishing"(v. 9). It is something that makes their ordinary routine pale by comparison. So they do that most difficult thing, the thing that many people think about doing, but that only a few actually manage: they leave everything and follow him.

Martin Buber once said, "Real life is meeting."[25] In this case, Peter, James, John, and a host of followers have met face-to-face the answer to their deepest existential and historical longing. C. S. Lewis closed his fable *Till We Have Faces* with these words: "I know now, Lord, why you utter no answer. You are yourself the answer. Before your face questions die away. What other answer would suffice? Only words, words."[26] I like to imagine that at the very depth of Peter's fear, amid the chaos of this "net breaking, boat sinking" moment, when Jesus turns to him and says, "Do not be afraid," he is lifted beyond words. I imagine that the chaos stops for a moment in his face-to-face encounter with Jesus. Fear, falsity of being, and anxiety roll away, and the presence of the New Creation is experienced in all of its mystery and hopefulness. In this moment, Simon Peter realizes that the catching of fish is not the miracle that day. Meeting this person is the miracle.

SIXTH SUNDAY AFTER THE EPIPHANY

FEBRUARY 15, 2004
SIXTH SUNDAY IN ORDINARY TIME / PROPER I

REVISED COMMON	EPISCOPAL (BCP)	ROMAN CATHOLIC
Jer. 17:5-10	Jer. 17:5-10	Jer. 17:5-8
Psalm 1	Psalm 1	Ps. 1:1-2, 3, 4-6
1 Cor. 15:12-20	1 Cor. 15:12-20	1 Cor. 15:12, 16-20
Luke 6:17-26	Luke 6:17-26	Luke 6:17, 20-26

According to Jeremiah, God is writing God's covenant on our hearts (Jer. 31:31-34). Indeed, this Sunday's texts go straight to the heart of the matter: the fact that God has already ushered in an entirely new form of life in Jesus Christ. Paul speaks of this in terms of resurrection—real life against the powers of death. Jesus, in the Sermon on the Plain, continues to develop a vision of God's new reign of Jubilee justice. Within all of these frameworks, the core message is that this new reality is *already here.*

FIRST READING

JEREMIAH 17:5-10 (RCL, BCP);
JEREMIAH 17:5-8 (RC)

Interpreting the Text

The days of special rights and privileges have come to an end. According to Jeremiah, the people of Judah will be held accountable for the condition of their hearts toward God. They cannot presume that they will receive special treatment based on the old covenant. If they cave in to "devious" and "perverse" ways of the heart, then God will give to them "according to their way, according to the fruit of their doings" (v. 10).

In the Old Testament, the "heart" is at the center of a person's motivations and actions. It is the deepest fiber and sinew of the human willpower. Jeremiah's words anticipate the words of the apostle Paul when he speaks of minds that are "set on the flesh" (Rom. 8:5-6). Just as Jeremiah holds that such an orientation of the heart is "cursed" (v. 5), Paul acknowledges that it is "death." It is entirely possible for the people of Judah to turn to idols, to "trust in mere mortals and make mere flesh their strength" (v. 5). When this happens, their hearts literally turn away from God so that both motivations and actions are ruled by that which is finite, human, and apart from God's design.

In order to establish a contrast between those who "trust in mere mortals" and those who "trust in the Lord," Jeremiah poetically compares a mere "shrub in the desert" with a "tree planted by water" (vv. 6, 8). The shrub in the desert is overcome by the heat, unable to find relief and preoccupied with its own idolatrous attempts to secure itself against the elements. Those who trust in the Lord, on the other hand, do not worry about the heat because they have roots that extend into the life of God, which, as Jeremiah tells us in 2:13, is the "fountain of living water."

The word "trust" in these sentences is something like the word "faith" as it is used in the New Testament. The word indicates a deep and abiding relationship rather than a certain doctrinal position or affirmation. Any gardener will tell you that a well-tended relationship with one's plants is essential for bearing fruit. This relationship requires that the plant be rooted in the best soil, with a good water source nearby. Jeremiah desires this same kind of deep, organic relationship between Judah and God.

Finally, this passage, with its emphasis on the heart, with its treacherous aptitude for deception, anticipates Jeremiah's ultimate assertion that God will write God's covenant on the heart (31:31-34). Ultimately this problem of the heart will have to be solved by God.

Responding to the Text

Will Campbell, a writer, "bootleg" preacher, Kentucky farmer, and social activist recalls some years ago being given the "prestigious position" of cook on Waylon Jennings's tour bus. Late one night he asked Waylon, "Waylon, what do you believe?" Waylon answered, "Yeah." After a long silence, Campbell pursued him: "Yeah? What's that supposed to mean?" After more silence, Waylon again just said, "Uh-huh." Campbell goes on to write these words:

> Today we are bombarded with a theology of certitude. I don't find much biblical support for the stance of "God told me and I'm telling you, and if you don't believe as I do, you're doomed." A sort of "My god can whip your god" posture. From Abraham, going out by faith not knowing where he was being sent, to Jesus on the cross, beseeching the Father for a better way, there was always more inquiring faith than conceited certainty.

It occurs to me that the troubadour's response that late night might have been the most profound affirmation of faith I had ever heard.[27]

It was Judah's "theology of certitude," among other things, that troubled Jeremiah. Theologian Stephen Ray, in a sermon preached after September 11, 2001, said: "There is a little girl somewhere who woke up this morning without a mother because a few days back nineteen men were *certain* that they knew the will and the ways of God."[28] It is treacherous and sometimes dangerous to presume that one knows the will of God, especially when one uses that as license to "trust in mere mortals and make mere flesh their strength" (v. 5). The juxtaposition between "theological certitude" and idolatries of power does not escape God's scrutiny and judgment. That is the promise of Jeremiah. God sees

> THE JUXTAPOSITION BETWEEN "THEOLOGICAL CERTITUDE" AND IDOLATRIES OF POWER DOES NOT ESCAPE GOD'S SCRUTINY AND JUDGMENT.

through these "devious" and "perverse" ways of the heart. God will "test the mind and search the heart" (v. 10). Is the heart really turned toward God? Is the heart really set on righteousness, steadfast love, faithfulness, and peace? God knows.

RESPONSIVE READING

PSALM 1 (RCL, BCP);
PSALM 1:1-2, 3, 4-6 (RC)

Abraham Heschel once wrote: "The Bible is a seed, God is the sun, but we are the soil. Every generation is expected to bring forth new understanding and new realization."[29] Psalm 1 begins with a similar exhortation in the form of a beatitude: "Happy are those . . . (whose) delight is in the law of the Lord, and on his law they meditate day and night" (v. 1). The law to which the psalmist refers is not merely a dry code of moral precepts. According to James L. Mays, *torah* "is used in a comprehensive sense to refer to the whole body of tradition through which instruction in the way of and the will of the Lord is given to Israel."[30] Constant "delight" in *torah* opens up a "way" in life through which one turns from wickedness and finds the deeper sustenance that God promises. The psalmist contrasts the life of those who meditate on *torah* with the life of the wicked. Whereas the wicked are "chaff that the wind drives away," those whose lives are shaped by *torah* "are like trees planted by streams of water."

As an introduction to the psalms, Psalm 1 encourages the reader in a way of life that is literally saturated with Scripture. The psalms themselves are meant to direct the reader along this way of renewal and enriched Bible-shaped living.

SECOND READING

1 CORINTHIANS 15:12-20 (RCL, BCP);
1 CORINTHIANS 15:12, 16-20 (RC)

JOHN S.
MCCLURE

Interpreting the Text

All of the conditional qualifiers ("if . . . then . . .") that Paul uses in these verses must be read in light of the glad affirmation in v. 20: "But in fact Christ has been raised from the dead, the first fruits of those who have died." For Paul, the great fact of the Christian faith is that Christ has been raised. This has begun a great apocalyptic age in which those who are in Christ will be resurrected. The resurrection is the bedrock, the foundation, of what we proclaim (v. 14) and of our new life of faith and forgiveness (v. 17). It is also the sign of our hope as those who "die in Christ" (v. 18).

Paul drives a hard bargain. Christian faith requires an unconditional acceptance and testimony to *sarkos anastasin*, literally: resurrection of the flesh. This is not a metaphysical statement for Paul; rather, it is an apocalyptic statement. The new age has begun, and the "first fruits of those who have died" can be seen in the resurrection of Jesus Christ.

> PAUL DRIVES A HARD BARGAIN. CHRISTIAN FAITH REQUIRES AN UNCONDITIONAL ACCEPTANCE AND TESTIMONY TO THE RESURRECTION OF THE FLESH.

Responding to the Text

I can recall in a seminar in college a student arguing in agreement with Carl Jung that Christ is a "symbol of the self." My professor, who was near retirement and who had heard many similar arguments, responded firmly but patiently: "I wonder if this does not place Christ in a rather small box." Paul faced a similar problem in the Corinthian congregation, the tendency of the more cultured within the church to take the resurrection of Christ and treat it as if it were a symbol or metaphor of some numinous or psychic phenomenon.

I once taught a Sunday school class for teenagers in which we were discussing the resurrection. I asked them for an analogy or picture. One of the young women said that the resurrection reminded her of a "jack-in-the-box" that she still had on a shelf in her room from childhood. She said that this jack-in-the-box was not the usual kind. It had a problem: the latch was broken. This meant that she could push "jack" into the box and close the lid, but it didn't matter, he'd just spring back up. "After a while," she said, "I just got tired of trying to keep him in the box!"

I sometimes think about her box and the box that my professor was speaking about. It's true, Christ just won't stay there. Christ is about real life beyond death, real life in spite of death and real life against the powers of death.

The Gospel
LUKE 6:17-26 (RCL, BCP);
LUKE 6:17, 20-26 (RC)

Interpreting the Text

The Sermon on the Plain is commonly held to be a collection of loosely related teachings designed as a kind of seminary education-in-brief for the disciples and for all of those who care to listen in. The curriculum that Luke sets forth in this collection includes four components: blessings and woes (6:20-26), relational ethics (6:27-35), a plea for mercy instead of judgment as the norm for discipleship (6:36-42), and a call for depth of character (6:43-49). Some scholars wonder whether this "sermon" might, in fact, be the sermon on Isa. 61:1-2 that Jesus began to preach in the synagogue (Luke 4:16-21). This is especially true of vv. 20-26, in which the theme of Jubilee for the poor is strongly reasserted.

Unlike Matthew's Gospel, where this sermon takes place on the mount (Matthew 5: 1—7:29), here Jesus comes and stands "on a level place" (v. 17). He is surrounded by a great crowd, both his disciples and those who come in search of healing or restoration (v. 18-19). As usual in Luke's Gospel, Jesus' healing actions and his words are closely interrelated. The good news of Jesus Christ is not to be found exclusively on either side of this equation. Words and actions are wrapped together.

The Sermon on the Plain is far shorter than the Sermon on the Mount. Luke does not restrict himself to teachings found only in the Sermon on the Mount. He also includes teachings from other parts of Matthew as well. All in all, Luke's collection of these teachings seems to accentuate the material and physical conditions of those who follow Jesus, whereas Matthew uses language that appears to focus more on spiritual mat-

> JESUS HERALDS A NEW ORDER IN WHICH THE ENTRENCHED PATTERNS OF WEALTH, PRIVILEGE, AND WELL-BEING ARE BROKEN OPEN AND, IN SOME CASES, REVERSED.

ters. This distinction, however, should not be too sharply drawn. The focus on the material and physical dimensions of people's lives may have something to do with Luke's interest in Jesus as a harbinger of Jubilee, as we have already seen (Luke

4:18-19). Jesus heralds a new order in which the entrenched patterns of wealth, privilege, and well-being are broken open and, in some cases, reversed.

This reversal of fortune is nowhere more evident than in vv. 20-26. In vv. 20-23, Jesus indicates that those who have suffered economically and personally are indeed blessed within the realm of God's Jubilee (vv. 20-21). Likewise, anyone who suffers "on account of the Son of Man," who suffers because of association with Jesus himself, will find a reward that is "great in heaven" (vv. 22-23). On the other hand, those who are rich, full of food, and happy have already taken their turn as "blessed." Their place will be assumed by those who have suffered (vv. 24-25).

It is helpful to make note of the style of communication in this passage. Jesus uses the second person plural, indicating that he is speaking directly and perhaps conversationally to people that he knows. This is not to say that he knows them all personally, but it is clear that he knows their personal condition in life and the deeper expectations that they bring with them. These are people with whom he can identify. Here, at the beginning of his public ministry, Jesus pauses to offer a brief homily designed to draw his hearers into a more personal and intimate relationship with himself and his mission. The great reversal of fortune heralded in this sermon is for those whom Jesus *knows* both personally and existentially. In other words, there can be no doubt that God's Jubilee has come, and that it is for *you*.

Responding to the Text

There is always a tendency, when preaching this passage, to reduce it to a set of moral precepts. The poor and suffering are confirmed in their life status and go away with encouragement to accept their condition in life, since it will one day be redeemed in an other-worldly kingdom. Those who are more comfortable and prosperous are encouraged to feel a heavy shadow of guilt and looming judgment. Embarrassed by their riches, they grasp hold of a futile works-righteousness, seizing on small, individual things to do that will, perhaps, add up to something in the eyes of God and make up for their status in life. The bottom line for this text, however, is theological, not moral. In the words of Sharon H. Ringe, these blessings and woes "announce a truth about the divine agenda rather than a mandate for human morality." She goes on to say that "the list of woes is not one of behaviors to be avoided or changed in order to avert disaster. Instead, it states facts: People who are rich, well fed, laughing, and enjoying good reputations will also experience the alternative. They are not being punished for their actions; rather, they have enjoyed the blessings, and now the turn passes to others."[31] Jesus in Luke's Gospel is communicating through his actions and his words the end of the system of privilege that underpins all social relationships as we know them. He announces the great social reversal that accompanies God's Jubilee: guests become hosts, hosts become guests, rich take their turn in poverty, the poor have an opportunity to prosper, those in prison are released, those who are suffering, blind, or ill experience release and restoration. God's agenda is one of hope, healing, and dramatic change in status.

Who needs to hear this message? Consider some of these people: those who have experienced sexual or domestic abuse; nations that have experienced invasion, occupation, or devastation; a single mother trying to eke out a living on minimum wage for her three children; persons suffering from chronic pain or disability; anyone suffering under the weight of oppressive systems of privilege in society, including classism, sexism, and racism. The Sermon on the Plain communicates that, in the last analysis, these conditions are intolerable to God, and God in Jesus Christ has acted and is acting to reverse these conditions. The mission of Jesus Christ is not to tolerate the status quo, but to usher in a world literally turned topsy-turvy. According to Stanley Hauerwas and William Willimon, "Christians begin our ethics not with anxious, self-serving questions about what we ought to do as individuals to make history come out right, because in Christ, God has already made history come out right. The sermon is the inauguration manifesto of how the world looks now that God in Christ has taken matters in hand."[32] In other words, these blessings and woes announce that God, in Jesus Christ, *already* sees the world in a strikingly different way than we do. The "real world," for all those who are in Christ, is one in which most of the major status roles in life are utterly reversed. Our task, in the words of Dietrich Bonhoeffer, is "to be what in the reality of God (we) are already."[33]

Without a doubt, one of the most fundamental impulses structuring all of our social relationships is status or privilege. All that you need to do is to walk into a junior high school or high school or talk to a young person who is not a member of the "in-crowd" to know how painful and, at times, dehumanizing an explicit or implicit social caste system can be. At the same time, challenges to the system of privilege in society often bring about violent backlashes. The assassination of Martin Luther King Jr. should remind us that it is dangerous to resist the systems of social privilege engrained within social structures. When I was in college, a friend of mine wrote an article for the campus newspaper challenging the racism within the fraternity system on campus. Several days later he was badly beaten, covered with molasses and chicken feathers, and left with his hands and feet tied in the parking lot of the student center. Those who benefit from a system of privilege will often go to extremes to insure their status and power.

Nevertheless, the message of Jesus is resoundingly clear: God sees the world differently—and this Jubilee vision is now *our vision* as disciples. More than anything else, Jubilee vision values each human life infinitely. In the words of Bruce Cockburn, in his song "Cry of a Tiny Babe," in Jesus Christ, "the humblest of people catch a glimpse of their worth."[34] "Blessed are you," means "you are valuable," "you are esteemed." If this is true, then, in the Epiphany of Jesus Christ, we see the end of the world as we know it and the beginning of the world as God knows it. Blessed are those who have been pushed to the margins by an evil system of privilege! Woe to those who have reaped the benefits of this system and have tolerated the structures of violence and oppression that have propped this system up. If we can catch this theological vision, then we have begun to catch the vision of the reign of God in Luke's Gospel.

THE TRANSFIGURATION OF OUR LORD / LAST SUNDAY AFTER THE EPIPHANY

123

FEBRUARY 22, 2004
SEVENTH SUNDAY IN ORDINARY TIME

REVISED COMMON	EPISCOPAL (BCP)	ROMAN CATHOLIC
Exod. 34:29-35	Exod. 34:29-35	1 Sam. 26:2, 7-9, 12-13, 22-23
Psalm 99	Psalm 99	Ps. 103:1-2, 3-4, 8-10, 12-13
2 Cor. 3:12—4:2	1 Cor. 12:27—13:13	1 Cor. 15:45-49
Luke 9:28-36 (37-43)	Luke 9:28-36	Luke 6:27-38

At the pinnacle of the season of Epiphany is the great manifestation of God's presence in Jesus during the theophany that occurs on the Mount of Trans-figuration. In this event, Jesus' message and actions are both legitimated and graced with new power. The disciples, and we latter-day followers of Jesus, begin to see that we are caught up in something that God is doing in history and beyond history. New dimensions of glory and divine power are added into the equation. Yet we will be tempted to misunderstand this glory and power right at the moment when we turn to squarely face the cross.

FIRST READING
EXODUS 34:29-35 (RCL, BCP)

Interpreting the Text

The mysterious story of Moses and his shining face is the culmination of the restoration of the covenant following the Hebrew people's sinful episode with the golden calf (Exodus 32). The story of the golden calf ends with a word of judg-ment (32:34) and a plague falls upon the people (32:35). Exodus 33 continues this attitude of judgment, though there are some signs that Yahweh may be softening (33:2, 19-23). Moses becomes an intercessor before God, arguing with God on behalf of the people. Exodus 34 therefore becomes a climactic moment in which the covenant made at Horeb/Sinai is reaffirmed.

What seems to emerge from this picture of Moses is his role as mediator between the people and God and between God and the people. Moses is given special qualities and status by the narrator. The people appear at some distance, and Moses alone accepts the new covenant. His shining face accentuates this separate and now glorious quality of Moses' leadership. The Hebrew verb translated "shine" is associated with the word *horn,* which symbolizes military power. Not only is Moses God's emissary, but he has other qualities that now make him *fearful* to the people.

It is important to note the nature of this renewed covenant. In Exod. 34:11-16 the covenant is presented in a way that emphasizes its exclusivity. The Israelites are separated off from other peoples and are not to worship in their shrines or intermarry. Above all else, they are to be a holy and distinct people among all nations. Yahweh is a jealous God who will not tolerate any more golden calf idolatry. They are to focus their attention on their leader, Moses, who is divinely authorized to mediate between them and God.

In the story of Moses' shining face, Moses seems to realize that all of this emphasis on him is likely to be interpreted incorrectly. After all, since the people have found it so easy to worship a golden calf, how simple it would be to make Moses into an idol. In order to keep this from happening, Moses covered his face with a veil, removing it only when he spoke with Yahweh or to the people on Yahweh's behalf (vv. 34-35). This emphasizes how important it is for charismatic religious leaders to guard against potential abuses of their power or misunderstandings concerning the source of their authority.

All in all, the renewal of the covenant and Moses' shining face offer capstones for the entire book of Exodus. The basic message is clear: when God's judgment and God's mercy come into conflict, God's mercy can and will prevail. God does not and will not forsake God's special people, no matter how dismal and insidious their sinfulness may have become. God listens to God's people when their leaders cry out for mercy, and God responds with a new covenant and a shining new presence in their midst.

Responding to the Text

Frederick Buechner once aptly said of Moses that "he became in the end a kind of burning bush himself."[35] From humble and all-too-human beginnings,

> MOSES BECAME A DIRECT SIGN TO THE HEBREW PEOPLE THAT GOD WAS FAITHFULLY SEEKING THEM OUT AND GUIDING THEM THROUGH THE PERILS OF LIFE.

Moses became a direct sign to the Hebrew people that God was faithfully seeking them out and guiding them through the perils of life. His shining presence meant that God was with them, and that God's message to them was one of mercy and not judgment. If his life began floating aimlessly in the waters of the Nile, it ended reflecting the burning fire of God's presence and glory.

The idea that in the face of their inadequacy to deal with their sinfulness human beings need some kind of mediator between themselves and God has deep roots in the Hebrew Scriptures and in the theology of the Christian church. It is no accident that the need for a mediator in this story falls so closely on the heels of golden calf-building. Sin, breaking covenant with God, is not something that human beings are capable of overcoming on their own. They need a God who is committed to mercy and a mediator capable of changing God's mind regarding judgment. They also need someone who will be able to communicate God's law and intentions for mercy in new and appropriate ways.

It is important, however, to be very cautious when speaking of "mediators" between God and humanity. To some extent, all of the baptized share in this role, especially by virtue of the church's intercessory prayer. All of us go before God in prayer, beseeching God on behalf of a world torn apart by idolatry, conflict, and violence. On the other hand, the face-to-face encounter with God has been reserved in the Bible for a select few.

In spite of this, when considering these special forms of mediation as they appear in the Bible, it is crucial to underscore the *reality that such mediation actually does occur!* God does listen to our stuttering pleas for help and provide a way. God does offer redemption through human agents who become burning testimonies to God's presence, power, and love in our lives. We are not left to struggle with our sinfulness alone. God has spoken to us and offered to us new covenants through the agency of those whom God has decided to speak through. There is every reason to believe that this pattern will continue.

1 SAMUEL 26:2, 7-9, 12-13, 22-23 (RC)

Interpreting the Text

What are we to make of David's act of mercy in this story? Surely the most pragmatic decision for David would have been to kill Saul while he had the chance. Saul has grown increasingly irrational, half-crazed by his own paranoia, desperate in his own mind to cling to power. The words of David in v. 20 describe Saul's strange obsession clearly: "for the king of Israel has come out to seek a single flea, like one who hunts a partridge in the mountains." Wouldn't it make more sense for everyone concerned if David simply rid the kingdom of this overzealous warlord?

Saul arrives in the Wilderness of Ziph with three thousand men, seeking David (v. 2). David and Abishai sneak into Saul's camp at night and find themselves standing next to the sleeping Saul. When Abishai asks David if he may kill Saul with Saul's own spear, David shocks the reader by saying: "Do not destroy him; for who can raise his hand against the LORD's anointed, and be guiltless?" (v. 9). So David and Abishai retreat, taking with them Saul's spear and water jar (v. 12). David then calls to Abner, the king's bodyguard, and berates him for not protecting the king better (vv. 15-16). When Saul discovers that David has had the opportunity to kill him and yet has relented, he is smitten with temporary remorse for pursuing David (v. 21). Then David outlines his theological rationale for sparing Saul—his desire to honor God's anointing of Saul, and his hope that this will bring him God's favor and blessing (v. 23).

Clearly David's motives are mixed. On the one hand, there seems to be some emotional attachment between David and Saul so that David cannot act out of personal obligation to the king (v. 24). On the other hand, David acknowledges that the king should die, albeit at someone else's hands (v. 10). Ultimately, however, he appeals to a theological motive for sparing God's life. After all, this is God's anointed king. To raise one's hand against God's anointed would be to act against God. David knows that the people of Israel will question his motives and ultimately question his divine authority should he raise his hand against Saul.

Responding to the Text

It is somewhat ironic on Transfiguration Sunday to have before us this rather quirky story in which two of God's "anointed" are entwined in an all-too-human power struggle. If nothing else, this story makes it clear that those whom God has chosen are not immune from the plots and intrigues of all human relationships and politics. Like David, Jesus would soon be hunted by those motivated by irrational fear and a single-minded desire to maintain power. Again, the temptation for Jesus would be to return evil for evil, to seek power through the assertion of power, instead of attempting to persuade one's enemies through expressions of care and love. We cannot extend this analogy too far, however, because we know the rest of the story. David's motives are far from pure and Saul's days are numbered. In David's actions, however, we can glimpse something of God's mercy—staying the hand of deserved judgment, showing respect where none is due, and appealing for reconciliation to those who are blinded by the pursuit of power.

PSALM 99 (RCL, BCP)

Psalm 99 is an enthronement psalm that reminds us of the power of God to deliver and save. God is "great in Zion," "exalted over all the peoples" (v. 2) with an "awesome name" (v. 3). God is "holy" (v. 3), a "lover of justice" (v. 4), and worthy to be worshiped (v. 5). Clearly this is the same God who delivered the people in Exodus—the God who has all power and is able to do all things.

At the heart of this psalm is a short list of three of the great mediators between God and the people: Moses, Aaron, and Samuel. According to the psalmist, "they cried to the Lord, and he answered them. He spoke to them in the pillar of cloud" (vv. 6-7). Again, in v. 8, it is accented that God "answered them." More importantly, the nature of this God is underlined. God is a "forgiving God" but also "an avenger of their wrongdoings" (v. 7). God does not forget wrongdoing. There are consequences for sin. And yet God is forgiving and merciful.

Finally, God is worthy to be worshiped "at his holy mountain." This suggests the mountain where Moses beheld God, and also the mount of Transfiguration. Both are places of prayer and worship, of struggling with God, interceding before God, meeting God. Mountains are places where God and God's intermediaries meet, mindful of the power of God and of the depths of human need.

PSALM 103:1-2, 3-4, 8-10, 12-13 (RC)

James L. Mays calls Psalm 103 a "profoundly evangelical hymn."[36] This is due to its message of unmerited salvation from sins. The sinner is overwhelmed with joy and gratitude to God who forgives, heals, and redeems (vv. 3-4). Anticipating the Sermon on the Plain, in which believers are invited to emulate God's mercy in their relationships with one another (Luke 6:36), this text describes what God's mercy looks like. It involves patience, steadfast love, letting go of anger, and a policy of unequal repayment for sins (vv. 8-10). At the root of this mercy is God's compassion. God knows that human beings are made of dust, fragile and limited, and makes allowances for these things so long as they "fear him" (vv. 12-14). We can rejoice, therefore, that if our hearts are given over to God, God will deal with us according to the measure of God's abundant compassion and mercy, and not according to our sins.

SECOND READING

2 CORINTHIANS 3:12—4:2 (RCL)

Interpreting the Text

Evidently, a group of Jewish Christians in the Corinthian church are granting more credence to the old covenant given to Moses than they are to the new covenant that Paul understands to be mediated in the person and work of Jesus Christ. Since Paul's own conversion was one of having a veil lifted from his own eyes, his argument is based directly on Exod. 34:29-35, in which the veil over Moses' face was a central theme. Although Moses wore the veil to keep the Israelites from becoming too afraid, Paul incorporates the veil into his rhetorical argument in two very different ways. First, according to Paul, Moses wore the veil so that the people would not discover that the glory of God was only temporary. Moses did not want the people to see the glory of the old covenant fade away from his face. Second, Paul takes the veil from the face of Moses and places it onto the minds of those Jews in the church who are failing to accept Christ boldly as the bearer of a radical new covenant.

In order to avoid a tacit or explicit form of anti-Judaism when preaching on this text, it is important to note three things. First, in Paul's day, Christianity was the smaller and more beleaguered faith. The strength of Paul's rhetoric was tempered by the odds he was up against. This situation has dramatically changed in our world and culture, in which Christianity is the dominant presence. Second, it is important to remember that Paul himself draws from the ancient scriptures the authority and vision to help him gain some understanding of who Jesus Christ is, and how to understand his life, death, and resurrection. The use of covenant language itself betrays Paul's fundamental commitment to a Jewish framework for thinking about Christ. Third, Paul in this passage is not making a historical and theological argument about the relationship between Old and New Testaments such as one might expect from a twentieth-century biblical scholar. Paul is making an internal, *pastoral* argument that is probably informed by a form of textual interpretation that would have been found in much of the rabbinical literature of his day. Paul is trying to persuade the Jewish Christians in the Corinthian congregation to make a still bolder and more radical confession of faith in Jesus Christ (v. 12). In order to accomplish this task, he makes use of a literary conceit of contrast in which one thing (faith in the old covenant) should be fading, while another thing (faith in Christ) should be becoming brighter and brighter (v. 18). Paul is seeking unity in the Corinthian church around one thing, and one thing alone:

that Jesus Christ is their one true mediator, who has delivered a new covenant for the salvation of all people. On account of this covenant, Paul insists upon a quality of boldness and single-mindedness in the Christian life that forsakes all other commitments as diminishing in importance.

Responding to the Text

Adopting Paul's pastoral agenda in today's congregations requires some rethinking. After all, what are the fading covenants, religious or otherwise, that exist in our congregations today? Do any of us have a congregation full of Jewish Christians, as was the case in Corinth? How many of us, in the North American context, find ourselves preaching Jesus Christ in a situation where we are a beleaguered religious minority attempting to make a stand in the face of a far larger (in Paul's case Jewish) religious hegemony?

> HOW MANY OF US, IN THE NORTH AMERICAN CONTEXT, FIND OURSELVES PREACHING JESUS CHRIST IN A SITUATION WHERE WE ARE A BELEAGUERED RELIGIOUS MINORITY ATTEMPTING TO MAKE A STAND IN THE FACE OF A FAR LARGER (IN PAUL'S CASE JEWISH) RELIGIOUS HEGEMONY?

What we can adopt, it seems, is Paul's single-minded testimony that we as Christians stand before Christ with unveiled faces, experiencing his glory in our lives. Frederick Buechner wrote of Paul, he "never in his life forgot the sheer lunatic joy and astonishment" of the moment of his conversion. Indeed, "everything he ever said or wrote or did from that day forward was an attempt to bowl over the human race as he'd been bowled over himself while he lay there with dust in his mouth and road apples down the front of his shirt."[37] Whether we encounter Christ through the reading of scriptures, Old and New, through proclamation and worship, or through engagement with others in the fellowship of the body of Christ, we can testify boldly that we have been "bowled over" by Christ's glory, that Christ's glory is "working on us" transforming us "from one degree of glory to another" (v. 18), and that we'd also like to "bowl over" others who are hanging around the edges of that glory, only partly persuaded.

We might also adopt Paul's strategy for persuasion. Something relied upon has to fade, and Christ has to grow brighter and take its place. What usually reliable religious practices are nonetheless proving inadequate to meet the needs for meaning, hope, and "transformation" today? Could it be that some are relying on a legalistic fundamentalism that has turned into empty, doctrinaire gnosticism? Could it be that some are relying on forms of lukewarm ritualism that have grown stale and repetitive? Maybe some are relying on activism devoid of spiritual empowerment.

No matter what it is, the strategy is the same: these things must fade as they are transformed by the absolute "freedom" that is found in Christ (v. 17).

1 CORINTHIANS 12:27—13:13 (BCP)

(See the comments on 1 Corinthians 13 for the Fourth Sunday after the Epiphany, above.)

1 CORINTHIANS 15:45-49 (RC)

The resurrection body is quite different from the prevailing Greek idea of immortality, in which the body is not transformed, but escaped. This Greek idea seems to be what Paul is arguing against, though he does not explicitly say so. In this passage, Paul completes his arguments concerning the transformation of the body that takes place through the resurrection. Paul is speaking eschatologically about the nature of the personal and individual resurrection. His argument is fairly straightforward, if not always simple.

By virtue of their new life in Christ, believers partake of the life-giving Spirit of the "last Adam" (v. 45). Those who belong to Christ are literally "of heaven" (v. 48). By virtue of their participation in Christ they are being transformed. The final transformation of their bodies is an eschatological event in which their resurrection into the likeness of "the man of heaven" will be complete (vv. 48-49). The resurrection body is not perishable (v. 42) or physical (v. 44). It is a body that God makes available in and through the "last Adam," Christ. The Christian life in the physical body is nonetheless lived in the deepest and closest possible conformity to the likeness of Jesus Christ, conformity to the one who ultimately became a "life-giving Spirit." This conformity to the image of the Christ of heaven leads to the transformation of the body in resurrection into an "imperishable" and "immortal" *body* (not soul), the final hope that defines the Christian's personal and individual future expectations (v. 53).

THE GOSPEL
LUKE 9:28-36 (37-43) (RCL);
LUKE 9:28-36 (BCP)

Interpreting the Text

The story of the Transfiguration begins with an affirmation that this event took place "about eight days" after Peter's confession. These words could indicate that Transfiguration should be connected somehow in our theological imagination to the resurrection, which occurred on the eighth day. It could also indicate that this is a story designed specifically for worship, since Christian worship occurred on the day after the Sabbath, or the eighth day. Further warrant for this interpretation is the fact that Jesus goes up onto the mountain to *pray*. The Transfiguration, then, has its origins as an event of worship or prayer (v. 28).

It is during this prayer that Jesus' appearance is changed and his clothes become dazzling white (v. 29). The glowing face and Jesus' dazzling appearance hark back to Moses in Exod. 24:12-18 and Exod. 34:29-35. The Transfiguration story gathers together various aspects of these events: the mountain, the cloud, the voice, the glory, and Moses' shining face, and now associates these symbols and manifestations of God's presence with Jesus himself. The issue at stake here seems to be the confirmation of Jesus' identity. It is important to note that this confirmation takes place immediately following the revelation by Jesus that he would undergo great suffering (9:22). It is this suffering, it appears, that Jesus is discussing with Moses and Elijah, who appear in glory with him (v. 30). The narrative confirmation of Jesus' messianic identity in these verses therefore affirms that his passion should be interpreted as a part of his identity and not as something extraneous or in contradiction to this mission.

It is significant that Peter, John, and James are witnesses to this transfiguration and to the connection between Jesus, Moses, and Elijah. In order for testimony to be valid within Hebrew tradition, this testimony must be verified by more than one individual (Deut. 19:15). Peter, John, and James are the "big three" when it comes to apostolic witness. They are the same three who witnessed the healing of Jairus's daughter (8:51). It is clear, however, that nothing could have prepared these disciples for what they saw on the Mount of Transfiguration. Perhaps the greatest understatement in this text comes in v. 33 after Peter stammers his response to these events "not knowing what he said" (v. 33). Both the Transfiguration story and the exorcism that follows make it painfully clear that the disciples are stumbling about in the dark when it comes to understanding and appropriating the meaning and purpose of Jesus' life. There is something poignant in Peter's desire to "make three dwellings" for Jesus, Moses, and Elijah. It is no small confession, once again, that he has now elevated Jesus to the stature of these holiest of all mediators between God and the people of God. It makes perfect sense that he would want to hang on to this encounter, marking its significance for himself and for others who will come later.

Perhaps to remind Peter—and us—that this event, and indeed this person, Jesus Christ, cannot be contained within our narrow preconceptions, a cloud appears, as if to scare these preconceptions out of us once and for all. The words spoken by the voice from the cloud remind of Jesus' baptism. Once again, a heavenly voice announces Jesus' identity: "This is my Son, my Chosen; listen to him!" (v. 35). Just as the beginning of Jesus' public ministry was marked by a divine voice confirming his identity, so here at the beginning of his difficult journey toward Jerusalem a voice from heaven reminds the disciples and us that, not only is this God's Chosen, but that we are to pay special attention so that we will not miss the meaning of his life during the days that lie ahead. So it is that we are told: "Listen to him!" After this acclamation, Jesus is "found alone" (v. 36). With these words, Luke accentuates the unique and separate nature of Jesus' person

> PERHAPS TO REMIND PETER—AND US—THAT THIS EVENT, AND INDEED THIS PERSON, JESUS CHRIST, CANNOT BE CONTAINED WITHIN OUR NARROW PRECONCEPTIONS, A CLOUD APPEARS, AS IF TO SCARE THESE PRECONCEPTIONS OUT OF US ONCE AND FOR ALL.

and work. He also highlights the ensuing loneliness in Jesus' life as he begins his final pilgrimage to the cross.

The following day, Jesus emerges from isolation and is immediately enmeshed in a situation of desperate need (v. 37). Evidently, the disciples had been unable to exorcise an evil spirit that had been convulsing a young man, the only child of a man in the crowd (vv. 38-40). Remember that in 9:1 the disciples were given "power and authority over all demons." Because of this, it is at least partially understandable that Jesus becomes perturbed and impatient, crying out, "How much longer must I be with you and bear with you?" We confront head-on the fact that during the short amount of time that Jesus has left with his disciples they will not easily be able to "rise to the occasion." Rather, they will continue to be inept, hesitant, even faithless. Jesus' words cut to the quick. He is dealing with less faith and more sin than either he expected or the disciples are willing to admit.

Nonetheless, Jesus heals the boy in another act, which, like the Transfiguration, insures that "all were astounded at the greatness of God" (v. 42). In inverse proportion to the unimpeded glory of the Transfiguration, the glory of God is here revealed in the power that Jesus ultimately has over the evil in the world that wants to destroy God's creation. Again, one cannot help but conclude that the Jesus' (glorious) confrontation with the dangerous and life-denying forces of evil in this child's life foreshadow Jesus' final encounter with evil and sin at the cross.

Responding to the Text

The problem with something as radical as Jubilee is that it is not likely to occur without divine assistance. Jesus could go about announcing that he was bringing in the year of the Lord's Jubilee, proclaiming release of captives, recovery of sight, the forgiveness of debts, and the restoration of the land. But who would take him seriously? As a matter of fact, for all of the biblical references to Jubilee, it is still uncertain whether, in fact, the practice of Jubilee ever really took place. Jubilee, therefore, seems highly unlikely, without some kind of divine "assist." This was true when the Law was given to Moses. It took a shining face and a mysterious veiling to get everyone's attention. If people were to "listen" to this word of Jubilee from Jesus, therefore, they needed to hear from God in as straightforward a manner as possible. They needed to *see* and *hear* that this was indeed God's person and God's plan. They needed to see both the glory of God in the person of Jesus and the liberating, healing power of God in the actions of Jesus. Both scenes—on the mountain and down from the mountain—give us this picture of Jesus as God's person with God's plan. He is not messing around. He is "for real."

But the fact is that we have traveled a long way from this mountaintop. If the world was a violent and frightening place in Jesus' day, it is no less so in our day. The healing and restorative power of Jubilee seems, perhaps, even more remote for us than it did for Jesus' followers. Perhaps this is the reason that the prophets of apocalyptic rapture and tribulation are selling so many books and movies. At least they can offer the hope of some kind of final rescue or judgment. Jubilee—a reordering of human relations to express righteousness and love—is so profoundly different from the "way things are done." It just seems to be a pipe dream. How deeply we can identify with those disciples. We, like they, have bought into the system. We, like they, are simply part and parcel of another "perverse and faithless generation."

And yet, what are we to make of this strange mixture of God and humanity? In fact, isn't it really a picture of God *for* humanity? How can we give up hope when God has so clearly and dramatically not given up hope on us? How dare we? The story of the Transfiguration, if nothing else, shouts at us that God is *with us and for us.* God's glory and healing power are available to us, not in order that we might build "booths" or apocalyptic schemes, but to blind our straining eyes with visions and fill our listening ears with booming acclamations and sometimes exasperated pleas that will encourage us to continue to cultivate our faith and to follow Christ in transforming the world in which we live.

> HOW CAN WE GIVE UP HOPE WHEN GOD HAS SO CLEARLY AND DRAMATICALLY NOT GIVEN UP HOPE ON US?

It is crucial for the preacher to remember that the Transfiguration takes place during, and perhaps because of, the *prayer* of Jesus. Jesus' intercessions on our behalf, his being *for* us, is precisely the origin of his glory, a glory that ends at the cross with Jesus' final prayers for us. This should give us a clue to the commitment that Jesus has to us and to Jubilee. Jesus' prayer for the reordering of human relations, for the undoing of our violent and "perverse" ways, is relentless and brings him face-to-face with the "powers." Michael Ramsay, speaking about this prayer, says that "although we do not know much about this prayer, we know that it is a prayer near to the radiance of God and a prayer of one who has chosen the way of death."[38] Jesus will not relent until Jubilee is accomplished—even if it means that he must die in order to face down the powers in this world that keep Jubilee from happening.

Who are we in all of this? We are those who, in all our ineptness, nonetheless "listen." We are those who, in utter amazement and paltry faith, pay attention to the words and ways of God's love, justice, and Jubilee incarnate: Jesus Christ. Where are people bound by the power of evil? Listen and go. Where are people held captive by self-made conflicts, wars, and ideologies? Listen and go. Where does healing need to take place? Listen and go. Where are the cynics and inventers of farcical apocalypses who have given up on the world? Listen and go. Where does prayer to God for the world become our way of life? Listen and go. The pattern is simple, and yet it calls for all of the resources for attending and following that we can muster. In short, we have this vision: God is for us and with us in power and glory. And we have this word: "Listen!" And that, if we are to believe Luke's Jesus, is more than enough.

LUKE 6:27-38 (RC)

Interpreting the Text

In this section of the Sermon on the Plain, Jesus moves on to discuss relationships with enemies. The key to our response to our enemies, those who would have us continue to live under the old non-Jubilee order of patronage, enslavement, and abuse, is that we are not to allow their actions toward us to determine our actions toward them. Under the Jubilee plan, those captives who *are released*, those who have long been debtors, those who have been long abused or oppressed by certain individuals or groups in society, are not to simply turn around and begin to imprison, oppress, abuse, and enslave either their oppressors or others. This does not mean that they are not to seek justice for violent abuses. It is presumed that the great reversal heralded by Jubilee has at its core the judgment and prosecution of those who have destroyed human life and God's creation.

If, however, the followers of Jesus are *already* living within God's Jubilee, in the presence of the Messiah, then they should begin to behave as Jubilee people now, even before the great reversal heralded by the blessings and woes fully arrives. Victims under the old order can already begin to act in new ways. They are not to remain victims. It is assumed that by following the Messiah, they will leave these cycles of abuse—they will not stay in relationships that perpetuate non-Jubilee behavior. Once they are safe, outside the system of abuse and oppression, their unexpected, nonaggressive actions break the cycle of violence, oppression, and enslavement in which they find themselves. Once they have left, they are not to turn around and reinstitute the cycle. They return good for hate, blessings for curses, prayer for abuse, and so on (vv. 27-30, 33-35). These actions communicate that they will no longer play by the rules of the old order. They do this not to stay in the cycle of violence and to support the system of patronage and social stratification. Rather, from beyond that cycle, they break the cycle's power—they refuse to continue to live their lives on the terms set by their oppressors.

Responding to the Text

The great paradox of this passage is that, although it seems to be a self-denying capitulation to the old order, it is in fact a self-affirming manifesto of the new order in which relations are reordered by Jubilee justice. It is absolutely crucial to remember that this passage is not a plea for victims of violence, oppression, and abuse to stay in abusive relationships, *literally* "offering the other cheek" in an endless cycle of personal, social, or economic sadomasochism. The Sermon on the Plain presumes a reordering of human relations, in which certain "woes" have been and will be meted out to evildoers and oppressors, and certain "blessings" are already being communicated to their victims. Judgment and justice for abusive behavior is presumed.

Preachers must therefore make it clear that these rules for behavior operate at a deeper level as a way in which victims of oppression and violence can resist, and indeed overcome, the entire worldview of their previous life in the old order. How are they to slam the door on the way of violence and oppression? How are they to seize a new and separate identity for their lives? By being and behaving in a way that violates every rule established in the old order! By operating from and toward an entirely different vision for what human life should be: a vision of love and mercy (v. 36).[39]

Notes

1. Ann Weems, *Kneeling in Bethlehem,* large-print ed. (Louisville: Westminster John Knox, 1993), 95.

2. Parker Palmer, *The Courage to Teach* (San Francisco: Jossey-Bass, 1998), 38.

3. Søren Kierkegaard, *Purity of Heart Is to Will One Thing: Spiritual Preparation for the Office of Confession,* trans. Douglas V. Steeres (New York: Harper Torchbooks, 1956).

4. Madeleine Sweeney Miller, "How Far to Bethlehem?" in *Masterpieces of Religious Verse* (New York: Harper and Brothers, 1948), 156.

5. George Macdonald, *Diary of an Old Soul* (Minneapolis: Augsburg, 1994), 81.

6. Johannes Baptist Metz, "Gotteskrise: Versuch zur 'geistigen Situation der Seit,'" in idem, *Diagnosen zur Seit* (Düsseldorf, 1994), 84–85. Quoted from Erich Zenger, *A God of Vengeance? Understanding the Psalms of Divine Wrath,* trans. Linda M. Maloney (Louisville: Westminster John Knox, 1996), 75–76.

7. Bernard of Clairvaux, *In Epiphania Domini,* I, trans. a religious of CSMV, in *St Bernard on the Christian Year* (London: A. R. Mowbray, 1954), 37–38. Quoted in *The Westminster Collection of Christian Meditations*, compiled by Hannah Ward and Jennifer Wild (Louisville: Westminster John Knox, 1998), 122.

8. John R. Colt, *Becoming a Millionaire within a Year with No Effort* (e-book, Millionairethisyear.com, 1999); *Jesus of Nazareth, CEO*, coauthored with Angus MacFarlane (R. J. Sabongui, 2001).

9. Maria Harris, *Proclaim Jubilee: A Spirituality for the Twenty-first Century* (Louisville: Westminster John Knox, 1996), 86–87.

10. For more on this definition of biblical justice, see Walter Brueggemann, "Voices of the Night," in W. Brueggemann, S. Parks, and T. Groome, *To Act Justly, Love Tenderly, Walk Humbly: An Agenda for Ministers* (New York: Wipf & Stock, 1997), 5.

11. John Calvin, *Institutes of the Christian Religion*, I.xvii., ed. John T. McNeill, trans. Ford Lewis Battles (Philadelphia: Westminster, 1960), 10–11.

12. Sister Helen Prejean, C.S.J., *Dead Man Walking* (New York: Vintage, 1993), 244.

13. In *The Best of Peter Marshall,* compiled and ed. Catherine Marshall (Chosen Books, Guideposts edition; Grand Rapids: Zondervan, 1983), 186–87.

14. See John S. McClure, *Best Advice for Preaching* (Minneapolis: Fortress Press, 1998), 78.

15. Paul Byers, *Christian Worship: Glorifying and Enjoying God* (Louisville: Westminster John Knox, 2000), 11.

16. Alexander Schmemann, *For the Life of the World: Sacraments and Orthodoxy* (Crestwood, N.Y.: St. Vladimir's Seminary Press, 1973; reprinted, 1997).

17. C. S. Lewis, *Miracles* (New York: Macmillan, 1947), 177.

18. Ibid., 183.

19. Ibid., 185.

20. Ibid., 184.

21. Ibid.

22. Ibid., 184–85.

23. William James, *Varieties of Religious Experience* (New York: Collier, 1961), 77.

24. Ibid., 140.

25. Martin Buber, *I and Thou*, trans. Ronald Gregor Smith (New York: Scribners 1958), 11.

26. C. S. Lewis, *Till We Have Faces*, from *Time Magazine*, 1966, quoted in Ralph Harper, *On Presence: Variations and Reflections* (Philadelphia: Trinity Press International, 1991), 115.

27. Will D. Campbell, *Soul among Lions: Musings of a Bootleg Preacher* (Louisville: Westminster John Knox, 1999), 8–9.

28. From a sermon preached in the seminary chapel, Louisville Theological Seminary, on Sept. 28, 2001.

29. Abraham Heschel, *God in Search of Man: A Philosophy of Judaism* (San Francisco: Harper and Row, 1966), 274.

30. James L. Mays, *Psalms* (Interpretation: A Bible Commentary for Teaching and Preaching; Louisville: Westminster John Knox, 1994), 41.

31. Sharon H. Ringe, *Luke* (Westminster Bible Companion; Louisville: Westminster John Knox, 1995), 93.

32. Stanley Hauerwas and William Willimon, *Resident Aliens: Life in the Christian Colony* (Nashville: Abingdon, 1989), 87.

33. Dietrich Bonhoeffer, *The Cost of Discipleship*, trans. R.H. Fuller (London: SCM, 1959, New York: Simon and Schuster, 1995), 107.

34. Bruce Cockburn, *Nothing but a Burning Light*; compact disk (Sony Music Entertainment/Columbia Records, 1991).

35. Frederick Buechner, *Peculiar Treasures: A Biblical Who's Who* (New York: Harper and Row, 1979), 112.

36. Mays, *Psalms,* 326.

37. Buechner, *Peculiar Treasures,* 129.

38. Michael Ramsay, *Be Still and Know* (London: Collins Fount/Faith Press, 1982), 64–65; quoted in *The Westminster Collection of Christian Meditations,* 136.

39. For further resources on preaching this text, see John McClure and Nancy Ramsay, eds. *Telling the Truth: Preaching about Sexual and Domestic Violence* (Cleveland: United Church Press, 1998).

THE SEASON OF LENT

FREDERICK A. NIEDNER

Every year near the beginning of Lent, a seafood restaurant chain that is popular throughout Chicago and northwest Indiana advertises a special menu for the season. "For your sumptuous Lenten pleasure," says the heading meant to catch a newspaper reader's eye. This awkward oxymoron most likely issues not from a fear that a season of fasting represents a threat to capitalism but rather from something closer to unfinished catechesis.

Some within the church also misunderstand or shy away from the serious business of Lent. Once on Ash Wednesday, after speaking to members of a Protestant congregation about the traditions of Lent, I stayed for the imposition of ashes. The pastor who marked a cross of ashes on my forehead did so with these words: "Always remember that every ending is a new beginning." *Perhaps,* I thought, *but we came here this evening to die, not to philosophize.*

Lent is a forty-day wilderness journey in which we engage in the serious spiritual practices of fasting, almsgiving, and prayer. We have accumulated all sorts of household gods, workplace gods, and national gods since our last stretch of time out here, and it's high time we divorced them and put them away. Lent is spring cleaning for the soul and spirit as well as the body. Lent is spring training, a practice session for the rest of our lives.

> LENT IS SPRING CLEANING FOR THE SOUL AND SPIRIT AS WELL AS THE BODY. LENT IS SPRING TRAINING, A PRACTICE SESSION FOR THE REST OF OUR LIVES.

In earlier times, the church did its catechesis in Lent, then baptized neophytes at the Vigil of Easter. Dressed in new white garments, the newcomers witnessed to their faith in the risen Lord on Easter morning. Only then did they receive instruction in the deeper mysteries of the faith, like the Lord's Prayer, for example.

Regular catechesis has value for the whole congregation, not just the neophytes, so a return to certain basics in preaching and teaching during Lent has become a longstanding habit for many. The lections of Year C don't survey as wide a range of topics common to most catechetical instruction as do those for the other two years, but they provide especially good entry points for probing the first commandment of the Decalogue.

This year's lessons also prove rich in wilderness imagery. We don't like the wilderness much these days, unless we can go in our SUVs to a wilderness patrolled by the U.S. Forest Service and enjoy some sumptuous pleasures far from the madding crowds. As church, however, we go to the wilderness every year in Lent because the truth is that we live our whole lives in the wilderness. Always, and repeatedly, we move from some bondage or attachment through a time of transition in which we leave our old selves behind and move toward a new life. We never arrive in the promised land, however. Before the last transition ends, some new grief or change always thrusts us into the wordless void where familiar habits fail or even betray us.

The baptized will always find one sure word in the wilderness, the incarnate Word who travels with us, is tempted just as we are, dies with us on the rise overlooking paradise, and rests his life with ours in the very hands that have formed us all—and will again, over and over and over.

ASH WEDNESDAY

FEBRUARY 25, 2004

REVISED COMMON	EPISCOPAL (BCP)	ROMAN CATHOLIC
Joel 2:1-2, 12-17	Joel 2:1-2, 12-17	Joel 2:12-18
or Isa. 58:1-12	or Isa. 58:1-12	
Ps. 51:1-17	Psalm 103 or 103:8-14	Ps. 51:3-6, 12-14, 17
2 Cor. 5:20b—6:10	2 Cor. 5:20b—6:10	2 Cor. 5:20—6:2
Matt. 6:1-6, 16-21	Matt. 6:1-6,16-21	Matt. 6:1-6, 16-18

Ambiguities and paradox characterize the day of ashes that marks the beginning of Lent. The prophet's call to repent really means, "Return!" The ashes on our faces confront us with another sobering return, our inevitable return to the dust from which we have come. We learn anew today, and all through this season, that the return of repentance entails our dying, while the return to dust signaled on our foreheads means new life.

FIRST READING
JOEL 2:1-2, 12-17 (RCL, BCP);
JOEL 2:12-18 (RC)

The prophet describes in vivid detail an army that swarms over the land like a plague of locusts. Or is it an insect infestation that proves as destructive as an army? To the poet who crafted these lines, it made little difference. Continually, it seemed, some malevolent host or another marched with ruinous intent through the homeland of God's people.

Moreover, whether clouds of locusts invade from the south or hordes of soldiers descend from the north, the meaning of such events remains constant, as does the most important response. Assaults on God's people mean a day of the Lord approaches (2:1, 11). Indeed, no invading legion comes to visit except the Lord commands and leads it.

Repentance remains the appropriate preparation for and response to any and all invasions. From infants to bridal parties to bent-over aging ones, the prophet bids all to don sackcloth and assemble for a festival of weeping and fasting. As the vast throng of Ninevites respond to a single itinerant's cry of warning in the story of Jonah (Jon. 3:1-10; 4:4), so Joel envisions a full repentance among God's people. Who knows but what God, "gracious and merciful, slow to anger and abounding in steadfast love," might relent from the punishing onslaught that seems unavoidable.

ISAIAH 58:1-12 (RCL, BCP alt.)

Interpreting the Text

Once upon a time, Cain invented religion and apparently expected a return on all he had invested and sacrificed in the way of time and produce. Eventually his failed expectations turned to resentment and murderous spite (Genesis 4). Now "the house of Jacob" attempts to draw God into the same timeless game by means of rituals and pious observances in the era of reconstruction that came after exile in Babylon. The prophet hears his people pouting. "Why do we fast, and you do not see? Why humble ourselves, and you do not notice?" (58:3).

As always, God wants no part of such a worship contract. Indeed, God reacts with disgust toward self-serving fasts that produce only quarrels, factions, and even fistfights.

God does stand ready, however, to respond with favor toward those who engage in other kinds of fasting, the sort that forgoes the usual controls we maintain over others and the distances we keep from the hungry, the homeless, and the naked. Those who fast in that manner don't seek a reward for their voluntary emptiness. When they call, God responds in a spirit of servanthood. "Here I am," God says (58:9)—a most astonishing reversal of roles.

Responding to the Text

When we suffer attacks of almost any sort today, we quickly respond with a litany of "re-'s." Our leaders hasten to reassure us that they have a strong resolve to find those responsible, and when they do, we shall repay our assailants with a strong measure of reprisal, retribution, retaliation, and revenge. At such times, we rarely hear the word Joel urges upon us: "Repent!" Even when someone dares mention it, we react with yet another round of outrage and brand the speaker a nut case.

Perhaps we resist the prophet's word because, given the way we understand repenting and repentance, we resent certain implications. Our repentance might imply, for example, that we deserved the suffering and horror that came with invasion or attack. The perpetrators—not the victims—should repent, we protest.

The prophets call for a time of turning and returning, however, not a rite of blaming. In their view, a healthy life routine would include the daily exercise of repentance. We never lack for occasions to turn back from some evil way or another and then to aim ourselves once more toward our home in God's embrace.

This day, however, a "day of the Lord," calls for more than routine. Today we conduct a great festival of repentance. We know not what the great cloud on the horizon might bring, but the approaching darkness seems like a threat. When in doubt, we run straight to the arms of God. Ah, but God comes into the picture at the head of the storming host that alarms us, says Joel. Nevertheless, we have nowhere else to seek refuge. Even if God marches before a column of invaders, it makes better sense to turn to God, even should God slay us, than to run away or seek relief in our own devices.

God, too, repents. That remains a key element of God's reputation as one "gracious and merciful, slow to anger, abounding in steadfast love, and who repents of evil" with which God threatens when finally pushed to wrath. Yes, better to trust God than our own hiding places.

What does repentance look like, especially the festival-strength version? Sackcloth, ashes, weeping, and even some gnashing of teeth have their place, at least as a preparatory exercise. God really wants, however, a heart torn to rags.

In repentance we offer God a broken heart, a heart emptied of pained resentment and cleared even of its own favorite virtues. Such an offering God finds most precious, for from hearts like this come the loosening of oppression's bonds. In a heart rent asunder there is room for others, enough even for the homeless poor, and rags enough to clothe the naked in kindness.

> IN REPENTANCE WE OFFER GOD A BROKEN HEART, A HEART EMPTIED OF PAINED RESENTMENT AND CLEARED EVEN OF ITS OWN FAVORITE VIRTUES.

Repentance isn't a blaming game. Rather, for the baptized it becomes a habit—a *habitus,* a habitat, a place to live, a place with room for everyone.

RESPONSIVE READING

PSALM 51:1–17 (RCL);
PSALM 51:3–6, 12–14, 17 (RC);
PSALM 103 or 103:8–14 (BCP)

The psalmist here offers up in sacrifice precisely what the prophets of repentance called for—a broken and contrite heart. According to ancient tradition embedded in the superscription, this is a psalm of David that comes in the aftermath of Nathan's rebuke of David over the unseemly affair with Bathsheba. So thorough is the humiliation expressed here and so deep the shame that our instincts would have us turn away in embarrassment. Instead, we stand with the psalmist, individually and collectively stripped bare, with every secret of our hearts exposed before God and counting solely on the Holy One's mercy. We have only emptiness to give as our gift. In return, we seek a clean heart and the simple joy that comes from knowing that despite everything, God preserves for us a place of belonging.

Second Reading
2 CORINTHIANS 5:20B—6:10 (RCL, BCP);
2 CORINTHIANS 5:20B—6:2 (RC)

Interpreting the Text

When Paul urges his readers, "on behalf of Christ, be reconciled to God," he uses a verb that has its roots in the business of currency exchange. Eventually, the term came to describe a change in human relationships for which "reconciliation" serves as an apt translation. Accordingly, Paul uses the same word in 1 Cor. 7:11 when speaking of estranged spouses choosing to reconcile. In 2 Cor. 5:19, the imagery of marital reconciliation may apply, with God as the marriage partner who, for the sake of living again as one flesh, chooses to put aside the infidelities and violations of trust that have broken the relationship.

In subsequent verses, however, the notion of a currency exchange helps us to picture what God has done in Jesus Christ. From one perspective, it seems God makes a most foolish exchange, trading good currency of infinite value for worthless tokens no one else would ever redeem. Christ for us—the remarkable "sweet swap," as Luther sometimes called it.

THE NOTION OF A CURRENCY EXCHANGE HELPS US TO PICTURE WHAT GOD HAS DONE IN JESUS CHRIST.

Now Paul bids us, simply but urgently, to accept the reality of our exchanged state. "Be reconciled!" he beseeches his audience. "Now is the day of salvation." You have become in God's hands new money, a fortune beyond telling. Trust me, says Paul.

And why should we trust Paul? The credentials he offers fit the sort of currency exchange for which he is spokesman. "Let me tell you about my afflictions, hardships, calamities, beatings, imprisonment, sleepless nights, and hunger," he begins. "From out of these have come whatever purity, knowledge, holiness of spirit, or truthful speech I have to offer."

If we trust that kind of sales agent, then we can also believe his promises about the new economy. "Though poor, we make many rich. Though we have nothing, we possess everything."

Responding to the Text

As we begin a season of penitence and renewal, we behave sometimes as though we must go out of our way to experience the sort of emptiness, sorrow, or deprivation that would properly lead us to spend a season in sackcloth or go about with ashes on our faces. Hence, we silence our alleluias and fast from sweets or cocktails. If we must lie in the dust for God to find us, then we'll find our way to the ditch.

This seems a bit like play-acting, however, because most of us feel or assume we're closest to God when things go well for us, when we're at the top of our game, and when our family's overall condition remains sound. (Have you ever seen an athlete point gratefully to the heavens after striking out or fumbling away the team's last hope for a win?)

For those whose lives lie hidden with Christ in God, the realities Paul describes become those in which we see our true wealth and find our most remarkable reasons for giving thanks. We certainly don't seek suffering, romanticize it, or name it a gift of God. Nor do we suggest, like Job's pious friends, that others should suffer gladly (Job 5:17).

Yet the baptized keep in their hearts a remarkable secret. In the yawning desolation of a death-watch, in the godforsakenness of places where we face up to the truth that we have forfeited not only our virtues but also our integrity, precisely there we find ourselves in the company of the crucified. In such circumstances we have nothing, but we possess everything.

In this season of ashes, we needn't seek out artificial emptiness or invent ersatz suffering. We need only face the truth of our everyday lives. In the midst of life we are in death, and we pass through hell several times a day. But the worst that could happen to us already has. We have died with Christ in baptism.

The ashes, the shame, and the stench of death become Christ's, thanks to the great exchange. Meanwhile, we tread the halls of hell as the righteousness of God in action.

THE GOSPEL
MATTHEW 6:1-6, 16-21 (RCL, BCP);
MATTHEW 6:1-6, 16-18 (RC)

Interpreting the Text

This middle section of the Sermon on the Mount echoes prophetic calls to repentance like those from today's readings from Joel or Isaiah. The public exercise of piety meant to impress others will surely have its intended impact. People will praise the generosity of liberal donors, the eloquence of those who direct their rhetoric to heaven, and the remarkable stamina of spiritual athletes who can make a marathon of fasting.

God, however, does not grant similar performance points. "Hypocrites," Jesus calls those who practice their piety in this way. The word comes directly from the Greek and in our language means a phony, a pretender or dissembler. It first came by way of the stage, however, and once referred to play-actors, particularly those who adore their own costumes and love nothing more than the roar of the crowd.

Truly just and pious worship consists of remaining off-stage, while leaving one's beneficence, prayer, and self-denial a secret between oneself and God. Moreover, if credit should go to anyone for the outcomes of such discipline, that belongs to God. A bit earlier in this sermon, Jesus called his followers the "light of the world" and bade them, "Let your light shine before others, so that they may see your good works and give glory to your Father in heaven" (Matt. 5:15-16).

Understood together, these things mean that our secret disciplines of giving, prayer, and fasting issue in works that bring no attention to ourselves but instead leave others rejoicing. Recipients cannot tell from whence or from whom an unexpected blessing has come. They can only lift their hands to God in wonderment, surprise, and thanks.

The truth behind such blessing remains the secret of God and the soul in the prayer closet. Meanwhile, to those who give, pray, and fast in secret, Jesus promises a reward. The word here suggests repayment, or perhaps a yield of the sort that seeds planted in the ground finally produce. Someone, somewhere prays, fasts, and makes offerings on our behalf—and all that in secret. We may never know who. That leaves us with one option. Thank God.

Responding to the Text

All this talk of repentance, or "return," and the secret disciplines Jesus urges on us have their necessity in yet another secret and a return we seldom name except on this day. "Dust you are, and unto dust you shall return," we say aloud today as the gritty ashes of last year's hosannas somberly adorn our faces. The ashes expose our most terrible secret. We are dust. And we have so short a time as flesh and blood sons and daughters, wives and husbands, mothers and fathers, and all the other roles we play.

It takes most of that time to learn our part, and just when we know our lines, the curtain closes. Darkness descends. No one applauds. It's no wonder we give in to every temptation to seize the stage and seek praise for our generosity, our piety—or something that shows that our lives have proved more than a rush of vanity signifying nothing.

Today we retreat to the practice studio, alone or nearly alone. Here we face the secret of mortality and the truth of all our other secrets, the ones we could lump together and call our sins. Here we pray about those secrets to our Father who art in secret. We confess the secrets of our prejudices and addictions, of the betrayals that damn our most intimate relationships, of our petty fears and honest dreads. Beneath the uniform of every vocation, including the clerical collar, beats one more heart filled with deadly secrets.

Bearing all of that, we pray in the closet, surely not on the street corner. As words for our praying we take the ones Jesus himself taught and then used himself when he went off alone with a heart full of the same things that beat us down. That Abba-prayer is a prayer of return. It returns one to the moment of baptism and brings to mind the truest thing any of us need remember. We are the children of God, the delight of God's soul.

> BENEATH THE UNIFORM OF EVERY VOCATION, INCLUDING THE CLERICAL COLLAR, BEATS ONE MORE HEART FILLED WITH DEADLY SECRETS.

God, too, keeps a dear secret. Each of us means more to God than any offerings could measure, prayers declare, or self-denial prove. God's heart, too, aches to the point of breaking over our dread secrets. In the battered, crucified flesh of Christ, we see God's secret.

The dust on our faces comes from the cross, from the crucified one. With him, we return as dust to the same hands where he would lie in death. And the last secret? The dust began in those hands, remember? And there it remains. In the beginning God gave life to the dust. Let us return to the Lord our God; who knows but what God will give us life once more?

Prayer

"Almighty and ever-living God, you hate nothing you have made and you forgive the sins of all who are penitent. Create in us new and honest hearts, so that, truly repenting of our sins, we may obtain from you, the God of all mercy, full pardon and forgiveness."[1] Fill us with a measure of your own holy love for those whose faces we mark this night with the sign of your Son's cross. From our own newly broken and continually mended hearts, bring words to carry news of your goodness and mercy to all who embark this day upon a journey of renewal; through your Son, Jesus Christ our Lord, who lives and reigns with you, and the Holy Spirit, one God, now and forever.

FIRST SUNDAY OF LENT

FEBRUARY 29, 2004

REVISED COMMON	EPISCOPAL (BCP)	ROMAN CATHOLIC
Deut. 26:1-11	Deut. 26:(1-4), 5-11	Deut. 26:4-10
Ps. 91:1-2, 9-16	Ps. 91 or 91:9-15	Ps. 91:1-2, 10-15
Rom. 10:8b-13	Rom. 10:(5-8a), 8b-13	Rom. 10:8-13
Luke 4:1-13	Luke 4:1-13	Luke 4:1-13

We cannot return to God except through the wilderness, and Lent's wilderness journey begins amid voices of temptation, testing, and trial. Here we face the emptiness and deceptions of our own expectations and the false promises to which we so easily give our hearts. We do not come here alone, however. God's people have passed this way before, as has the baptized one, Jesus Christ. The same Spirit that sustained them on their perilous journeys travels every step of the way with us.

FIRST READING

DEUTERONOMY 26:1-11 (RCL);
DEUTERONOMY 26:(1-4), 5-11 (BCP);
DEUTERONOMY 26:4-10 (RC)

Interpreting the Text

These directives for a ritual by which pilgrims to the Jerusalem temple should make an offering of their produce come to us by way of the wilderness. The whole of Deuteronomy, including the second law or new covenant at its core, presents itself as a series of discourses that make up Moses' farewell address to the Israelites he has led through the wilderness. Soon the people would enter the promised land, but first God would end Moses' life (Deuteronomy 34).

In the new land, the people must remember to give thanks for all they have as gifts from God, and the ritual prescribed here instructs them how to do that. They will give thanks for having become a mighty and populous nation (v. 5); for release from affliction, toil, and oppression (v. 7); for the inheritance of "a land flowing with milk and honey" (vv.1, 9); and for the fruit of that land and of their own labors upon it (v. 10).

The ritual of thanks does not end at the temple, however. It concludes with a feast of rejoicing that involves one's own household and family as well as "the Levites and the aliens who reside among you" (v. 11). The importance of including these two groups stems from their having no inheritance in the land (18:1-8), and Deuteronomy frequently stipulates that the people of Israel as a whole must look out for these groups who can claim no land of their own (12:18; 14:26-29; 16:11, 14).

This last directive brings the rite full-circle, for it begins with a statement of remembrance that "a wandering Aramean was my ancestor; he went down into Egypt and lived there as an alien" (v. 5). The English "wandering" fails to capture completely the plight of the ancient ancestor. The Hebrew word here literally means "perishing," on the verge of being completely lost. Moreover, the worshiper speaks in first-person discourse, as one who came from the wilderness and entered the land (v. 3) and not as one for whom that endangered state now resides in some hazy past. "I nearly perished. We wandered about lost. In addition, we knew affliction and bondage."

From such a threatened place and condition, God's mighty hand and outstretched arm rescued us from extinction. Surely all we have is purely a gift.

Responding to the Text

No matter how prosperous or settled we may find ourselves at any given moment, we always remain but a single step from the wilderness. It behooves us to give thanks for the security of home and homeland, for health and a good reward for our labors. Our gratitude, when genuine, also translates into generosity, particularly toward those whose present state of residence remains more wilderness than land of milk and honey.

It also behooves us, however, to consider who we would be or become if we found ourselves once more a wandering, near-to-perishing Aramean, or even a bond servant stuck again in Egypt. Part of Lent's discipline consists of returning to such places through prayer, fasting, and the giving of alms. We engage in these practices because we so easily forget how we got from the hungering loneliness of slavery and wilderness to the satiety of our current homeland. It comes naturally to think we brought ourselves here with our own mighty hand and determined arm. A sojourn in the wilderness reminds us of our dependence. We engage in fatal deception when we allow ourselves to become gods and guarantors of life in the land of our own promises.

> IT COMES NATURALLY TO THINK WE BROUGHT OUR-SELVES HERE WITH OUR OWN MIGHTY HAND AND DETERMINED ARM. A SOJOURN IN THE WILDERNESS REMINDS US OF OUR DEPENDENCE.

The importance of returning deliberately to the wilderness and its difficult but salutary lessons rests also in the truth that each of us will return there against our own will. Sooner or later, illness, death, injury, or incapacity will take us to the wilderness, that wild place beyond meaning and words. Who—and whose—shall we be then?

As we traverse the wilderness throughout this season we set aside the gods of our own making and illusion. We learn again the truth of simple gifts, of trust in God's promises regarding our identities and future, and of thankfulness as our response.

RESPONSIVE READING
PSALM 91:1-2, 9-16 (RCL);
PSALM 91 or 91:9-15 (BCP);
PSALM 91:1-2, 10-15 (RC)

Renowned biblical scholar Claus Westermann spent part of his early adulthood in a Nazi concentration camp. Prior to that time, he had memorized many of the Bible's psalms, and he credited his sanity and the spiritual strength he retained during that terrible experience to the gift of being able to pray and study the psalms that lived in his heart and mind.

After the war, Westermann wrote several scholarly works based on the reflection he had done in the concentration camp without benefit of a Bible or writing materials. Psalm 91 is one of the very few psalms not treated in those studies. We can only wonder how Westermann made sense of the promises God makes to the faithful in Psalm 91. Did these words seem hollow as he watched other prisoners, including those who loved God and knew God's name, dashed to pieces and trampled underfoot? Did his own suffering seem a cruel joke, or evidence, perhaps, that something in his love for God fell short?

The tempter can easily enough throw this psalm in the face of all who love God and still suffer, including Jesus Christ. To what in this psalm can the tested and already broken heart cling?

"When they call to me, I will answer them; I will be with them in trouble" (v. 15). On that, and perhaps only that, can the scourged and mauled pin some hope, but only if the voice that speaks this promise calls out from the direction of Golgotha.

SECOND READING

ROMANS 10:8b-13 (RCL);
ROMANS 10:(5-8a), 8b-13 (BCP);
ROMANS 10:8-13 (RC)

Interpreting the Text

These verses come from the portion of the letter to the Romans in which Paul deems it necessary to declare God's promises trustworthy. "No one who believes in him will be put to shame," says the old book (v. 11; cf. Isa. 28:16), and, "Everyone who calls on the name of the Lord shall be saved" (v. 13; cf. Joel 2:32). Trouble was, it now appeared, at least according to some strands of Christian proclamation, that the very people to whom God directed those promises had become lost to God.

With few exceptions, the Jews, Paul's own people, had not accepted Jesus as the Messiah nor believed the gospel. Many Christians, including Gentiles, who now identified themselves as God's chosen people, denied the continuance of that election to the Jews. Does this mean, some would surely have asked, that God has reneged on the ancient promises? Has God rejected God's people?

At stake here is the readers' confidence in God's trustworthiness. If God has rejected a group that had formerly been God's own people, how do we know the same won't happen to us? How can anyone trust God's promises if those promises can be withdrawn?

> AT STAKE HERE IS THE READERS' CONFIDENCE IN GOD'S TRUSTWORTHINESS. IF GOD HAS REJECTED A GROUP THAT HAD FORMERLY BEEN GOD'S OWN PEOPLE, HOW DO WE KNOW THE SAME WON'T HAPPEN TO US? HOW CAN ANYONE TRUST GOD'S PROMISES IF THOSE PROMISES CAN BE WITHDRAWN?

In response to such questions, Paul pushes further the assertion he made in 8:31-39 and applies it now to all those God has chosen, called, or given the status of "elect," including Israel. God never, ever revokes a promise.

This line of thinking will ultimately stretch Paul's theology nearly to the breaking point. He will not, and cannot, give up his assertion of God's trustworthiness. In the end, Paul declares God's handling of this whole matter a mystery beyond his own explaining (11:25). Paul finds himself left with one response to grace such as this—a hymn (11:33-36).

Responding to the Text

One of the deadliest stretches of wilderness the baptized traverse comes when they hear the inevitable voice that asks, "Did God really say . . . ?" The quote that comes next, whether slightly amended or not, needn't speak about the tree in the midst of the garden. No, we have our antenna ready for that one. Many other sayings, however, when rehearsed in this context, easily enough lead us into idolatry, despair, and ruin.

"Not everyone who says to me, 'Lord, Lord,' will enter the kingdom of heaven" (Matt. 7:21) works rather well. So does, "God is faithful, and he will not let you be tested beyond your strength" (1 Cor. 10:13). How do you know you won't come awake with a start at midnight after some dreadful stretch of nonsense, and when you pray, "Lord, Lord," the voice from the other side will say only, "Sorry, I never knew you"? As for your crushed spirit, you'll have to handle that on your own. God would never let things get too heavy to bear, so get a grip.

The temptations best able to poison our trust in God come in the guise of God's own words. Though always subject to such attacks, we find ourselves especially vulnerable when alone in a time of trial. In such moments we obviously need an ally, an attorney who can aid us with words of response. The Holy Spirit plays this role and thus rightly gets from us the name Paraclete, an ancient term for a defense counsel. For the Christians of Rome, Paul took up that task, working in concert with the Spirit.

Their defense tactic? As much as possible, quote God against those who use God's words to threaten the strong and terrify the weak. Indeed, as Moses and others had done before him, Paul dares to quote God against God. "No one who believes in him will be put to shame" (v. 11). "Everyone who calls on the name of the Lord shall be saved" (v. 13). Period.

Isn't that right, God?

Yes, and we'll keep on saying it, and likely put those words to music as well, though we have holes in our hands, a deep gash square in the middle of our strength, and a thirst as great as the parched wilderness itself.

The Gospel
LUKE 4:1-13

Interpreting the Text

In each Synoptic Gospel, Jesus undergoes a period of temptation in the wilderness immediately following the baptismal scene in which the Holy Spirit descends upon him and a voice from the heavens names him God's beloved Son. Luke follows Mark in suggesting that the testing occurred throughout the forty-day wilderness sojourn, though details of specific temptations Luke shares with Matthew come after the note concerning how hungry, and thus vulnerable, Jesus had become on account of his long fast.

An abundance of allusions to older narratives nearly overwhelms the recipient of Luke's story. Forty days of fasting in the wilderness recalls parallel episodes in the lives of Moses (Exod. 34:28), Elijah (1 Kings 19:8), and the people of Israel as they journeyed from the sea crossing to the land of promise. All three older stories include a visit to the same holy mountain. In the liturgical sequence of reading Luke, the recent visit to the Mount of Transfiguration, with its conversation between Jesus, Moses, and Elijah about completing the Exodus Moses never finished, adds still more to the weight of these allusions.

Luke identifies the tempter with the Greek term *diabolos,* equivalent to the Hebrew term *satan,* which can refer to anyone who brings charges against another. Here the prosecutor doesn't so much accuse as he pushes Jesus to define the way he will live out his identity as God's Son and pursue his mission as Messiah.

Some interpreters suggest that the tempter tries here to drag Jesus into politics but Jesus resists. Luke's Jesus, however, unlike the more solitary, publicity-shunning figure in Mark, is clearly a popular figure whose political weight cannot be ignored by other politicians of his day. Friendly crowds and a host of loyal disciples surround him continually (cf. 19:37; 22:6; 23:48). Jesus will lead a people, Luke teaches, but where will he take them, and by what sort of power or force?

Each of the tempter's three proposals corresponds to elements of popular messianic hope among Jews living under Roman domination. One who could turn even a single stone to bread shows promise of providing plenty for God's people. That one could bring an end to hunger and want, and unlike the wilderness experience of every other age, in this Messiah's reign we could indeed collect and eat tomorrow's bread today.

The Messiah would also rule peacefully over all the nations of the world—with headquarters in Jerusalem, of course. To make this happen, Jesus need only fall down before the threatening accuser and admit that his way of making and keeping peace held the world's only realistic hope. Finally, surviving intact a leap of more than four hundred feet from the temple pinnacle to the Kidron Valley below would not only prove the worth of God's promises, but offer hope as well for an age in which life was no longer so nasty, brutish, and short.

Jesus rejects these proposals and responds in turn with three wilderness words from Deuteronomy. Nevertheless, Jesus will soon enough do a miraculous feeding (9:12-17), ride into Jerusalem as peacemaker and king (19:28-38), and defy death (7:11-17; 8:40-56). Ultimately, however, his politics take him inexorably to the cross. Indeed, these measures make no sense apart from the cross, and Jesus leads his loyal throng of disciples on the path of daily cross-bearing (9:23-25).

Responding to the Text

Like our ancient forbears, we dream of a world in which everyone has enough bread—and plenty of everything else, for that matter. We imagine a time when no one ever again must compete with a neighbor for scarce resources. Have-nots would all become haves. Hunger and deprivation would end, as would envy and class struggle.

We would give most anything for peace and homeland security, too, for that, along with plenty, would make for a mostly perfect world. Never mind that we must bend the knee for the moment to the gods of this world who have pretty much proved over the centuries that the only way to make or keep peace is by means of threat and intimidation. "Either do things our way, or we'll nuke you. You choose." Thus did the world come to live in *Pax Romana,* and now *Pax Americana,* such as it is.

What's missing? Even with peace and plenty, we still bury too many of our young thanks to accidents, disease, or plain foolishness. Hence, we yearn for a Messiah who could leap not only the Kidron Valley, but also the Valley of the Shadow of Death, the Chasm of Cancer, and the Abyss of Accident and Tragedy, all with us on his back of course, so we could each get our three-score years and ten and die peacefully in our beds with grandchildren all about to sing us a sweet benediction.

We not only want and dream of such things. In subtle ways we expect they should be our rightful heritage as the sons and daughters of God. When we find ourselves, therefore, in some poverty, war, or wilderness of grief, the voice of the tempter comes stalking us sarcastically. "If you are a child of God, what in the world are you doing on that ugly cross? Is that how God treats loved ones?"

Surely there must be some sign that proves our worth and gives meaning to our brief and fragile lives. All the bread in the world—and everything else to go with it, including peace and longevity—cannot do these things, however, and not merely because there's ultimately no such thing as enough stuff, enough years of life, or the perfect peace. We always, always want more.

> SURELY THERE MUST BE SOME SIGN THAT PROVES OUR WORTH AND GIVES MEANING TO OUR BRIEF AND FRAGILE LIVES.

We do well to come with Jesus to the wilderness to wrestle with these matters once again under the watchful eye and shielding wing of the Holy Spirit. Our deep hungers lead us to trust in a kitchen full of gods that cannot support or sustain us in a true time of crisis. But out here in a barren place of prayer and fasting, we cling to the one word and the sole truth that breathes life even in the darkest moments of our countless sad and sorry endings.

"You are my beloved child." There our story begins. It seems to end at a place called The Skull, where the young Messiah who refused the tempter's proposals hangs out with an unlikely but loyal subject (Luke 23:39-43). Together they ponder not what they've lost, but even in that dread wilderness they speak of what lies ahead. Together they trust that something does. And so do we.

Prayer

"Lord God, our strength, the battle of good and evil rages within and around us, and our ancient foe tempts us with his deceits and empty promises. Keep us steadfast in your Word and, when we fall, raise us again and restore us through your Son."[2] Let the memories of our own scars and the credulity from which you have redeemed us fill us with thanks and hope that will translate into a faithful word of warning and even stronger words of trust in your faithful grip on us all, through Jesus Christ our Lord, who lives and reigns with you and the Holy Spirit, one God, now and forever.

SECOND SUNDAY OF LENT

MARCH 7, 2004

REVISED COMMON	EPISCOPAL (BCP)	ROMAN CATHOLIC
Gen. 15:1-12, 17-18	Gen. 15:1-12, 17-18	Gen. 15:5-12, 17-18
Psalm 27	Psalm 27 or 27:10-18	Ps. 27:1, 7-9, 13-14
Phil. 3:17—4:1	Phil. 3:17—4:1	Phil. 3:17—4:1
		or 3:20—4:1
Luke 13:31-35	Luke 13:(22-30), 31-35	Luke 9:28b-36
or Luke 9:28-36		

In this next stretch of our wilderness sojourn, testing and temptation continue. To whom do we entrust our personal and communal identities and destinies? We hear God's calls to trust and faithfulness, but we also see frightening specters on all sides that we're not sure God has anticipated and accounted for in the resources given us for this journey. In any case, we can't stop now. In the face of continual threats, we trust as our Shield the wings of a determined Hen.

FIRST READING

GENESIS 15:1-12, 17-18 (RCL, BCP);
GENESIS 15:5-12, 17-18 (RC)

Interpreting the Text

In response to God's call, Abram and Sarai had given up the familiarity of a homeland to become wanderers in a place not their own. They set out with four promises to sustain them. God would make of them a great nation, bless them, make their name great, and through them bless all the families of the earth (Gen. 12:1-3). They had sought no clarification about these matters and ventured forth, it seems, without any suggestion from God or preconception of their own concerning what the fulfillment of God's promises might look like.

Now, some time later, God appears to Abram and speaks in a manner normally associated with angels who call prophets and others to special tasks. "Fear not! I am your Shield. I bring good news." God may have intended a longer speech, but Abram interrupts. He and Sarai don't have as yet a single heir, much less made strides toward becoming a great nation, though Abram does not specifically mention that latter point.

To answer Abram's worry, "the word of the LORD came to him" (v. 4) much as it would come later on to countless prophets among Abram's progeny. "Not to worry, Abram; you will have an heir from your own body. Indeed, your offspring will outnumber the stars."

Abram believed, and, although this leap of faith mightily impressed the narrator, God, Paul, Luther, and perhaps others, this confidence didn't suppress Abram's disbelieving questions for long. In the very next scene, when God appears to Abram as the one who brought him from his old homeland to give him a new one (see the promise of land in 13:14-17), Abram demands a sign of assurance that he will indeed possess the land on which he sojourns.

> ABRAM BELIEVED, AND, ALTHOUGH THIS LEAP OF FAITH MIGHTILY IMPRESSED THE NARRATOR, GOD, PAUL, LUTHER, AND PERHAPS OTHERS, THIS CONFIDENCE DIDN'T SUPPRESS ABRAM'S DISBELIEVING QUESTIONS FOR LONG.

Without hesitation or reproof, God responds to this request by instigating a covenant ceremony of an ancient type in which parties pledge to keep their word to one another on penalty of death. After Abram cuts in half the animals God has directed him to collect, God in effect declares, "If I fail to keep my word about your having all this land, you may do to me as we have done to these animals here slaughtered."

The scene ends without mention of Abram's response. The next episode begins, however, with Abram and Sarai devising their own way to make the promise of progeny come to fruition.

Responding to the Text

The mix of faith and uncertainty evident in Abram manifests itself in every generation of God's people, including our own. Among the ancients, Moses would grow discouraged about the progress and potential success of Israel's wilderness journey and, much like Abram, would seek from God some sign that might reveal the future and prove God's faithfulness (Exod. 33:12-23). Even the most single-minded prophets secretly longed for personal vindication and assurance of their work's success (Jer. 15:15-21). And what parent has not prayed tearfully over a sick and vulnerable child, "Lord, I believe; help my unbelief!" (Mark 9:24)?

Some among us embark on a thoroughly serious journey of repentance in the season of Lent. We may need to make some radical change in the direction or pattern of our lives, and we count on the disciplines of prayer, fasting, and almsgiving to assist us in what may be our last, best chance at reform or renewal. We enter a wilderness of difficult transition with the promise of God's faithfulness, but we long to know if the journey will succeed. Will the results at the end prove the worth of the pain we must endure?

Through much of our lives, our hopes remain clouded as those of the current dwellers on the land Abram surveyed when God promised him and his descendants everything between Egypt's great river and the Euphrates (15:18). Everyone striving to live there understands that land as a gift of God, a sacred inheritance given to the seed of Abram—some through Ishmael, and some through Isaac. None can leave the fulfillment of these promises strictly in God's hands. All must help God, it seems, with bombs and guns as well as prayers, for surely God's vision of the future must correspond to their own.

What will become of us? What sign have we that God's promises will take us to a future we shall find truly inhabitable?

"I am your Shield," God declares. The Hebrew for "shield" comes from the same root as the word for "garden" or "enclosure." Though we rest secure in no other place or destination, we have a place in God.

We also have the covenant God cuts with us, wherein God offers up God's own life as the pledge of faithfulness, which at the very least means God cannot quit any more than we can on the painful journeys we must somehow finish.

Responsive Reading
Psalm 27 (rcl, bcp);
Psalm 27:10-18 (bcp alt.);
Psalm 27:1, 7-9, 13-14 (rc)

"I trust" (am confident, v. 3) and "I believe" (v. 13). On a line strung between these two anchoring points hang the manifold reasons any one of us could have to be afraid. "Evildoers" may chew on us like wild animals. Armies may array against us or war envelop us. Loved ones may abandon us. It may appear that God, too, hides from us.

We live with confidence, however, because we dwell in God's temple. That remains our hiding place. Where is this temple? The psalmist calls it God's "tent." For the original wilderness generation, God's tent went with them everywhere. For later exiles far from sanctuary in Jerusalem, the heavens became God's tent (Isa. 40:22). Either way, we never lack shelter in a world where hostile forces roam at will. God's tent will conceal us, too. We trust. And we believe.

Second Reading
Philippians 3:17—4:1; 3:20—4:1 (rc alt.)

Interpreting the Text

From a cell in some prison we can no longer locate with certainty, Paul follows his own advice as he addresses dear friends in Philippi. "Beloved," he wrote, "whatever is true, honorable, just, pure, or commendable, if there is any excellence and if there is anything worthy of praise, think about these things" (4:8). Accordingly, Paul thought plenty about the Philippians themselves and how much he loved them and entrusted his heart to them (1:3-11).

Perhaps because they meant so much to him, Paul also feared for the Philippians. Multiple temptations threatened them, but few so troublesome to Paul as those that came from "enemies of the cross" (v. 18) who urged in Philippi a false gospel that apparently resembled the faith-plus-circumcision version that so exercised Paul when he wrote to the Galatians. "Beware of the dogs . . . who mutilate the flesh!" he warns the Philippians in a spirit of polemical tirade (3:2), and proceeds to caution them sternly about putting their confidence in ritual practices such as circumcision.

Paul likens those who trust in ritual cleanness to gluttons and libertines. On the surface, the latter types seem a complete, spiritual opposite to the strict, legalistic practitioners of religion. For both, however, the "belly" serves as their god. They put their confidence not in God but in practices they control and enforce and that give them occasion to become judges over others.

Paul and his readers find their lives and vocations in a different sort of community. Translated "citizenship" in NRSV and "commonwealth" in RSV, Paul's word for that community in 3:20 depicts the baptized as a colony of displaced persons that lives within or alongside some dominant culture. Compared to the larger group, this little colony looks humble, lowly in every way. The one who claims this weak, little band as his own, however, already now has begun to transform it into something glorious. Crouched in a ghetto the world scarcely notices, the body of Christ awaits the fulfillment of God's promises.

> THEY PUT THEIR CONFIDENCE NOT IN GOD BUT IN PRACTICES THEY CONTROL AND ENFORCE AND THAT GIVE THEM OCCASION TO BECOME JUDGES OVER OTHERS.

Responding to the Text

We think first of Esau, perhaps, when assembling a list of prototypes for the category "belly-servers." He sold everything for a single bowl of soup (Gen. 25:29-34). At the other end of the list we must place ourselves, for we entrust our welfare to an economic system addicted to unnecessary consumption. Moreover, obesity has reached epidemic proportions in our society. Esau, after all, ate to live. We live to eat.

Hungry as we may be for food, sex, and the delights we receive from all our gadgets, we still crave nothing more than a belly full of righteousness. More than anything, we love being right. We are right about the environment, the economy, the state of the world, the issues in our marriage, the trouble with young people today, and the complete idiocy of all those who drive either slower or faster than we do.

When it comes to religion, theology, and the church, we have even greater hungers and thirsts for rightness. For one thing, the music those other folks love sticks in our craw. We can't swallow it. The same goes for their views on sexuality, gender roles, and relations with others outside our fellowship. We smile politely, as we think we must, but we know in our hearts those others will some day be on the outside looking in. Given our druthers, that would happen here and now.

The god of our own belly seduces us so cunningly, playing mostly on our virtues. So easily we trust our need of something more than the gospel's simple promise to satisfy our righteous hungers. For some in Paul's day, old laws concerning circumcision offered that something extra that might prove the sign of certainty, but every community of believers struggles with some issue of rightness that threatens to split them up and destroy their gospel-centered community.

> HUNGRY AS WE MAY BE FOR FOOD, SEX, AND THE DELIGHTS WE RECEIVE FROM ALL OUR GADGETS, WE STILL CRAVE NOTHING MORE THAN A BELLY FULL OF RIGHTEOUSNESS.

"Slaves to the belly" Paul calls those who foment division and lay stumbling blocks in others' paths by adding requirements to God's simple promise of grace in the cross and resurrection of Jesus Christ (Rom. 16:17-18). Their god is their own rightness (Phil. 3:19). Most of the time, we assume Paul was talking about someone else. During Lent, we assume he means us. Accordingly, we submit to the only known cure for belly-serving. We repent.

THE GOSPEL

LUKE 13:31-35 (RCL);
LUKE 13:(22-30), 31-35 (BCP);
LUKE 9:28B-36 (RC); 9:28-36 (RCL alt.)

Interpreting the Text

The bulk of Luke's Gospel consists of Jesus' journey to Jerusalem that begins in 9:51 and stretches all the way to the cross that awaits him there. Nothing can detain Jesus from the way he has chosen nor redirect him toward some other destination.

Jesus prepares for his journey by going to "the mountain" for a time of prayer, much as he will later retreat to Gethsemane to ready himself for the trip's last, fateful leg. The preparatory moment becomes an occasion of revelation. Jesus' face and clothing change in appearance, and the disciples witness him in conversation with Moses and Elijah. These three speak of "the exodus Jesus was about to complete in Jerusalem." Both Elijah and Moses had come to the end of their mission on God's behalf atop a mountain (Deuteronomy 34; 1 Kings 19), but in some sense neither had finished his work when God declared his season ended. The Law and the Prophets now pass the baton to Jesus, as it were. On the cross he will complete the journey to freedom that they had begun.

For sustenance along the way, Jesus sets out with a single word of promise—the baptismal identity (cf. 3:22), this time voiced from within the cloud of God's presence (cf. Exod. 24:15; 1 Kings 8:10-11).

Quite a way into Jesus' journey, some Pharisees warn him of a death warrant Herod has published against him (13:31). For once, Jesus sounds almost like the kind of dramatic hero we expect to find in a story of rivals approaching a climactic face-off. "Go tell that so-and-so that I'm not about to back down from him. I have places to go and things to do." Even when he speaks of the inevitable cruelty that awaits him in the city famous for killing prophets and stoning messengers of ill news, Jesus still sounds like a conventional, though tragic, hero.

> BOTH ELIJAH AND MOSES HAD COME TO THE END OF THEIR MISSION ON GOD'S BEHALF ATOP A MOUNTAIN, BUT IN SOME SENSE NEITHER HAD FINISHED HIS WORK WHEN GOD DECLARED HIS SEASON ENDED. THE LAW AND THE PROPHETS NOW PASS THE BATON TO JESUS.

In the image Jesus chooses for describing himself in his lament over Jerusalem, namely, a mother hen who wants nothing more than to gather under her wing the people and nation he loves with all his heart, we see at last a different kind of Messiah. And only then do we catch on to something deeper in the subtle sarcasm of calling Herod a fox. The hen dares the fox to come into the chicken coop and do his dirty work.

We know this scene. It appears in many a cartoon, and somehow the chicken always wins while the fox falls prey to some trick. In Luke's story, the fox will eventually take a pass on his chance for a slaughter (23:6-12), and the hen will face a lion instead. The hen will die, though the chicks will live to tell the story.

Responding to the Text

Who will rule God's people, and to which chosen one do we listen—the fox or the hen? Many a prophet had promised Israel freedom and glory after a messiah would stomp their enemies as the great King David had done. It made sense to reject any alleged messiah who didn't meet those expectations.

Jesus had faced this issue in the wilderness when offered an empire if he would only honor the tempter's rightful hold on power. How would Jesus rule? The fox's way—with intimidation, fast horses, and crackerjack armies? Or another way?

We tread the wilderness of Lent, tempted as Christ was, while seeking to depose the false gods that seek to own our souls. We, too, face the god of fast horses and smart bombs, along with his prophet, the fox.

Their program entices us, as theirs is the only kind of peace most of us have ever seen work. In the hardball games of government and international relations, but also in our neighborhoods and families, the fox keeps the peace by making everyone afraid. He walks menacingly about our homes, teeth slightly bared, sometimes wearing our own skin. No one wants to feel the fox's bite.

Other prophets, like Isaiah, offered an alternative peace. "In returning and rest you shall be saved; in quietness and in trust shall be your strength," says God, though no one trusts this and all opt instead for fast horses (Isa. 30:15-20). Isaiah says God waits until after the ensuing debacle, then steps in to comfort the survivors. The fox and lion will always come around, and we grant them the mantle of necessity, but God's ultimate way with humankind, the way of the Lord's Messiah, is the way of the hen—the chicken—not the fox or the lion.

As for us, our money says, "In God we trust." But we find it easier to trust the money instead—or the missiles, stealth bombers, and aircraft carriers money can buy. Even at home, we trust loud, sharp words more than the value of repentance and quietness.

The patient Lord, however, waits until the din of fighting ceases, then rises up to heal the broken and slaughtered. Such is the story of Jesus, the mother-hen Messiah. He would have gathered the crowds, but the crowds turned against him, siding with the fox and calling out, "Crucify him!" Later, he, too, would rise up in mercy when the racket ended. First he was raised up on the cross, a sign of what the fox always does to the hen.

The Father waited for one last rising, the resurrection of the Great Chicken. That one is our Lord. Now we are his (her?) wings. We gather the threatened, the broken, the scattered, the weary, the lonely, the frightened, including those sick and tired of being sly foxes, ready now for rest and quiet under the wings of the patient Lord who waits while we play our deadly games of chicken. That one calls us home.

Go tell that fox this hen has a long journey ahead. We're on our way to Jerusalem!

Prayer

"Heavenly Father, it is your glory always to have mercy. Bring back all who have erred and strayed from your ways; lead them again to embrace in faith the truth of your Word and to hold it fast."[3] By your Spirit, fill us with courage so that through our words and actions, we and all your people might find our way to shelter beneath protecting wings. Make us also your shield for those who waver, doubt, stumble, and fall; through Jesus Christ your Son our Lord, who lives and reigns with you and the Holy Spirit, one God, now and forever.

THIRD SUNDAY OF LENT

MARCH 14, 2004

Revised Common	Episcopal (BCP)	Roman Catholic
Isa. 55:1-9	Exod. 3:1-15	Exod. 3:1-8a, 13-15
Ps. 63:1-8	Psalm 103 or 103:1-11	Ps. 103:1-4, 6-11
1 Cor. 10:1-13	1 Cor. 10:1-13	1 Cor. 10:1-6, 10-12
Luke 13:1-9	Luke 13:1-9	Luke 13:1-9

Accommodation to our various forms of imprisonment plus our own wisdom regarding suffering and tragedy often prove the most serious impediments to faithful trust in God. Once more, God calls us to repentance. Come home from all your places of exile, God's messengers declare, and leave behind the gods you there have made of and for yourselves.

FIRST READING

ISAIAH 55:1-9 (RCL);
EXODUS 3:1-15 (BCP);
EXODUS 3:1-8a, 13-15 (RC)

Interpreting the Text

The poetry of Isaiah 55 speaks meaningfully to people in a host of circumstances, particularly those dispirited or despairing over dashed hopes for a meaningful future. These verses first came as encouragement to the exilic community in Babylon near the time when Cyrus of Persia conquered Babylon and let that fallen empire's captives return to their homelands.

Isaiah 40 begins and sets the tone for the prophecy that stretches through chapter 55. The time of punishment has ended, a day of rebirth has come (40:1-2). Citizens of Jerusalem shall return to Zion, and this will bring great glory to God (40:3-5). Israel shall have again its ancient vocation as blessing to all the families of the earth and as light to the nations (42:6-7). God will see to it that even the people's terrible suffering proves to have meaning (52:13—53:12).

The tiny community of exiles, with their painful memories of Jerusalem's fall and a sense of themselves as scattered like dust in the wind, cannot easily trust God or themselves to make good on a promise of glorious return to the homeland (40:6-8,

27). The exilic prophet answered the call to sing to this broken, dispirited people that they might know God's comforting breath once more, trust in God's strength and faithfulness, and find as God's gift to them strength for renewal and return.

The final stanzas (55:1-13) begin with an invitation to a feast of God's providing. No one could pay for what gets served at this table. The nourishment received there has no price and does not come in jars or bowls. The wine is the joy of reunion, and the end of war and imprisonment the priceless, satisfying bread (vv. 1-2).

At this feast God also gives the exiles work and weight in the world, and God renews their vocation (vv. 3-5). They have reason to live.

But the time is too short to sit in despondence wondering how these things might work (vv. 6-7). While all this sounds unfathomable to human ears, God's ways and designs far surpass our most hopeful imaginings (vv. 8-9). Shall we forfeit a chance for renewal because we deem such a notion too good to be true?

A much earlier prophet, Moses, also had the task of convincing a captive and skeptical people that they could return in freedom to the land of promise. Exodus 3:1-12 sets the story of Moses' call in the form for narrating every genuine prophet's calling (e.g., Isa. 6:1-13; Jer. 1:4-10; Luke 1:26-38). Each prophet receives the summons to serve, but then demurs. "Who, me? Aren't you overlooking something in this choice of personnel?" The messenger in charge responds with assurances, and finally the prophet consents, usually with a simple, "Here I am."

In Moses' case, the call comes in the region of Mount Horeb, a place that will become the center of Moses' role as leader and prophet to Israel (v. 1). The sequence of events here differs from most, as Moses responds, "Here I am," before the rest of the typical sequence unfolds. This prophet signs on without a clue as to what God will ultimately require of him. This moment will cost Moses his life. Yet, like the bush that burns but is not consumed, so will Moses find himself ablaze with God's word and work without burning out along the way.

Moses understands from the outset that he lacks credibility in the palace as well as among those in the slave ghetto whose trust he must win. He asks the name of the God who has called him, for he knows everyone, from Pharaoh to the slaves, will ask in whose name he comes. God says, "Tell them, 'I AM sent me.'"

Volumes have been written on this mysterious disclosure and the way it plays on the sacred name YHWH. Mixed in with all the serious implications we also see a bit of humor. Imagine Pharaoh's response as Moses offers the authorized answer to the powerful king's question, "Tell me Moses, who is the God who sent you?"

"I AM."

Pharaoh may have the first laugh, but God will get the last, as God soon makes good on Moses' strange claim (7:1).

Responding to the Text

The journey from exile or bondage to freedom always runs through the wilderness, and despite all our rhetoric about loving freedom, we never want to risk the journey. We think we do, but in truth, we fear the cost, the dangers, and the loss of all we know for certain. Even slavery and exile have their payoffs.

Slaves don't have to make choices. They follow orders, or they suffer and die under the lash. Exiles can always blame their misfortune or misery on the dominant culture that surrounds them. They live with certainty that once upon a time, back in the old country, life was better.

Liberation and freedom bring choice and responsibility. Inevitably, they bring shortage and hardship as well, at least through the period of transition as slaves learn to quit thinking like slaves and exiles wrap their brains around the notion of "home." To Israelite slaves in the wilderness of transition, Egypt began to seem like a paradise lost, a land of free food and plentiful water. How soon they forgot that the price of that menu was bondage—a few leeks, some garlic, a melon in exchange for one's soul.

Anything that holds us in some bondage relies on our addiction to the very things that enslave us, as well as on our powers of denial and self-deception concerning the payoffs we get for remaining captive. Such things depend as well on our inability to imagine a life without certainties of the one we know now, wretched though it may be. Alcohol, medications, relationships, work, and patterned behaviors of many other kinds can make any of us slaves. We sometimes call such things "habits," a name that derives from older words for a home or dwelling place.

Every such place has its god, and that god feeds and sustains us for the price of our devotion. All these gods prove highly jealous. They must keep us from contact with the outside, so they weaken or sever our ties to family and friends. In the end, we sacrifice to them our health, our sanity, our lives. We would escape, but to whom shall we go? These things have the words of the only life we know!

> IN THE BUSH THAT BURNS AND YET REMAINS, WE MEET UP WITH THE MYSTERIOUS I AM WHO SIMPLY WILL NOT LET US REMAIN PRISONERS OF OUR IDOLATRIES AND IMPOVERISHED IMAGINATIONS.

"Why do you spend your money for that which is not bread, and your labor for that which does not satisfy? Listen carefully to me, and eat what is good, and delight yourselves in rich food. Incline your ear, and come to me; listen, so that you may live," says the voice that interrupts the dulling din of the slave-master's music.

We would listen so we might live. But first we must die. No one escapes the wilderness alive, not even Christ. Here in Lent's wilderness we face these things, but not alone. God knows our sufferings. We are buried with Christ, marked with the gritty ashes of his cross. In the bush that burns and yet remains, we meet up with the mysterious I AM who simply will not let us remain prisoners of our idolatries and impoverished imaginations.

PSALM 63:1-8 (rcl);
PSALM 103 or 103:1-11 (bcp);
PSALM 103:1-4, 6-11 (rc)

Psalm 63 identifies itself as "A Psalm of David, when he was in the Wilderness of Judah." The psalm gives thanks for the gift of sanctuary and rich, satisfying nourishment even in a dry and weary place. These words come as witness to the truth that we needn't return to bondage in order to find what sustains and gives life. Here is a song meant precisely for singing in the wordless wilderness, in the place we feared no music could reach save for the sounds of mourning and emptiness.

Psalm 103 gives thanks for God's forgiveness and healing. Rather than leave us in "the Pit" or insisting that we toil forever in an economy of paying for our sins and iniquities, God shows us love and faithfulness beyond our wildest imaginings. Even as God revealed such boundless mercy to Moses and Israel, so God will also treat us with infinite compassion.

Second Reading

1 CORINTHIANS 10:1-13 (rcl, bcp);
1 CORINTHIANS 10:1-6, 10-12 (rc)

Interpreting the Text

The prophet Hosea (2:14-15) viewed the wilderness sojourn as a honeymoon period for God and Israel. The Pentateuch and Psalm 78, however, depict the journey through the wilderness as a time when Israel complained, rebelled, suffered, and died miserably. Paul takes the latter view when he holds up the Exodus generation as a negative example the Corinthian church should by all means avoid.

God had provided Israel with everything necessary for safe and sane passage, including the cloud of divine presence, protected passage at the sea, and miraculous food and drink (1 Cor. 10:1-4). Ultimately, however, the people met with catastrophe that also came from God's hands.

Why? Idolatry brought this reaction from God.

Paul alludes in turn (vv. 7-10) to the incident of the golden calf reported in Exodus 32, the mix of idolatry and sexual promiscuity described in Num. 25:1-9, and the rebellion that warranted the plague of "fiery serpents" of Num. 21:4-9. All these things, Paul asserts, show a link between idolatry and disaster, and this should serve as a lesson to all future generations. Even strong people who think themselves immune from temptations to seductive offers of other gods should take special heed.

Paul's word of encouragement in v. 13 has suffered serious abuse over the centuries. Read in this context, the claim that temptations are common to everyone and do not come upon the helpless with overwhelming force applies specifically to idolatry, not to everything in life that proves a test of one's strength, character, and identity as a child of God. Moreover, Paul does not claim here that God sets up the tests of thirst, hunger, and accompanying discouragement that become the occasions for idolatry.

> EVEN STRONG PEOPLE WHO THINK THEMSELVES IMMUNE FROM THE TEMPTATIONS TO THE SEDUCTIVE OFFERS OF OTHER GODS SHOULD TAKE SPECIAL HEED.

Paul concludes his warning with a word of promise and comfort. We fail tests, even when warned. God, however, remains faithful (v. 13). No matter how many ways we might reasonably interpret the "way of escape," the point is that God's faithfulness proves stronger than any temptation and remains valid despite the outcome, however disastrous, of any round of testing.

Responding to the Text

Most of the idolatry discussed here occurs as people in transition replace the God they can't see with one they can. By introducing the golden calf episode (Exodus 32), Paul brings to mind the prototypical temptation of that sort. The absence of Moses, who stood for God in the sight of both Israel and Pharaoh, prompted the people to seek some alternative assurance of God's presence in their midst. Contrary to popular opinion, the people didn't set out to worship cows, golden or otherwise. They made for themselves a cherub, like the ones that would eventually perch atop the ark of the covenant and serve as God's throne (cf. 1 Sam. 4:4).

Eventually, such signs of God's presence begin to attract the reverence and trust that belongs to God alone. In our day, things like the stock market, or even the entire free market system we choose to live by, may well serve as a golden calf. We trust prosperity and financial security as signs of God's presence and providence. All too easily, however, the market becomes our god. Market forces dictate our every move. Even as church, we quake before the awesome and inescapable power of the market as we make decisions about worship, mission, and bang for our bucks. We dare not defy the Market, else we surely face ruin.

The Israelites in the wilderness, Paul reminds us, had copious signs of God's presence. They had the cloud and all that miraculous bread (manna) and water (from the rock). But apparently they didn't have everything they wanted, which to them meant God had failed them. At this same point, amid the emptiness of crushed expectations, we all find our temptations to idolatry. How could God leave us in such a spot? Where is God when we need God?

Curiously, Paul alludes to the presence of Christ in the wilderness with the Exodus generation (v. 4 and perhaps v. 9). Though the ancients didn't see Christ in their midst, from his vantage point, Paul could discern the shadow of the cross on those ancient wilderness scenes.

The cross is our sign of God's presence throughout the wilderness stretches of our lives. Our sufferings, emptiness, and sense of godforsakenness don't mean God has abandoned us or that we must find another god. Just the opposite. Precisely there, in the crucified Christ, God remains a faithful companion—our Rock—through the darkness of the wilderness trek.

THE GOSPEL
LUKE 13:1-9

Interpreting the Text

With the transitional phrase translated, "At that very time," Luke links the conversation in this lesson to the teachings that immediately precede it. There Jesus has sternly warned the disciples to remain watchful despite the Son of Man's delayed return (12:35-48), and he chides the crowds who can skillfully read the signs of earth and sky to predict the weather, but they cannot interpret "the present time" (12:54-56).

Some of those present report a piece of breaking news. Pilate has murdered some Galilean worshipers. What does this mean?

Jesus presumes the crowds will read this sign in the most common way. Even the scriptures—Psalm 1, for example—support such a reading. Surely the victims of this massacre must have done something to deserve it. For good measure, Jesus adds an example of his own, an apparently well-known story of eighteen people crushed accidentally in the fall of a tower. Did these unfortunates owe God some bigger debt than anyone else in Jerusalem at the time?

No, Jesus answers. These signs of the times suggest only one thing for certain. It's high time for repentance, just in case the rest of us should perish as did those in the news. Curiously, hard upon his critique of the crowd's unsophisticated way of understanding the signs around them, Jesus seems to say that all signs mean the same thing: It's time to repent.

> JESUS SEEMS TO SAY THAT ALL SIGNS MEAN THE SAME THING: IT'S TIME TO REPENT.

The teaching that follows this assertion (vv. 6-9) offers a simple but profound bad news/good news take on the occurrence of tragedy and suffering. Given the proximity of warnings about the Son of Man's coming (12:40), this parable of the failed fig tree may represent in Luke a softening of the mysteriously harsh story of the cursing of a similarly unfruitful fig tree in Mark 11 and Matt. 21:18-20. After waiting three years for his fig tree to yield a crop, the vineyard owner decides to have it destroyed. The gardener, however, pleads for patience. "Give me—and the tree—one more cycle of seasons. Let's see if some digging and a load of manure can make this tree produce."

We have little evidence that the ancients thought or joked as we do about the prospect of standing ankle-deep in manure. Nevertheless, Jesus seems to teach here that we might well find some painful disturbing of our surroundings and roots, not to mention a pungent load of dung, more as opportunity than curse.

Responding to the Text

Most of us practice a measure of circumspection as we read the signs of our times. Accordingly, we recoil at the suggestion some Christians have offered that AIDS is a sign of God's judgment on the sexual practices common to some population groups. The cruelty of this claim puts it in a category similar to the assertion that Jews somehow deserved what happened in the Holocaust.

Even if we don't share in these judgments, we instinctively look for a cause-and-effect relationship between catastrophe and the lifestyle or specific behaviors of those we see struck down. We cannot abide the notion that such things happen randomly, apart from any higher order by which the universe operates. Hence, we seek to discern that order. Those who suffer or die must have done something that brought this result on themselves—they drove drunk, perhaps, or had unprotected sex, or didn't pay attention to their diet. There must be some reason. And when we establish the reason, we resolve to avoid such mistakes and thus avoid the fate of those who didn't live as carefully as they might have.

As for fallen towers and crushed lives, we know more than we like about such things, though ours have not come down by accident. We have responded habitually to that circumstance with oaths to track down those responsible so we might visit upon them a reward of revenge, reprisal, retribution, and retaliation. This response, too, comes from our need for finding meaning and exerting control.

So much of our meaning-making apparatus has as its true purpose the establishment of our own innocence, justification, and rightness. Whatever happened, it wasn't my fault, or our responsibility. I'm clean. We remain the good guys, and if victims, innocent ones.

Jesus has a "re-word" for those who think along these lines. "Re-pent," he says. Never mind whose fault things are. Truth be told, our lives are so tangled and enmeshed, not only in our families but on this tiny globe of a world as well, we can never determine exactly who's to blame for what.

Besides, all the goodness and righteousness we can muster will never make us exempt from falling towers or killers on the loose.

So don't go further into the darkness of seeking your own control, Jesus warns. Instead, repent. Stop. Look at your situation. Turn around. Come home.

At the very least, stop long enough to turn around and face the one who comes to seek you in the dust, rubble, and darkness—Jesus Christ, who also fell victim to Pilate's bloody games, and on whom the vaunted towers of Roman justice and Israel's holy *torah* came crashing down in a heap of stones and nails that killed him.

He enters our darkness as well, to die with us beneath the horror of what we've all together made of this world. Renewal comes through dying with him instead of insisting on choosing our own rewards of retributive righteousness.

The same Spirit that raised Christ from the dead fills us, too, in each new year of life we're granted daily by the gardener who comes with shovel and manure bucket to give us one more chance.

Many of us live our whole lives in the span of that year.

Prayer

"Eternal Lord, your kingdom has broken into our troubled world through the life, death, and resurrection of your Son. Help us to hear your Word and obey it, so that we become instruments of your redeeming love."[4] Grant us who proclaim your Word with words that we may not stumble over the fallen icons, broken visions, and ripped assumptions that come with your breaking into our world. Let us find and speak your good news in the rubble of these days; through your Son, Jesus Christ our Lord, who lives and reigns with you and the Holy Spirit, one God, now and forever.

FOURTH SUNDAY OF LENT

MARCH 21, 2004

REVISED COMMON	EPISCOPAL (BCP)	ROMAN CATHOLIC
Josh. 5:9-12	Josh. (4:19-24); 5:9-12	Josh. 5:9a, 10-12
Psalm 32	Psalm 34 or 34:1-8	Ps. 34:2-7
2 Cor. 5:16-21	2 Cor. 5:17-21	2 Cor. 5:17-21
Luke 15:1-3, 11b-32	Luke 15:11-32	Luke 15:1-3, 11-32

Technically, Sundays are not numbered among the forty days of Lent, and today we break the fast of the season for a taste of the feast of reconciliation that awaits us at the end of our journey. A Passover behind and one ahead tell the meaning of our wilderness sojourn, though we have much within us still to kill before we can join in the feast of the final homecoming.

FIRST READING
JOSHUA 5:9-12 (RCL);
JOSHUA (4:19-24); 5:9-12 (BCP);
JOSHUA 5:9A, 10-12 (RC)

Interpreting the Text

The Deuteronomistic history here notes the signposts marking the beginning and end of Israel's wilderness journey. The stones in Gilgal where the people finally cross the Jordan serve as a kind of catechism for future generations. When children ask concerning them, "What does this mean?" the answer will come as a story of water-crossings at the beginning and end of Israel's long journey. God accomplished both passages, through sea and river, so all the earth may know and fear the Lord.

Others besides the children hear these stories. In 5:1, a verse outside the reading, nations that find themselves in the path of the people who have come from the wilderness also hear these remarkable tales and respond with fear. A sense of doom overwhelms them and their hearts melt.

The "disgrace of Egypt" that Joshua declares "rolled away" (5:9) refers to the renewal of ritual circumcision reported in 5:2-8. The Deuteronomistic history

assumes that the tribes of Israel practiced circumcision before their descent to
Egypt but not during the centuries of bondage. Perhaps the narrator understands
the cessation of a people's central rites and covenant symbols as the greatest disgrace or shame of a people fallen into slavery. The Deuteronomistic writer surely
knew as well the subsequent tradition concerning Gilgal. Named for this "rolling
away" of shame, it would later become a place known for shameful apostasy and
idolatry (cf. Amos 4:4; 5:5; Hos. 9:15; 12:11).

With the circumcision complete and the men of Israel healed, the people prepare to observe the Passover in the plains of Jericho (5:10). Passover, with its shedding of blood and ritual meal, had launched them on their journey to freedom.
This initial commemoration of that event now marks the people's arrival in the
land of promise.

That Passover also signaled the end of manna, the miraculous bread and staple
of the wilderness diet. From this day on, Israel would eat the crops of Canaan.

In important ways, these verses say more about the wilderness sojourn than they
do about the beginning and end of the journey. For all its wonders and occasional
moments of drama, Israel remembered the days of transition in the wilderness as a
time devoid of the punctuation that ritual affords. They knew neither fast nor feast,
only manna. All time proved ordinary, and every day resembled the last. Life differed
little from slavery, except no one knew for sure who ruled now as taskmaster.

Responding to the Text

Along with other observances of fasting in Lent, many Christians forgo
their expressions of "Alleluia!" during this time. This practice not only signals the
sobriety appropriate to serious repentance, it also helps to teach us the deep wisdom of living with rhythms. Even as we live by more than bread alone, so also we
cannot thrive on a diet of high time without low time—or the reverse.

Transition periods in our lives as individuals and communities usually find us
experiencing a breakdown of traditions. Newlyweds often discover that each of
their singleton's ways of observing holidays no longer work for a couple. The
newly sober must approach every festival with great caution and perhaps skip some
altogether. Similarly, those who bear in their hearts a fresh grief find all their old
feasts a scene of glaring absence that renders all times and places desolate.

All these and many others who have left their old lives behind on some far bor-
der will live again, sing again, and despite occasional tears rejoice and give thanks
once more. While for now it behooves them to trust in the supply of one-day-at-
a-time bread, memories of feasts and of ritual beginnings and ends have their place
in the wilderness. When the people of Jerusalem first received the Deuteronomistic historian's work, they had once more lost the land of promise. Another
wilderness lay between them and a time or place of rejoicing. But for now they

could comfort themselves with the promise that God had seen them through this before and surely would do so again.

During Lent we practice this oft-repeated cycle in our lives. Time after time we slip into some unexpected wilderness of flat time and common space. We can't sing "Alleluia!" out here. But we trust the Spirit will again give us words and songs and set us at some table of feasting. The God who met us once in the water will one more time birth us into a family that gathers to sing.

RESPONSIVE READING

PSALM 32 (RCL); PSALM 34 or 34:1-8 (BCP); PSALM 34:2-7 (RC)

Psalm 32 gives thanks for forgiveness received and reflects on the pain and folly of clinging fearfully to unconfessed iniquity (vv. 1-5). Rather than hiding from God, the absolved find safe sanctuary in God (vv. 6-7). The wicked live in torment from which trust in God's steadfast love offers the only release (v. 10). This freedom in turn brings songs of praise to the lips and hearts of the forgiven (v. 11).

Psalm 34 proceeds in the same pattern, in this case giving thanks for protection from danger rather than pardon for one's sins. The exhortation, "O taste and see that the LORD is good" (v. 8), provides a clear, thematic link to the Passover festival in Joshua 5 as well as the meal of a fatted calf in Luke 15.

Either of these psalms easily could serve as the prayer of thanks one would offer at the meal that celebrated the presence of one we thought was dead but somehow, by God's mercy, returned to us alive.

SECOND READING

2 CORINTHIANS 5:16-21 (RCL); 2 CORINTHIANS 5:17-21 (BCP, RC)

Interpreting the Text

A sorely strained relationship between Paul and the congregation in Corinth lurks behind the somewhat defensive tone of this letter's early chapters. The troubled relationship has taken a toll on Paul and pushed him close to a bankruptcy of discouragement. He protests once too often, as it were, with his repeated assertions, "We have confidence," and "We do not lose heart" (3:4,12; 4:1, 8, 16; 5:6).

Paul's desire to reconcile with the Corinthians (6:11-13; 7:2-3) prompts him in 5:11-21 to define his entire ministry as a mission of reconciliation. The love of Christ who died for all has taken Paul's heart and soul captive (vv. 14-15). Hence, Paul no longer lives for himself or even as himself. He lives for Christ and, more astonishingly, as Christ.

Christ's crucifixion and resurrection changed forever the way his followers regard him. Similarly, Paul now views everything and everyone differently than before his own moment of dying with Christ (v. 16). Such is the consequence and power of baptism. The statement translated, "If anyone is in Christ, there is a new creation" (v. 17) refers to the fruit or effect of baptism. (Cf. Rom. 12:5; Gal. 3:27-28 on baptism and being "in Christ.") This claim also has roots in Paul's Jewish upbringing. In rabbinical tradition, a Gentile converting to Judaism could not change and "become a Jew." Rather, this step requires the making of a new person, a whole new act of creation on God's part. Here Paul asserts the same of baptism. In baptism, God makes new persons in place of the old.

> PAUL NOW VIEWS EVERYTHING AND EVERYONE DIF-FERENTLY THAN BEFORE HIS OWN MOMENT OF DYING WITH CHRIST (V. 16). SUCH IS THE CONSEQUENCE AND POWER OF BAPTISM.

This, in turn, allows Paul to assert that even as God was in Christ working a reconciliation that would restore the whole world to God, so also Christ now lives in all the baptized. Once we lived as sinners and worked to tear the world apart. In Christ, those old sinners have all died, and as "new creatures" we have now become in this world the reconciling righteousness of God in action.

Responding to the Text

A whole category of humor plays on the observation that some people mistake themselves as God. To wit, this old office joke: Q. What's the difference between God and Mr. Z.? A. God never acts like he thinks he's Mr. Z.

Paul had lived the mocked pattern in this joke as he traveled about the Mediterranean world driven by a holy zeal to divide up the world into the righteous and unrighteous, God's people on one side and everyone else on the other. All who accepted Jesus as the Messiah of Israel fell into the latter group, and Paul did his best to prove them wrong and make them outsiders.

We easily mistake Paul's efforts following his conversion as the same basic work but with the categories now reversed. The feisty former Pharisee seems to have gone about trying to argue folks into the kingdom by proving himself right and others wrong about God and the gospel. Many today seem only too eager to adopt that approach to the church's mission and message.

In his sanest moments, however, Paul understood and preached that being right about everything did not put anyone right with God or heal the divisions between human beings. Only the love of God, and particularly the sacrificial love incarnate in the crucified Christ, could do these things. This meant a whole new outlook on the Galilean teacher whom Paul once persecuted, but also a new view of himself. Paul lived now as the product and captive of God's redeeming love. The God who would reconcile all the world in a single embrace now went about clothed in Paul.

The same goes for all who die in the baptismal waters. Christ takes to his cross all our precious, self-defined rightness along with every other virtue that in our minds distinguishes us from others. For our part, we awaken to a new creation with a different kind of sight. We do not keep count of transgressions nor divide the world into two kinds of people. Our hearts open wide as Christ's arms in his cruciform embrace. Despite all appearances to the contrary, we are indeed God's holy and peculiar righteousness in action.

What's the difference between God and Mr. Z.? It's hard to say.

THE GOSPEL
LUKE 15:1-3, 11b-32 (RCL, RC);
LUKE 15:11-32 (BCP)

Interpreting the Text

Luke sets up this most familiar of Jesus' parables as a response to criticism Pharisees and scribes aim at Jesus because of his association and table fellowship with tax collectors and sinners (15:1-2). Between this murmured but malevolent charge and the parable of the two brothers Luke places his version of the parable of the lost sheep and its parallel, the parable of the lost coin.

Each parable depicts God as unwilling to tolerate the permanent loss of anyone. They also play on the natural human tendency to find greater joy in recovering a lost treasure than in resting assured over some favorite thing that never left one's sight. The suggestion that heaven shares the same tendency (v. 7) anticipates the chilly standoff between the father and the older brother in the Gospel. Both the ninety-nine who "need no repentance" and the brother who never left home remain outside the circle of rejoicing as the respective parables close.

In requesting his inheritance while his father remains alive, the younger brother merely asks for what rightfully belongs to him by the traditions of that time. He has come of age and wishes to make his way in the world, which he does as far from home as possible. By summarizing all but the last days of the young man's life in the far country as a time of throwing everything away in "dissolute living," the parable highlights the mindless way the son wasted what the father had worked a lifetime to save.

The parable then spends six verses (vv. 14-19) detailing the prodigal's progress of repentance. His waste leaves him wanting. The only work he can get leaves him no better off than the swine he feeds. In a sober moment, he sees the truth of his plight and resolves to go home, no longer as a son and heir, but as a hired hand.

The parable then shifts to the father's perspective (vv. 20-24). He sees with the eyes of compassion. For one thing, these eyes see "from afar," which means the young profligate never got so far from home as he thought. For another, they see from within a loving parent's insides, so the father sees not the failed beggar staggering home but the child who once moved inside his mother's womb, the lad the father had taught to walk on that same road.

The father runs to greet the boy—a most undignified and outrageous behavior for an old man—and gathers him in. The son begins the penitent speech he has rehearsed all the way home, but the father interrupts with directions to the servants for preparing a long-awaited celebration.

In the final scene (vv. 25-32) the parable contrasts the father's perspective with that of the older brother—and by implication the scribes and Pharisees who listen. Unlike his father, the older brother has disowned the younger. "Your son," he calls the other (v. 30), not "my brother." Astonishingly, he has long since renounced his own place in the family as well. "I have been working like a slave for you," he whines (v. 29). The fields close to home proved for this son a far country just as remote as the region of the other boy's folly.

The story ends with the father's plea that the elder son recognize his place in the family, but along with that unconditional status goes the utter necessity of celebrating the return of the family's stray as one would rejoice over resurrection from the dead. At that point, the father who waited so long for one son to return can only wait again for the other to come in from a self-imposed exile.

Responding to the Text

Some who hear this parable may listen with ears that know all too well the seductive songs of the far country and the shaming self-talk that comes after waking up some morning after a binge to find oneself among grunting swine. Such listeners likely receive this teaching with gratitude and may remain oblivious to the upset their rehabilitation precipitates among other family members.

Most of us, however, find that the music and dancing of the prodigal's party makes our blood boil. In our minds we dutifully affirm both justice and mercy. In the secret chambers of our hearts, however, we despise mercy except for that which we ourselves receive. By our calculations, we have earned it.

Few, if any, can see and listen from the father's perspective, but the parable means to give us the eyes and ears that can know satisfaction only when all members of the family sit together gladly at a meal of thanksgiving.

Journalists occasionally talk of news stories that write themselves. This parable preaches itself. Even without our help, it does its job. All that remains is to find in the parable a place for the one who told it—the soon-to-be-crucified Christ.

Using the same expression the parable's merciful father employs to name the "necessity" of rejoicing (v. 32), Luke's Jesus describes the necessity of the Son of Man's suffering and rising from the dead (24:26; cf. also 22:7; Acts 17:3). Thus, while celebration must eventually come, and one day all will welcome the music and dancing that greets us as we come in from the fields, for now Christ's place in the larger scheme of things remains on the fringes of the home place, out where the lost ones linger. His cross is fixed in the far country where the lost look like the found and the found like the lost. He hands over his life not only for those who fall into obvious sin, but also for us righter than right souls who can't receive a gift because we must, and in our own eyes do, earn everything we could possibly need.

> JOURNALISTS OCCASIONALLY TALK OF NEWS STORIES THAT WRITE THEMSELVES. THIS PARABLE PREACHES ITSELF. EVEN WITHOUT OUR HELP, IT DOES ITS JOB.

Prayer

"God of all mercy, by your power to heal and to forgive, graciously cleanse us from all sin and make us strong."[5] Stir up in us your own compassion so that we may see your people as you do, the weak and the strong, the resentful and the pure in heart, the broken and those who live in denial, forgiven one and all in the cleansing blood of Jesus Christ our Lord, who lives and reigns with you and the Holy Spirit, one God, now and forever.

FIFTH SUNDAY OF LENT

MARCH 28, 2004

REVISED COMMON	EPISCOPAL (BCP)	ROMAN CATHOLIC
Isa. 43:16-21	Isa. 43:16-21	Isa. 43:16-21
Psalm 126	Psalm 126	Ps. 126:1-6
Phil. 3:4b-14	Phil. 3:8-14	Phil. 3:8-14
John 12:1-8	Luke 20:9-19	John 8:1-11

Though we deliberately leave most of our usual baggage behind as we proceed on our Lenten pilgrimage, too easily the memory of our sins becomes a wearying, even deadly burden. Today we handle this baggage. The ancient name for this Sunday was *Judica*. "Judge me, O God," began the day's introit. Yes, judge us, God. Get it over with. The Judge listens and responds, "Remember not the former things. Go your way."

FIRST READING
ISAIAH 43:16-21

Interpreting the Text

This lesson calls readers and listeners back to the period late in Israel's exile when the prophet urged God's people to rise up and prepare for the return to Jerusalem (Isa. 40:1-5; 55:10-13). The oracle begins with mention of the mighty acts associated with God's deliverance at the time Pharaoh's army had trapped Israel by the sea. The grammar of this remembrance presents these remarkable deeds as frequent or habitual, however, not as singular events in the past (vv. 16-17).

Having brought to mind these marvelous and salutary acts of God, the oracle then issues a strange command. "Do not remember the former things" (v. 18), for "I am about to do a new thing" (v. 19). Why forget the very things the prophet just recalled, pieces of sacred history that remained for this and every other prophet the centerpiece of Israel's story as God' people?

The answer lies apparently in the need for total readiness to God's "new thing," which will include a highway through the wilderness complete with a reliable water supply at all the rest stops (vv. 19-20). Perhaps this means the exiles must forget not only the mighty deeds of the Exodus but the subsequent forty years of hardship and testing that might discourage the current generation from ever setting out on yet another wilderness journey. The wonders of this journey will surpass even that one in the lore of God's saving acts.

Some of the rhetoric here suggests the need to "forget" not only the Exodus, but everything of the past. Understood literally, v. 18 says, "Remember not the *first* things. . . ." In addition, when v. 21 speaks of God "forming" a people to declare God's praise, it uses the same descriptive verb for shaping pottery that describes God's creation of humankind in Gen. 2:7. Thus, the oracle of Isaiah 43 urges hope and preparation for a new creation, not "merely" a repeat of the exodus.

Responding to the Text

In every generation, faith comes by hearing. Specifically, hearing the ancient stories of our people, particularly as our forebears came to know, struggle with, and trust God, most effectively gives birth to faith. The Holy Spirit works with words and creates through story.

HEARING THE ANCIENT STORIES OF OUR PEOPLE, PARTICULARLY AS OUR FOREBEARS CAME TO KNOW, STRUGGLE WITH, AND TRUST GOD, MOST EFFECTIVELY GIVES BIRTH TO FAITH.

As heirs to our people's story, we become a tribe of both faith and unfaith. We can remain the latter when we choose to live in or cling to the past, refusing to face either the dangers or the prospects of present circumstances. Similarly, we may rehearse and revere the glorious past in which God once upon a time delivered people from bondage, but do so in a way that relegates all God's saving power to the past. Maybe God acted once, but nothing could redeem us in our current mess.

Amid our own versions of such denial and discouragement, we hear a word of promise that hints at a whole, new world. Such news proves even more difficult to believe than a rerun of the Exodus, especially for people who listen to these same stories more than two millennia later. We know how hard it proved for Israel's exiles to return and how even their successes at rebuilding seemed so pathetic they couldn't distinguish the weeping from the sounds of rejoicing among those who watched (Ezra 3:12-13).

The new creation did not materialize then, at least not in a form anyone recognized. A few centuries later, its failure to appear in Jesus' day led almost everyone to reject him as Messiah. And still we wait, all the while telling the same old stories that call us both to remember and not remember the former things, or even the first things. We cannot live in the past or in some pretend version of the future. Neither can we thrive in a present bound to the limits of our imagination.

Faith comes through hearing, in the old stories, about God's habitual work of making paths through the deep, snuffing out the headlights on the empire's chariots, and reshaping each one of us over and over, like a potter with a vessel that's never been fired.

RESPONSIVE READING

PSALM 126 (RCL, BCP);
PSALM 126:1-6 (RC)

This psalm looks back on the return and restoration promised in Isa. 43:16-21. It offers no hint of the difficulties that accompanied these events, recalling them instead as a time so marvelous it seemed a wonderful dream.

Now, however, the psalmist looks for yet another period of comfort and renewal, for once again God's people have lived some nightmare. The community has returned to the wilderness and to the drought and thirst that always threaten travelers there. Fresh water in dry beds of the Negev comes at the end of winter. Like those who wait for a spring season they know will come, so God's people who have only tears to quench the thirst of hardship live even now with joy that wells up from trust in the one who has restored them so often in times past.

SECOND READING

PHILIPPIANS 3:4b-14 (RCL);
PHILIPPIANS 3:8-14 (BCP, RC)

Interpreting the Text

This section of Philippians sets up the argument for the paragraph the lectionary employed for the Second Sunday of Lent (Phil. 3:17-4:1). There Paul urged his friends to follow his example and to stand strong, lest they become enemies of God and "belly-servers," as some others have done. Here the apostle describes his former life as a pious and blameless man of God, but he renounces the whole of that piety and righteousness he once prized as nothing but "rubbish" (literally "excrement") compared to what he has come to possess through knowing Jesus Christ as his Lord.

Paul's older set of credentials become useful to him here as he seeks to counteract the efforts of those who worked to introduce required practices such as circumcision among the baptized in Philippi. Paul was circumcised; indeed, he embodied everything circumcision signified. He could boast of pure blood, unquestioned zeal, and perfect obedience. What did he gain from all this? Nothing. Actually, less than nothing. These things had allowed Paul to live with a deceptive illusion about a righteousness he could pursue and acquire on his own.

Such righteousness amounts to mere self-serving, Paul now believes in the wake of his coming to know Christ. The righteousness of God that comes as a gift far surpasses any righteousness of our own we can muster through obeying the law.

Paul remains something of a zealot, however. When he describes how he now pursues the goal of knowing Christ that he might become like him in his death, and through that dying might also know resurrection and the "heavenly call," Paul twice (vv. 12, 14) uses the same word translated earlier (v. 6) as "persecutor."

Paul had once devoted his life to circumcision. Now he had found in the suffering and death of Christ an infinitely more compelling reason to live.

Responding to the Text

The dogs against whom Paul warns the Philippians (3:2) still prowl today. They sniff around and bark their turf-marking messages all through the church. They don't urge circumcision, but they can quote plenty of other demands and prohibitions in minute detail from constitutions, by-laws, and handbooks. They are always right and sometimes righter than right.

If Paul and Luther are right about all this rightness, every one of us works instinctively and incessantly to do right and think rightly, or at least to look like we're in the right, and thereby to avoid criticism. Any who think they have put these habits to death once and for all need only recall the last time they realized they would be late for some appointment or deadline. Did a story begin to form that would explain—and justify—the imminent tardiness as a matter beyond my control?

> EVERY ONE OF US WORKS INSTINCTIVELY AND INCESSANTLY TO DO RIGHT AND THINK RIGHTLY, OR AT LEAST TO LOOK LIKE WE'RE IN THE RIGHT, AND THEREBY TO AVOID CRITICISM.

The pursuit of rightness is an all-consuming goal that leads to sickness, isolation, and death. Among the best extrabiblical treatments of this truth is Flannery O'Connor's story "Revelation,"[6] which tells of a rigidly pious small-town woman who has spent her life looking down on others she deems less right about things than herself. In the story's climactic, revelatory vision, this woman sees a great procession marching upward into the heavens where all appear to be welcomed. To her astonishment, all those she has despised march ahead of her and her husband in the grand procession. They go last. Moreover, even their virtues must be stripped away upon entry. All their rightness will become so much rubbish.

Remember not the former things (Phil. 3:13), Paul tells himself. Nothing in my past can lift me out of the endless cycles of criticism, excuse-making, and self-justifying. Nor does anything I have done or not done sink me forever in the rubbish of my countless shortcomings. God's love and acceptance remain sheer gift.

This we have come to know through the sufferings and death of Christ, which we share through baptism.

THE GOSPEL

JOHN 12:1-8 (RCL);
LUKE 20:9-19 (BCP);
JOHN 8:1-11 (RC)

Interpreting the Text

The account of Mary anointing Jesus at Bethany in John 12:1-8 has close parallels in Mark 14:3-9 and Matt. 26:6-13, in which a woman anoints Jesus in Bethany two days before Passover. John's placement of this event six days before Passover holds a key to its meaning in the Fourth Gospel. The soteriological depiction of Jesus as the Passover Lamb in John ultimately finds Jesus slaughtered at noon on the Day of Preparation (19:14), at precisely the same time the sacrifice of the festival lambs began at the temple in Jerusalem. According to Exod. 12:3, preparation for Passover includes selecting on the tenth day of the month of Nisan a lamb without blemish or spot to reserve for sacrifice. Passover itself came on the fifteenth. In all likelihood, John has located the anointing story in the sequence of days leading up to Passover so as to make this scene the moment of ritually selecting this Gospel's "lamb of God who takes away the sin of the world."

Other uniquely Johannine features characterize the story as well. Lazarus, newly raised from the dead in an episode recounted only in John, as well as the particularly mendacious Judas of the Fourth Gospel are present as well. Martha, whose confession in the previous chapter (11:27) parallels Peter's at Caesarea Philippi in the Synoptics, serves the meal, and sister Mary anoints Jesus' feet.

Jesus' parable in Luke 20:9-19 is commonly read as an allegory about Israel's history and the Jews' rejection of Jesus. God expects good fruit or produce from Israel, the chosen people, but gets none. Even worse, the people rejected and abused the former prophets, the latter prophets, and in these last days also the Son of God, the Lord's Messiah. As a consequence, suggests the usual line of reasoning, Jews deserved what happened when Rome attacked and destroyed Jerusalem.

Such a reading does not lead toward proclamation of good news. We gain nothing good by rejoicing in Israel's distress. A reading that would allegorize but substitute Christians of various eras as tenants who fail to produce fruit might prove more useful, but even then we still haven't heard gospel.

Where does the gospel reside in this parable? If Christ is the stone the builders reject, and that stone ultimately becomes a scandal to the builders, and it destroys them when it falls on them, how can this serve as good news for anyone?

Can we find another cornerstone? The rejected "cornerstone" that ultimately proves most foundational in Luke's Gospel is something no one can understand until after Easter and the resurrection. In Luke 24, Jesus, yet unrecognized by the

Emmaus pair, teaches that the key to understanding everything that had transpired resided in understanding that the Messiah must suffer and only then enter his peculiar sort of glory. Later, Jesus teaches the whole group of gathered disciples the same lesson in hermeneutics.

The stone must be rejected. All nearby will go down with it when it falls. "Heaven forbid!" say the people and their teachers. But crushed beneath that stone is the only condition that leaves one with hope. This is Luke's secret.

The well-known textual questions surrounding the placement and authenticity of John 8:1-11 have not kept it from holding a prominent place in popular theology. Even those who know little else of the tradition can quote Jesus' line, "Let anyone among you who is without sin be the first to throw a stone at her." Despite its familiarity, however, this remains the only occasion in any lectionary system that the story appears as a reading for the church.

> THE REJECTED "CORNERSTONE" THAT ULTIMATELY PROVES MOST FOUNDATIONAL IN LUKE'S GOSPEL IS SOMETHING NO ONE CAN UNDERSTAND UNTIL AFTER EASTER AND THE RESURRECTION.

While Jesus teaches "all the people" at the temple, scribes and Pharisees bring forward a woman they accuse of adultery. Indeed, she can only be charged if caught in the act by at least two witnesses other than the man involved. The implied scenario of her capture piques the reader's imagination, as does the obvious absence of the male sexual partner who has somehow vanished.

The accusers desire more to test Jesus than to prosecute the adulteress, although the various ways they expect Jesus to fail are not altogether obvious. The test by which Jesus tries the accusers becomes the focus of the story. All present find themselves convicted when they take Jesus' challenge, beginning with those with the longest life experience.

Much speculation, mostly fruitless, has focused on the content of what Jesus may have written "on the ground" (vv. 6, 8). Jesus' clear word to the woman in the closing interchange gets less attention. As the last potential executioner, he withholds condemnation and sends the woman off to live a new, or at least different, life.

Responding to the Text

John has assembled a highly significant cast of characters for the momentous event reported in 12:1-8. Each played a typical role within the community of the Fourth Gospel, and perhaps in our own communities as well. Lazarus has just shed his grave-clothes and begun a new life. He is the assembly's neophyte. Martha serves as deacon (see this word in v. 2), and Mary acts as the priest who performs the anointing. Judas is a thief, but the worst thing about his stealing becomes evident in the way John describes the treasury bag he carries. The bag

(v. 6) contains "what they collected," probably not for their own needs but as their offerings for the poor. Moreover, the verb used for Judas's action of carrying the bag also consistently names the action of cross-bearing, not only in the Synoptics, but also in John (cf. 19:17).

Together, this small gathering comprises a whole Christian community—the newcomers, the faithful proclaimers and servers, the worship committee, and the small contingent that sucks the community dry by betraying the mission. The mystery here is that together they select Jesus as their paschal lamb. Not only our faithfulness and worship make Christ our sacrifice, but also our sins and treachery call forth the need for his blood on our doorposts.

Later, when Jesus becomes the servant beneath the table, washing feet and wiping them dry (13:1-11), when he bears the cross by himself (19:17), when he ends up in Lazarus's grave-clothes, anointed in death with the fragrant substance meant to cover the stench of death (19:40), he does these things for the whole community. Judas was the traitor, but all of them together handed Jesus over on this day in Bethany when they selected him as God's lamb. Indeed, the words Jesus uses to instruct the group about Mary and her apparent waste of the ointment (12:7) could be translated, "Forgive her," just as accurately as, "Leave her alone."

Besides, the assembly will have plenty of time in the days to come for doing the work that the contents of the treasury bag were meant to aid. The poor are always with us, and in them we find our way to continue serving Bethany's guest.

The cornerstone in Luke 19:9-19 remains the stumbling stone over which folks fall yet today. Nobody gladly seeks or waits for a suffering messiah, for that puts us all in danger. We desire instead a clever leader or guru who can help us stay as far from blame, pain, and difficulty as possible. Yet, Luke's Gospel declares that a suffering Messiah becomes the orienting cornerstone by which to understand the older scriptures and to judge the preaching and teaching that grows out of the church.

When we reject the suffering Messiah and opt for the one that goes straight to glory, we end up crushed in a different way. Such a would-be savior inevitably leaves us behind. But the suffering Christ joins those crushed beneath the scandal of his own fate, and precisely there is the gospel. Luke's passion narrative carefully illustrates how Christ on his way to the cross attends to all those who are crushed by his own fate as well as their own. Even those who seem to perpetrate the worst of the crushing become this Messiah's concern. The mourning women, the executioners, and the fellow crucified (23:26-43)—all these the suffering Messiah comforts with his words and presence.

When our house falls on us because we have built and depended on something other than a suffering Christ, the devastation will be great indeed. But underneath the rubble, in the ruin of our lives, we shall meet again the stranger who walked

184

THE SEASON
OF LENT

─────────

FREDERICK A.
NIEDNER

the Emmaus road. He sits with us in our desolation and once more feeds us with his bread and cup.

While the once-free-floating story of the woman caught in adultery has appeared at the beginning of John 8 since the ninth century, some ancient manuscripts placed it after Luke 21:38, and many commentators point out that it fits more easily there than any place in John. The homiletical possibilities that stem from connections to Lukan themes prove richer, too.

In this narrative, Jesus proves himself a friend of sinners and the despised, as he does also in Luke's accounts of the woman with the ointment (7:36-50), the healings of a crippled woman (13:10-17) and ten lepers (17:11-19), and the visit to Zacchaeus's home (19:1-10).

Also, the narrator plays a bit with the family of Greek words that describe stooping and straightening up (vv. 6, 7, 8, and 10). The only other use of the simple form for bending or stooping in v. 6 appears in Mark 1:7, as John the Baptist explains his unworthiness to stoop and untie the coming one's sandal. The word for Jesus' unbending or straightening up in John 8:7 and 10 appears in Luke's story of the crippled woman (13:11) as a description of what the woman could not do. In Luke 21:28, an imperative of this same verb expresses faithful response to the Son of Man's coming.

Also, while Jesus does not say to the adulteress as he did to many others, "Your faith has saved you, go in peace," he does tell her, "Go your way, and from now on do not sin again." The first imperative is the same verb used throughout Luke and Acts for Jesus' having "set his face toward Jerusalem" and for "being on the way."

Taken together, the language of bending, rising up, and going one's way draws a picture of Jesus' joining his fame and fate to one humbled by her sins but invited by Christ to stand and join him on the way he alone could perfect.

Finally, many have used this story to dismiss in cavalier fashion all who serve as judges among human beings. Often this proves little more than a variation on other familiar themes of self-justification. The story does not render illegitimate all judging among human beings, but it does serve warning to all who set themselves up as judges over others or who rush to participate in every vigilante group that fixes on some sinner who deserves rebuke. By the end of the story, all those others have vanished. Only the accused remains, but in the company of the young man headed for Jerusalem.

Prayer

"Almighty God, our redeemer, in our weakness we have failed to be your messengers of forgiveness and hope in the world. Renew us by your Holy Spirit, that we may follow your commands and proclaim your reign of love."[7] Grant a strong measure of that Spirit to those of us called to the ministry of proclamation, for we know our own weakness and our failures weigh heavily upon us. Take the burden of our sins, fill us with hope, and give us words with which to proclaim the message of your daily miracle of resurrection in our lives; through your Son, Jesus Christ our Lord, who lives and reigns with you and the Holy Spirit, one God, now and forever.

Notes

1. *Lutheran Book of Worship* (Minneapolis: Augsburg Publishing House, and Philadelphia: Board of Publication, Lutheran Church in America, 1978), 17.

2. Ibid., 18.

3. Ibid.

4. Ibid.

5. Ibid.

6. Flannery O'Connor, *The Complete Stories* (New York: Farrar, Straus, and Giroux, 1971), 488–509.

7. *Lutheran Book of Worship,* 19.

HOLY WEEK

FOSTER R. MCCURLEY

Many people, especially those in the midst of sorrow or grief, confusion or fear, loss or anger, find particular meaning in the church's worship during Holy Week. While others around them—friends, family, clergy—offer well-intended advice and suggestions, those who are suffering often find more comfort in someone willing to walk with them in their darkness. The quick and easy answers to their difficult problems sometimes offend them, giving the impression that their friends do not take them seriously or their family members do not understand or their clergy are not listening.

Holy Week disallows quick and easy answers to life's challenges. Each day challenges even the most devout believers to recognize the complexity of Jesus' own experience and of ours as well. Each set of readings forces us to struggle with questions that profoundly affect the center of our faith and the core of our being. Throughout the week we face the utterly unfathomable issue about Jesus' identity, especially the tension between his humanity and his divinity. On the one hand, some of the texts will focus on the agony Jesus faced as a fearful human being, admitting, "my soul is troubled" (John 12:27; also 13:21), and on his identification with those centuries of worshipers who uttered their painful laments before an all-too-absent God ("I am thirsty"; John 19:28). On the other hand, we will hear Jesus state unequivocally his unique relationship with God and the purpose for which he was sent into the world (John 12:23, 27-28). The authors of the biblical books themselves will demonstrate their own struggles with the use of Old Testament prophecies and psalms to explain the meaning of the events of this Holy Week and to announce through their writings who this Jesus really is. Was he the servant of the Lord introduced to the world in four songs by the prophet Second

Isaiah, or did the early church reinterpret those ancient songs to explain the person and work of Jesus? Was he the expected Messiah, or did the events of this week render that possibility untenable?

Such questions and many others we will encounter this week force us to remain humble, for many of them cannot be resolved easily or at all. Yet it is precisely in their complexity that these issues provide comfort for those who suffer in the present. Jesus, the biblical writers, and—hopefully—contemporary preachers know that the life of faith stands in tension with the world, and in that tension faith is tested, challenged, and finally affirmed.

Walking with Jesus during this Holy Week is possible only because Jesus walked with us. We can follow in his footsteps only because he stood in our shoes and knows our pains, our grief, our fears, and even the darkness of death. Yet the journey is worth taking, because we know how the week will end. God will raise Jesus from the dead, exalt him to be our living Lord, and enable us to rise along with him to eternal life. In the meantime, we need not hasten through the week in order to find good news. It is already good that God has provided for us a living Lord who knows our sorrows and is present with us in the darkness of our lives.

> WALKING WITH JESUS DURING THIS HOLY WEEK IS POSSIBLE ONLY BECAUSE JESUS WALKED WITH US. WE CAN FOLLOW IN HIS FOOTSTEPS ONLY BECAUSE HE STOOD IN OUR SHOES AND KNOWS OUR PAINS, OUR GRIEF, OUR FEARS, AND EVEN THE DARKNESS OF DEATH.

SUNDAY OF THE PASSION / PALM SUNDAY

APRIL 4, 2004

REVISED COMMON	EPISCOPAL (BCP)	ROMAN CATHOLIC
Isa. 50:4-9a	Isa. 45:21-25	Isa. 50:4-7
	or Isa. 52:13—53:12	
Ps. 31:9-16	Ps. 22:1-21 or 22:1-11	Ps. 22:8-9, 17-20, 23-24
Phil. 2:5-11	Phil. 2:5-11	Phil. 2:6-11
Luke 22:14—23:56	Luke (22:39-71)	Luke 22:14—23:56
or 23:1-49	23:1-49 (50-56)	or 23:1-49

The challenge of preaching on Palm Sunday is inherent in the lessons assigned for the day. They seem to summarize the events and the message for the whole week right at the beginning, leaving the preacher grappling with variations on the theme as the following six days unfold. That is as it should be, because this final Sunday before Easter lays out not only the events of the week but questions about the identity of Jesus, apart from which the events bear no meaning at all.

FIRST READING

ISAIAH 50:4-9a (RCL);
ISAIAH 45:21-25 or 52:13—53:12 (BCP);
ISAIAH 50:4-7 (RC)

Interpreting the Text

The first half of Holy Week exposes us to the four "Servant Songs" in Second Isaiah. Today and Wednesday we hear the third one, Isa. 50:4-9a. On Monday the first song, Isa. 42:1-4, appears along with five additional verses, and on Tuesday the second song, Isa. 49:1-6, is extended by one verse to comprise the first reading. The fourth and most specifically "suffering servant" song, Isa. 52:13—53:12, takes its rightful place as the first reading for Good Friday.

Candidates for the position of the "servant" include the nation Israel, the people of Israel in exile, a prophet, the exiled king, some other unknown individual, and specifically the future Jesus. The debate occurs because the songs themselves present an inconsistent picture of whether the servant is an individual or a corporate body. The identity of the servant here will have to remain a scholarly mystery while we focus instead on the function of the servant in Isa. 50:4-9a.

The servant functions here as a wise person. The Lord has given the servant "the tongue of *limmûdîm*" (v. 4). The RSV followed the Hebrew word precisely and translated the plural adjective as "those who are taught," that is, pupils who have learned from a wise teacher. The NRSV has opted for the opposite side of the lectern by translating the Hebrew term as "a teacher." In light of the teaching role of the Lord in v. 5, "The LORD GOD has opened my ear" (see Prov. 2:2; 5:13), it would appear that the RSV was correct after all. The Lord is the teacher, and the servant is the pupil, the one preparing to be wise. (The reader will benefit from comparing Psalm 119 spoken by the Lord's "servant" [v. 17], who calls himself at v. 19 "an alien in the land" and includes at v. 80 the hope "that I may not be put to shame"—the same words that appear at Isa. 50:7.)

The servant of Isa. 50:4-9a is confident of the Lord's vindication. Indeed, it is because the Lord God helps him that he has not been disgraced and that he *knows* he shall not be put to shame (v. 7). He is willing to take on all adversaries without fear because he is confident that the Lord is near.

The lesson in the BCP from Isa. 45:21-25 is part of a "trial speech," a form common in Second Isaiah in which the Lord takes the idols of Babylon to court and charges them as imposters. Since the idols have not been able to speak beforehand regarding the events to come, they do not qualify as God whose word is effective (see Isa. 55:10-11). Contained in this pericope at v. 23 is the divine word:

> To me every knee shall bow,
> every tongue shall swear.

These words seem to provide the conclusion of the second reading, Phil. 2:5-11.

Responding to the Text

This third Servant Song appears to surface in discreet ways in the New Testament. The confident rhetorical questions, "Who will contend with me?" and "Who are my adversaries?" seem to have provided the apostle Paul with the ammunition to fire his question "Who shall bring any charge against God's elect?" at Rom. 8:33. His response, "It is God who justifies; who is to condemn," sounds very much like "he who vindicates me is near" (Isa. 50:8) and "Behold, the Lord God helps me; who will declare me guilty?" (vv. 8-9).

> THE USE OF THE SONG ON THIS PASSION SUNDAY CALLS US TO CONSIDER THE FAITHFUL SUFFERING OF JESUS IN TERMS OF THE SERVANT'S EXPERIENCE.

Further, the servant's claim that he "gave my back to those who struck me, and my cheeks to those who pulled out the beard" (v. 6) might have provided the general background for Jesus' instruction, "If anyone strikes you on the right cheek, turn the other also" (Matt. 5:39; see Neh. 13:25).

Strikingly, this Servant Song does not appear in the New Testament any more directly than through these few allusions. However, the use of the song on this Passion Sunday calls us to consider the faithful suffering of Jesus in terms of the servant's experience. While the song is not a prediction of the events of Holy Week, it is a description of the suffering that befalls the servant and of the confident trust that servant might have in the faithfulness of God to deliver.

RESPONSIVE READING
PSALM 31:9-16 (RCL)

Beginning with the plea that the Lord never allow the psalmist to "be put to shame" (v. 1), the psalm moves to the powerful words Jesus will one day utter from the cross: "Into your hand I commit my spirit" (v. 5; Luke 23:46). The psalmist laments his malady, indicating through his complaint the comprehensive nature of human suffering. His grief is so great that his emotional torment has increasingly affected him physically, losing strength and feeling his bones waste away. He has become such a sorry sight that even his friends dread his appearance (v. 11). Now, in addition to his chronic suffering, he appears to hover on the verge of a violent death (v. 13). The whispering, omnipresent terror, scheming and plotting to kill (v. 13) sound like the "confessions of Jeremiah" (Jer. 6:25; 20:3, 10; 46:5; 49:29). In the face of all this horror, the psalmist trusts in the Lord and confesses boldly, "You are my God" (v. 14). That confession leads to the plea for deliverance and salvation. The final verse selected for today (v. 16) contains the reason for its selection: "Let your face shine upon your *servant.*"

The power of the psalm on Palm Sunday lies in its description of human suffering. The agony over which body and soul attest their oneness, the grief that drives us to despair—all that human experience Jesus took on himself in order to become truly human, truly one with us, and then to rely on God to deliver him and to save us along with him.

SECOND READING
PHILIPPIANS 2:5-11 (RCL, BCP);
PHILIPPIANS 2:6-11 (RC)

Interpreting the Text

The apostle sometimes incorporated into his writings existing hymns and creeds in order to buttress his theological and ethical arguments. For example, Col.1:15-20 describes the creative and redeeming roles of Christ as a means of teaching the readers the role of Father and Son in redemption. The creed about the oneness of God as Father and Son in 1 Cor. 8:6 demonstrates the impossibility of idols and the implication of eating meant sacrificed to them.

Verses 6-11 of our text comprise an existing two-stanza hymn Paul incorporated into his letter. The first stanza (vv. 6-8) about Christ's humiliation contains expressions that contrast the divine *morphē* with Christ's willingness to take on the *morphē doulou*, the "form of a servant . . . born in human likeness . . . found in human form." So completely did he assume that servant-human form and so humbly and obediently did he follow his mission that he experienced death itself. Paul adds the means by which he died: "even death on a cross." Stanza two (vv. 9-11) begins with the profound word "therefore." The word connects the two stanzas in a causative way. The exaltation described in stanza two is directly dependent on the humility demonstrated by Christ in stanza one.

> SO COMPLETELY DID HE ASSUME THAT SERVANT-HUMAN FORM AND SO HUMBLY AND OBEDIENTLY DID HE FOLLOW HIS MISSION THAT HE EXPERIENCED DEATH ITSELF.

This exaltation includes God's gift of the highest name that we learn before the hymn ends: "Jesus Christ is Lord" (see Rom. 1:3-4; 10:9).

Everyone in the three-story universe—heaven, earth, and under the earth— will worship Jesus as exalted Lord. This universal acclaim will demonstrate the faithfulness of God to fulfill the divine promise of Isa. 45:22-23. Finally, the ultimate purpose of Christ's humiliation and exaltation becomes evident: "to the glory of God the Father" (v. 11). The hymn assumes that the death and resurrection of Christ have brought all creation into the worshipful and adoring position that God had intended in the first place.

Responding to the Text

Paul has used here a preexistent hymn about the exaltation and humiliation of Christ in the context of a discussion about lifestyle. Beginning the text with v. 5 leads the reader/preacher to follow that usage. However, the RC pericope starts with v. 6 rather than v. 5. As a result it focuses more on the christological and theological issues than on the ethical. In the context of Passion Sunday the RC position appears especially appropriate. The hermeneutical question, then, is whether we are limited by the apostle's use of an early hymn or free to employ it in its precanonical state. In this case, the hymn alone appears to carry the message of the week more directly than the focus on the humility of the Christian life.

The question of whether to use the text primarily as the basis for a sermon on humility or on Christology might be related to what we consider to be the basis for our ethics. If the basic principle for ethics is, "What would Jesus do?" then the inclusion of v. 5 into this text is essential. Christ was humble, and so should we be humble. That approach provides a "So what?" to the hymn. To base the sermonic emphasis on the Christology of the hymn, however, also allows a "So what?" to develop from the humiliation and exaltation of Christ. That question is not simply, "What would Jesus do?" but how we in our twenty-first-century lives worship Jesus as Lord to the glory of God the Father.

THE GOSPEL

LUKE 22:14—23:56 or 23:1-49 (RCL);
LUKE (22:39-71) 23:1-49 (50-56) (BCP);
LUKE 22:14—23:56 or 23:1-49 (RC)

Interpreting the Text

In its full form the Passion story includes almost two chapters of Luke's Gospel. In chapter 22 the evangelist reports the institution of the Lord's Supper (22:14-23), the dispute among the disciples about their relative greatness and Jesus' response (22:24-30), Jesus' prediction of Peter's denial three times before crowing time in the morning (22:31-34), Jesus' instruction to take up purse and bag and then go sword shopping (22:35-38), Jesus' prayer on the Mount of Olives submitting to God's will, undesirable as it may be (22:39-46), Judas's betrayal and Jesus' arrest (22:47-53), the fulfillment of Jesus' prediction regarding Peter's denial (22:54-62), the beating of Jesus by his captors (22:63-65), and Jesus' appearance before the council of Jewish leaders where they asked him about his identity: the Messiah or the Son of God (22:66-71). While every portion of this material from chapter 22 is essential to the Passion story, I will here discuss only two elements of the first part of the pericope, Jesus' prayer on the Mount of Olives (vv. 40-42) and Jesus' response to the identity issues before the council (vv. 67-70).

First, according to Luke the prayer occurs at "the place" that is located somewhere on the Mount of Olives. Typical of his practice, the author of Luke-Acts does not use Semitic words, and so he labels the spot not "Gethsemane" but simply "the place" (Greek: *ho topos*), which in this Gospel denotes a location where people show up who are not invited and then set an agenda different from what had been planned (prior to this text see 4:42; 9:12; 11:1). Encountering *topos* in v. 40 alerts the reader to the troops that will appear to arrest Jesus.

The content of Jesus' prayer at "the place" is briefly recorded: "Father, if you are willing, remove this cup from me; yet, not my will but yours be done" (v. 42). The reader is tempted to recall the words from the prayer that Jesus taught his disciples, "Your will be done on earth as it is in heaven." Those words, however, are not in Luke's version of the Lord's Prayer (Luke 11:2-4) but are in Matthew's (Matt. 6:10). The prayer of Luke 22:42, however, derives from Mark (see 14:36), who does not include the Lord's Prayer in any version, and so it is not appropriate to connect the prayer at "the place" directly with the prayer for disciples' use. Taking the three Gospels into account, however, enables us to recognize that the submission to God's will in the prayer taught by Jesus according to Matt. 6:10 does not include anything Jesus himself would not perform willingly: God's will replaces self will. Submitting to that divine will was the means by which Jesus proved faithful to the mission on which God had sent him.

Second, Luke's version of the accusations and questions before the council is interesting. Matthew and Mark report the question of identity in one question: ". . . tell us if you are the Messiah, the Son of God" (Matt. 26:63), "Are you the Messiah, the Son of the Blessed One?" (Mark 14:61), but Luke splits the question into two: "If you are the Messiah, tell us" (v. 67) and, "Are you, then, the Son of God?" (v. 70). To the first question Jesus answered by saying they would not believe him if he told them about the Messiah but immediately turned the title to "the Son of Man" who "will be seated at the right hand of the power of God." To the second question Jesus said simply, "You say that I am," leaving the identity issue quite ambiguous.

The titles presented here are ones that the church came to apply to Jesus, but only the Son of Man title is one Jesus generally used of himself. What he meant to convey with that title is not entirely clear, for the expression can be used (1) as the personal pronoun "I," (2) as a reference to a mortal (often in Ezekiel), (3) as a collective figure of martyrs (Daniel 7), or (4) as a victorious one who will appear at the last day (Enoch and elsewhere). It is probable that Jesus used the term in several or indeed all these ways, and perhaps because of its versatility the title was the one Jesus preferred when speaking of himself.

Chapter 23 describes Jesus' appearances before Pilate and then Herod (vv. 1-12), Pilate's death sentence on Jesus (vv. 13-25), the crucifixion (vv. 26-43), and Jesus' death (vv. 44-49). Within all this profound material we will discuss (1) the titles thrown at Jesus by the leaders and crowds, and (2) Luke's contributions to the last words of Jesus.

Having already encountered the titles "Messiah," "Son of God," and "Son of Man" in the earlier part of the pericope, we hear others hurled at him from the foot of the cross. The religious leaders challenged him to "save himself if he is the Messiah of God, his chosen one" (v. 35). Interestingly, those titles are used earlier in Luke's Gospel to describe Jesus. Peter used the words "Messiah of God" to respond to Jesus' question in 9:20: "But who do you say that I am?" The addition of "the chosen one" *(ho eklektos)* by the religious leaders is strikingly reminiscent of God's own definition of Jesus in Luke's version of the Transfiguration announcement, "This is my Son, my Chosen" *(ho eklelegmenos,* Luke 9:35). The religious leaders had all the right words, but in their own disbelief about Jesus' identity, they used the titles to mock him. Like the soldiers, they challenged Jesus to demonstrate proof in order to live up to his reputation as "King of the Jews" (vv. 37-38). The challenges to prove his identity, whoever made them here, are ones that the devil had already posed for Jesus (4:1-13). Either these mockeries at the cross were a déjà vu experience for Jesus, or else the so-called Q source that informed Matthew and Luke developed the narrative details of the Temptation to demonstrate what Jesus would face later in his life.

As for Jesus' verbal responses to the challenges and to the execution itself, Luke provides us with three of the "seven Last Words":

- "Father, forgive them; for they do not know what they are doing."
- "Truly I tell you, today you will be with me in Paradise."
- "Father, into your hands I commend my spirit."

That the first word Jesus speaks is "Father" is particularly striking in light of the preceding narrative words "when they came to the place. . . ." Is it possible that Luke is calling the reader's attention to the story about the testing of Abraham's faith in Genesis 22? There in v. 9 the narrator uses the words "when they came to *the place* [same words in Greek] that God had shown him," and in v. 7 he puts into the mouth of Isaac the address, "Father!" Perhaps the connection is not so farfetched when one recognizes that the expression "beloved son" *(huios agapētos)* used of Jesus at his baptism (Matt. 4:17; Mark 1:11; Luke 3:22) and at the Transfiguration (Matt. 17:5; Mark 9:7) appears in the entire Septuagint only in Genesis 22 in regard to Isaac on the day he was about to be sacrificed (vv. 2, 12, 16). That the sacrifice of Jesus occurs at "the place"

THAT THE SACRIFICE OF JESUS OCCURS AT "THE PLACE" IS ONCE AGAIN A DEMONSTRATION OF LUKE'S THEOLOGICAL GEOGRAPHY WHEREBY A "PLACE" IS WHERE NO ONE IS INVITED BUT THE CROWDS COME NEVERTHELESS AND WHERE THE CROWDS SET THE AGENDA.

is once again a demonstration of Luke's theological geography whereby a "place" is where no one is invited but the crowds come nevertheless and where the crowds set the agenda.

What follows Jesus' address to "Father" at Luke 23:34 is his prayer that God forgive those who are executing him on grounds that they do not know what they are doing. Jesus is demonstrating what he taught his followers in the sermon on the level place: "love your enemies," the demonstration of which leads to becoming "children of the Most High" (6:35). In the face of all the titles thrown at him during his trial and execution, Jesus proves faithful by doing what he asks of his disciples, nothing more or less dramatic than that.

Jesus' second word, promising the repentant thief, "Today you will be with me in Paradise," is the most confusing. If he meant that promise in its literal sense, then the thief must have been waiting a long time for Jesus to arrive in Paradise—in fact, forty days. The key, it seems, to understanding the use of "today" lies in the way Luke has been using the term *sēmeron* throughout the Gospel. At 2:11 the angel announced to the shepherds the eschatological arrival of the Messiah with the words "to you is born this day *(sēmeron)* in the city of David a Savior who is the Messiah, the Lord." At 4:21 Jesus preached the briefest sermon anyone ever delivered in one's hometown: "Today this scripture has been fulfilled in your hearing." In this case *sēmeron* explicitly connects the eschatological expectation of Isa. 61:1-2 with the ministry of Jesus. When Jesus said to Zacchaeus at 19:9, "Today salvation has come to this house," he indicated God's eschatological promise of bringing home the outcasts. By the time the readers reach the words from the cross, *sēmeron* is firmly planted as the signal that the end time was dawning.

The final words Luke reports, also put in terms of address to "Father," are part of the lament of Psalm 31: "Into your hands I commend my spirit" (v. 5). Facing persecution and both physical and spiritual pain, the psalmist places trust in the Lord. Other "words" from laments appear in the crucifixion accounts. Matthew follows Mark in reporting Jesus' words from Ps. 22:1: "My God, my God, why have you forsaken me?" the opening of an individual lament. (See the discussion of the psalm for Good Friday.)

The laments accomplish two purposes in the crucifixion story: first, to demonstrate that Jesus identified with the suffering of humanity, even to the point of feeling God-forsaken; and, second, to remind readers that these laments end with praise and thanksgiving for God's intervention. Along with the narrative details and the other "words" from laments, Luke's use of Ps. 31:5 points the reader to Jesus' faithful response in the midst of his suffering and beyond the suffering to deliverance and praise.

Responding to the Text

Throughout this text the question of Jesus' identity stands out above all else. The Romans crucified many thousands of people throughout their empire. Why this particular death is recorded, remembered, and interpreted as the salvation event for the world is based on Jesus' identity. Only the divine gift of faith can perceive that Jesus is the Messiah, the Son of God, the Son of Man, the Chosen One, even the Beloved Son. Without faith all these words and titles function as mere mockery, and apart from faith the events surrounding this Holy Week bear no meaning.

Coming to the conclusion that Jesus is all of the above is a challenge to human reason. While the Old Testament is used and quoted again and again, it is quite difficult, if not impossible, to find a specific Old Testament text in which the eschatological Messiah would suffer and die. To be sure, there is a suffering servant (whoever that might be); there is a suffering prophet (Ezekiel, for instance); there is a suffering group of martyrs during the Maccabean rebellion. There is not, however, a suffering Messiah in the Old Testament. Because Jesus is the suffering Messiah in the New Testament, confessing who he is requires a faith that surpasses reason and understanding, even tradition and exegetical skill.

Highlighting the identity of Jesus in a sermon this Passion Sunday places the emphasis on Christology rather than on the events themselves or solely on our response to them. The use of the laments both in the so-called Last Words and in the narrative describing the events enables the preacher to focus on the humanity of the one called Son of God. This Messiah, quite contrary to all the expectations, identified himself with the suffering of the earth and went to his death like the rest of us. He knew our lamentable situations. He knew also how the laments end—with praise and thanksgiving because of God's faithful listening.

HIGHLIGHTING THE IDENTITY OF JESUS IN A SERMON THIS PASSION SUNDAY PLACES THE EMPHASIS ON CHRISTOLOGY RATHER THAN ON THE EVENTS THEMSELVES OR SOLELY ON OUR RESPONSE TO THEM.

In the midst of that lament, stretched out on a cross, Jesus the suffering one promised Paradise to the thief suffering beside him. He also promised the same destiny to all of us who know what it is to lament the pain of the world and the apparent absence of God.

For the Preacher

William Shakespeare wrote of the way in which Henry V spent his time with his troops on the eve of the Battle of Agincourt. The following day they would face a French army that outnumbered them five to one. Henry walked

> from watch to watch, from tent to tent. . . .
> With cheerful semblance and sweet majesty;
> That every wretch, pining and pale before,
> Beholding him, plucks comfort from his looks.[1]

Such is the comfort Jesus provides for us preachers through this week. Jesus walks among with us with the confidence that he and his Father are in charge of the events. By his semblance and in his words, we pluck comfort for the days ahead.

MONDAY OF HOLY WEEK

REVISED COMMON	EPISCOPAL (BCP)	ROMAN CATHOLIC
Isa. 42:1-9	Isa. 42:1-9	Isa. 42:1-7
Ps. 36:5-11	Ps. 36:5-10	Ps. 27:1-3, 13-14
Heb. 9:11-15	Heb. 11:39—12:3	
John 12:1-11	John 12:1-11	John 12:1-11
	or Mark 14:3-9	

The sufferings of Jesus, while painful to recall, expand our vision of God's love far beyond individual or provincial understandings of God's love. They demonstrate the faithfulness and loyalty of God in all places and all times. Christ's passion benefits not certain folks, not even religious folks, but the world that humans and animals alike call home.

FIRST READING
ISAIAH 42:1-9 (RCL, BCP);
ISAIAH 42:1-7 (RC)

Interpreting the Text

Of the four so-called Servant Songs (see the discussion for Palm Sunday), the first is the beginning of this text, namely, vv. 1-4. As readers of Second Isaiah move their eyes from the previous chapter to this one, they have already been introduced to the term "servant" *('ebed)* at 41:8: "Israel, my servant//Jacob, whom I have chosen." With that passage still in mind, readers wander into this first Servant Song with the identity of the servant intact, and so the mind is open to ponder the relationship of the servant to the Lord and the function of the servant according to this text. The addition of vv. 5-9 emphasizes even more the worldwide context for the servant's work. These additional verses identify the Lord and continue to explore the servant's job description.

In the first verse the Lord introduces the servant as "my servant," claiming ownership of the *'ebed,* as in 41:8. In order to confirm the identity of the servant established in 41:8, the LXX reads here "Jacob is my servant." The Lord further defines the servant as one "whom I uphold." While worshipers elsewhere used the same term to confess their trust in the Lord's presence and protection (Ps. 41:12; 63:8), more relevant for our purposes is the previous chapter, where at 41:10 the Lord offers such support for "Israel, my servant." The second half of the parallelism at 42:1 defines the servant as "my chosen, in whom my soul delights." The specific form of the word "chosen" is used twelve times in the Old Testament, always with the Lord as the chooser. Obviously a favorite word for Second and Third Isaiah, "chosen" occurs six times for the people of Israel, a collective figure (apart from our text see 43:20; 45:4; 65:9, 15, 22).

> THE LORD DELIGHTS IN CHOOSING HUMAN AGENTS WHOSE ROLE IN THE WORLD IS TO MAKE A DIFFERENCE.

That the Lord "delights" in this servant calls to mind as the objects of delight the ancestors of Israel who may or may not have been pious or righteous (Ps. 44:3) and "those who fear him" (147:10-11). Beyond Psalm 147, it is difficult to prove what kind of human behavior delights the Lord. What is clear, however, is that the Lord delights in choosing human agents whose role in the world is to make a difference.

The difference the servant is to make lies in the function assigned in this text. One word summarizes this function: *justice*. The word (Heb.: *mišpat*) establishes a mission platform for the servant, since it appears in each of the four Servant Songs (here, 49:4; 50:8; 53:8). Apart from the Servant Songs, the word occurs repeatedly in the preaching of Second Isaiah (40:14, 27; 41:1; 51:4; 54:17). Often "justice" points to a positive order of existence; here that justice is God's goal for the world ("the nations") through the agency of Israel. Equipped with the Lord's assurance for success, the servant will have no need of complaining aloud, growing faint, or being crushed (vv. 2-4).

What gives the Lord the right to change life for the nations is the recognition of the Lord as the exclusive Creator of the universe and the source of human life (v. 5). This claim to exclusive divinity also gives the Lord the right to refuse glory and praise to the idols (v. 8). After all, they cannot, like the Lord, tell of things to come before they happen (v. 9).

Having asserted that claim, the Lord can now expand the job description of the servant to serve as "a light to the nations" (v. 6b). While that function will appear again in the third Servant Song at Isa. 49:6, here it serves to connect the servant to the world. The additional functions of changing the fortunes of the blind and the prisoners (v. 7) will occur again in the call of the prophet called Third Isaiah (Isa. 61:1). In the immediate context the reader might assume that the sufferers are not exiled Israelites alone but the poor of the nations to whom the servant will give light.

To whom the Lord presents the servant at the beginning of this text is not stated. The words "Here is my servant" and the explanation of the functions that follow assume a listener or listeners. The opening words of Second Isaiah, out of which issues the call to the prophet (Isa. 40:1-8), appear to be addressed to God's heavenly court. That audience might be the same in our text. Another possibility is the world itself. After all, the servant begins the second song by calling on the "coastlands" and "the peoples from far away" to listen to the story of the Lord's call and the functions assigned (Isa. 49:1). This is the same audience the Lord summons to heed at 41:1.

Responding to the Text

The New Testament writers use the imagery of the servant from this song to serve the purposes of Christology and missiology. On this Monday in Holy week it is the christological focus that deserves our attention. At the baptism of Jesus in all three Synoptic Gospels (Matt. 3:17; Mark 1:11; Luke 3:22) the divine voice from heaven describes Jesus, "my beloved Son," with the words from Isa. 42:1: "in whom my soul delights." Whether the origin of "beloved Son" is also Isa. 42:1 through some textual manipulation of "my chosen" or a more direct rendering of the description of Isaac in Genesis 22, the descriptive words "in whom my soul delights" are certainly derived from this first Servant Song. The net result is to identify Jesus as the servant in Second Isaiah. The significance of the connection between the servant of the song and Jesus lies in the worldwide task set before them. Like the servant, Jesus did not come to fulfill the wishes of Israel but to accomplish the will of God for the world.

RESPONSIVE READING
PSALM 36:5-11 (RCL);
PSALM 36:5-10 (BCP);
PSALM 27:1-3, 13-14 (RC)

As the first Servant Song casts the role of the servant into the context of the world, so Psalm 36 provides profound reflection on that universal theme. While the first part of the psalm (vv. 1-4) denounces the wicked in terms that recall proverbial wisdom teachings, the second part (vv. 5-9) continues the universal context of wisdom and connects quite directly to the servant's role to shine as "a light to the nations."

> For with you is the fountain of life;
> in your light we see light. (Ps. 36:9)

We saw the imagery of light in the context of the world in the first lesson, where the servant is to be a light to the nations. That light is, of course, always a reflected light. Psalm 27:1 brings that point home to the individual by opening with the confession "the LORD is my light and my salvation." That conviction enables the worshiper to withstand the onslaught of evildoers without fear.

SECOND READING
HEBREWS 9:11-15 (RCL);
HEBREWS 11:39—12:3 (BCP)

Interpreting the Text

The purpose of Hebrews, whether it is actually an epistle or a homily or something else, is to wake up readers from complacency and worn-out ideas to a vital understanding of the gospel of Jesus Christ and to the newness of what his sacrificial death and resurrection have achieved. In that newness the readers would find hope and courage in the face of hostilities against them in their time (see 12:3, BCP). Throughout chapter 1

> THE PURPOSE OF HEBREWS IS TO WAKE UP READERS FROM COMPLACENCY AND WORN-OUT IDEAS TO A VITAL UNDERSTANDING OF THE GOSPEL OF JESUS CHRIST AND TO THE NEWNESS OF WHAT HIS SACRIFICIAL DEATH AND RESURRECTION HAVE ACHIEVED.

the anonymous author demonstrated the superiority of the Son of God over the angels. In chapter 7 he argued for the superiority of Jesus' priesthood over the Levitical priesthood, which was apparently well known to his audience. Our text is couched in a section that runs from 8:1 through 10:18 in which the author demonstrates the superiority of the ministry of Jesus as high priest and of the sacrifice he offered (see also 11:39-40, BCP).

In the paragraphs immediately preceding our text, the author described the old covenant in which the earthly sanctuary (the Jerusalem temple) provided the space in which the high priest would annually enter the Holy of Holies, taking with him the blood of a sacrificed animal. That blood served the purpose of cleansing both himself and the people from defilement caused by proximity to corpses and other such bodily taints. Having argued that the old covenant was already seen to be in need of a new one (quoting Jer. 31:31-34 at 8:8-12), the author now wrote of the contrast with Jesus, taking into the new Holy Place his own blood for the purpose of securing "an eternal redemption." The result of his once-and-for-all sacrifice is not merely the cleansing of the body but the purifying of the conscience from dead works so that Christians might worship the living God. Further, since Christ offered that effective sacrifice, he is the mediator of a new covenant in which the redeemed might receive "the promised eternal inheritance" (9:15).

Preachers of every time and place face the challenge of shocking listeners out of their complacency to seize the gift God gives us in Jesus Christ and to see the opportunities from that gift for serving "the living God." One of the lessons the author provides us in this text and throughout his work is the use of creative language to convey the meaning of the gospel of Jesus Christ. There are no precise human analogies to communicate the uniqueness of who Jesus is and what God accomplished for us in his death, resurrection, and exaltation. Yet, piling up approximations through the use of language can come close to communicating that unparalleled message. In this text the author used language from the religious cultic system, from the marketing or commercial world, and from the legal system—in five verses. Taking from the cultic system the concept of sacrifice and cleansing, the

> IN THIS TEXT THE AUTHOR USED LANGUAGE FROM THE RELIGIOUS CULTIC SYSTEM, FROM THE MARKETING OR COMMERCIAL WORLD, AND FROM THE LEGAL SYSTEM—IN FIVE VERSES.

author demonstrated the uniqueness of Christ's death and the cross and its eternal benefits. Borrowing from the marketing or commercial world in which "redemption" meant the freeing of a slave through a business arrangement, he demonstrated the freedom that Christ's sacrifice acquired for us. From the legal system the author took the word *covenant* (consider "last will and testament" at Gal. 3:15) and the concept of "inheritance" in order to announce the unilateral act of God in giving us gifts that do not require our cooperation or even agreement.

In our day some of the biblical words have taken on different meanings that lead listeners of our preaching down different paths of thought. *Redemption* is the word used when I exchange frequent flyer miles for an airline ticket. *Covenant* is another word for a contract in which mutual obligations are laid out. Paul's favorite word *justification* determines how the lines of my manuscript line up—to the right, to the left, or not at all. Preaching is all about finding images and words, literature and movies, events contemporary and past, that by their accumulation can approximate the message of the gospel and its effects for us. One rather bizarre possibility is the movie *Slingblade*. It tells how a mentally challenged man, freed from an institution because he was deemed no longer a threat to society, sacrificed his new freedom (admittedly by a horrendous act) in order to give new life and a future to his young friend and the friend's mother. As with every illustration, there is much left to be desired, but it is in the culture of our day that we find preaching possibilities, just as Paul and the author of Hebrews did in their age.

THE GOSPEL

JOHN 12:1-11 (RCL, RC, BCP);
MARK 14:3-9 (BCP alt.)

Interpreting the Text

As readers of John begin chapter 12, they have just covered the story of Jesus raising Lazarus from the dead, and they have learned that that miracle sealed his death sentence. The miracle itself provided the stage for Jesus' teaching about his claim to be "the resurrection and the life," and that "I am" saying promised eternal life to all who believe in him. The sign that the promise is true takes the form of the stench-filled corpse of Lazarus walking out of the tomb at Jesus' command. At the same time the sign points forward to Jesus' own resurrection even while the miracle hastens his death. Caiaphas, the high priest that year, "prophesied that Jesus was about to die for the nation" (11:51). The chapter ends with the news that the Pharisees had sent out spies to ascertain Jesus' whereabouts "so that they might arrest him."

The story of Mary's anointing of Jesus rings familiar chimes for many readers, but probably few would be able to relate the details of the story without peeking. The problem with recalling the precise actions, words, and characters lies in the appearance of another anointing described in the Synoptic tradition. While differences abound between Mark 14:3-9 and Luke 7:36-38, those two evangelists report a story about an unnamed woman who enters the house of a man named Simon to anoint Jesus' head or feet; for her deed Jesus defends her use of expensive perfume or forgives her for her sin. While John seems aware of both these stories or another one with common details, our text stands out from the others in naming the woman as Mary, locating the home as belonging to Lazarus, reporting that dinner was served by Martha, and placing at the event the disciple named Judas.

More precisely, the roles of Mary, Lazarus, and Jesus enable us to focus on the uniqueness of this account, even in the midst of many parallels with the Synoptic traditions of Mark and Luke. First, the acts of Mary in anointing Jesus' feet with expensive perfume and wiping them with her hair are astonishing. Normally one anoints the head of another, as attested in the familiar Ps. 23:5 (see the parallel at Mark 14:3). Anointing the feet would be more appropriate as part of preparing an entire body for burial. Hosts certainly had their servants wash the feet of their guests after traveling through filthy streets in order to avoid unappetizing aromas at the meal, but the ingredient for such hygienic care was water (or tears, as in the Lukan parallel), not perfume, especially not "costly perfume" worth 300 denarii (vv. 3, 5). Surprising, then, is her wiping off this expensive perfume, and equally astonishing is the use of her hair as the towel. The sinful woman of Luke's version dried the water off Jesus' feet with her hair before anointing them with perfume, but we would not expect the straight-laced Mary to let her hair down and then brush it across Jesus' feet.

Second, the story reveals some new data about the character of Judas. He is described here as the one who kept the common purse for the group, but beyond his job description is the detail that he "used to steal what was put into it" (v. 6). The author includes this information in order to explain why Judas objected so strenuously to the extravagant act on Mary's part. Perfume worth three hundred denarii (according to Matt. 20:2 the equivalent of three hundred days of a laborer's work) could have been given to the poor (or to fill his own pocket, the author implies).

Third, Jesus puts the entire event and Judas's response in perspective. He explains Mary's act as one of anointing him for burial. Caiaphas has already "prophesied" Jesus death. The Pharisees are already hunting him down to arrest him. Jesus' fate is imminent and obvious, and so Mary is "prophetically" anointing him for his burial, an act in which she will not participate after his actual death. Jesus' words explain why she anointed his feet and not his head: she is symbolically preparing his body for placement in the tomb. With that explanation as the background, Jesus also puts Judas's comment in its place. The words he uses, however, catch the reader of the Bible by surprise. "You always have the poor with you, but you do not always have me" (v. 8). The first part of the sentence recalls the teaching of Moses at Deut. 15:11: "Since there will never cease to be some in need on the earth." Jesus acknowledged that reality, but at that moment his disciples should focus on the immediacy of his presence and on the imminence of his death.

The concluding vv. 9-11 provide the evangelist the opportunity to set the bookend at the other end of the story of vv. 1-8. The narrative about the crowd desiring to see both Jesus and Lazarus and about the chief priest's plan to kill Lazarus as well as Jesus because "many were believing in Jesus" does not add substantively to the material that preceded our text.

Responding to the Text

Readers of the Bible are accustomed to the word *anoint*. When the word appears in the Old Testament, it is often in the form of a verbal adjective, "the anointed one," the Messiah. As a result, the word bears royal overtones. Almost always in the Hebrew Bible, "the anointed one" is the Davidic king who rules on God's behalf from Jerusalem's throne. Twice the royal persons called "the Lord's messiah" are not of Davidic lineage. David himself twice uses that title for Saul (1 Sam. 24:6; 26:9). The prophet Isaiah of Babylon reports the Lord's use of the title for Cyrus, king of Persia (Isa. 45:1), and other kings are "anointed" without having the title applied to them (see, for example, 1 Kings 19:15-16). Admittedly, persons other than royalty are anointed. God orders Elijah to anoint not only Haz-ael and Jehu as kings but also Elisha as his prophetic successor (1 Kings 19:16).

With all that biblical baggage in hand, our present text catches us off guard. The anointing here has nothing to do with kingship or royalty. The anointing in our text was for his death and burial. That was the means by which he would serve God's purpose of defeating the foe. His resurrection after that burial would make clear who was the victor for the world and who would rule the world for all eter-nity.

As for Jesus' remark that "you always have the poor with you," we must never distort that description of the human condition into a prescription for neglect of the poor. In fact, God calls the post-Easter church to worship its resurrected Lord precisely by caring for the needy. While Holy Week provides the opportunity to remember the sufferings of Jesus and to walk with him to the cross, the time in which we live and move and pursue our ministry is not the beginning of the first century but the beginning of the twenty-first. Jesus is no longer in need of the anointing for burial that Mary pro-vided. If Mary honored Jesus by anointing him prophetically for his burial, we today honor the resurrected Lord precisely by caring for the poor who are always with us.

> IF MARY HONORED JESUS BY ANOINTING HIM PROPHETICALLY FOR HIS BURIAL, WE TODAY HONOR THE RESURRECTED LORD PRECISELY BY CARING FOR THE POOR WHO ARE ALWAYS WITH US.

Care for the poor, of course, is not the main thrust of our text. The focus lies in the faithfulness of Jesus to fulfill the mission on which God the Father had sent him. Jesus' journey to the Passover in Jerusalem provided the opportunity for him to visit Bethany where the action of our text occurs. Determined to proceed toward a sure and certain death sentence, Jesus accepted Mary's extravagant prepa-ration for his forthcoming death and burial. If we today acknowledge in faith that the purpose of his death was for our benefit, for our salvation, and for our eternal welfare, then we might indeed ask how we can honor him in our day as Mary honored him in hers. Perhaps Jesus provided the clue in his response to Judas regarding the poor, especially since we know how the passage he quoted from Deut. 15:11 ends: "open your hand to the poor and needy neighbor in your land." That would be the honorable thing to do.

For the Preacher

The well-known hymn "On Eagle's Wings" summons those who "dwell in the shelter of the Lord, who abide in this shadow for life" to confess the role of the Lord as "my refuge, my rock in whom I trust." The psalmist for the day prom-ises "refuge in the shadow of his wings" (Ps. 36:7) for people of faith who find themselves hip deep in alligators and to find light in the Lord.

TUESDAY OF HOLY WEEK

REVISED COMMON	EPISCOPAL (BCP)	ROMAN CATHOLIC
Isa. 49:1-7	Isa. 49:1-6	Isa. 49:1-6
Ps. 71:1-14	Ps. 71:1-12	Ps. 71:1-6, 15, 17
1 Cor. 1:18-31	1 Cor. 1:18-31	
John 12:20-36	John 12:37-38, 42-50	John 13:21-33, 36-38
	or Mark 11:15-19	

The world in which we live and move and have our being is for many people more dark than light. Nations fight against nations, citizens against citizens, gangs against gangs. The food we eat is not only junk but often poisonous. The air we breathe spreads diseases into our lungs. Futurists talk about the wonders of technology that will continue to change our lives, but along with toilet seats that take our temperatures and internet access to accomplish our shopping needs comes an awful price: loneliness. Clearly the world is in need of light, a light that will not only provide clearer direction for people listening to "the music of the night" but also hope for something different at the end of the tunnel. The light God provides might not even appear to be religious.

FIRST READING

ISAIAH 49:1-7 (RCL);
ISAIAH 49:1-6 (BCP, RC)

Interpreting the Text

The compiler of the material assigned to Second Isaiah has placed this second Servant Song between two speeches to the world that promise salvation for the exiled Israelites in Babylon (Isa. 48:20-22; 49:7-13). The redeeming of Israel has cosmic proportions: the world will hear and see the work of the Lord.

In this Servant Song, as in 42:1-4, the speaker is the servant rather than the Lord. Appropriately, therefore, the servant comes across as less lofty than in the first song or the fourth. First-person speakers are more effective when they are eating humble pie. Downplaying self, the servant focuses on the actions and speeches of the Lord. In doing so, the song supports the universal nature of the promises of salvation that surround it.

To begin with, the servant addresses the song to the "coastlands" and "the peoples from far away." Immediately the servant's story is set within the context of the known world, as are the Lord's own speeches at 41:1 (see also v. 5) and at 45:22-23. What the servant announces to that big wide world is the Lord's calling and his own function.

The calling took place before the servant's own birth. The Lord figuratively invaded the womb of his mother in order to elect the servant to a yet-unstated mission (v. 1) and to form him specifically "to be his servant" (v. 5). Similar imagery describes the formation of the nation as servant at 44:1-2. In preparation for this mission the Lord equipped the servant as a wisdom teacher prepares pupils for the world, making his mouth like a sharp sword. The servant admits that the Lord hid him in his quiver, apparently protecting him until the appointed time (see Ps. 17:8; 27:5; 31:20; 64:2). Then, as the Lord earlier introduced the servant to an unspecified audience with the words "Here is my servant" (Isa. 42:1), so here the Lord announced directly "to me, 'You are my servant, Israel, in whom I will be glorified.'" The servant now knows both his own identity and his ultimate purpose, although not yet his job description.

The function would have been difficult enough if it had been limited to bringing Jacob/Israel back to the Lord. Yet such a task "is too light a thing" in contrast to the Lord's actual goal for the servant: to be "a light to the nations, that my salvation may reach to the end of the earth" (v. 6). It is no wonder the servant addressed this song to the coastlands and to the peoples from far away. They have a vested interest in the function of the commissioned agent of light and salvation called the servant of the Lord.

Responding to the Text

Assigned for Tuesday in Holy Week, this text can hardly be read and heard without applying it to Jesus. Certainly the use of v. 6 as a portion of Simeon's song regarding the infant Jesus affirms the connection (Luke 2:32: "a light for the revelation to the Gentiles"). Strikingly, the application of the verse to Jesus affirms not only Jesus' identity but also his universal mission—exactly what readers would expect of Luke, sometimes called the Gospel for the Gentiles. In another sense, however, "the light to the nations/Gentiles" in the New Testament is the apostle Paul (see Acts 13:47; Gal. 1:15-16). Clearly Paul was citing here the prenatal election of Isa. 49:1 and his own role as the servant to be the basis for his mission among the Gentiles.

The use of Isa. 49:1-6 in the New Testament points us in two directions. The first is the christological issue in which the Servant Song adds its imagery to the baffling questions about Jesus' identity. The second is the role of the church in any age to carry the gospel of Jesus Christ beyond its "own kind" into the world of many peoples. While Christians worship the servant of the Lord, they also find their own identity as the servant church to give light for the world.

RESPONSIVE READING

PSALM 71:1-14 (RCL);
PSALM 71:1-12 (BCP);
PSALM 71:1-6, 15, 17 (RC)

Of all the psalms of lament that might have been chosen for this Tuesday in Holy Week, Psalm 71 stands out as the obvious choice, and all our lectionaries agree. Like many psalms of lament, this one consists of two parts. The first part, vv. 1-13, mingles the psalmist's confidence in the Lord with a present plight. Here the lamentable situation is the presence of enemies who are waiting to pounce on "this person whom God has forsaken, for there is no one to deliver" (v. 11). The perception of divine forsakenness in the hearts of the enemies (cf. Exod. 32:11-14) is a marketing issue. God's reputation is at stake, and witnessing to God's fidelity in difficult times is the means by which the world will know the incomparable nature of the Lord: "O God, who is like you?"

The second part of Psalm 71 (vv. 14-24) ends with praise and thanksgiving to God for having delivered the persecuted one with the result that the persecutors are put to shame by God's faithfulness. While the BCP lectionary (vv. 1-12) focuses exclusively on the first part of the psalm with its plea for deliverance, the RCL hints at the coming praise in the second part by including v. 14. Limiting the first part of the psalm to vv. 1-6, the RC lectionary thus omits the allusions to the specific lament about the enemies but provides two isolated verses (vv. 15, 17) that indicate how the story of Jesus' persecution will end.

SECOND READING

1 CORINTHIANS 1:18-31

Interpreting the Text

Perhaps no single passage from the New Testament defines the distinctiveness of the Christian faith and theology more precisely than this text. The content of these words is scandalous, foolish, illogical, unreasonable, and provocative—to name just a few of the possible reactions. Yet everything rides on these words.

Paul wrote these words to the Christians in Corinth in the context of his expression of heartbreak at the report of divisions within the congregation there (vv. 10-13). The apostle objected to such divisions, especially to a group founded in his name on the grounds that he baptized none of them. He concluded that paragraph with the clear statement of his function: "not . . . to baptize but to proclaim, and not with eloquent wisdom, so that the cross of Christ might not be emptied of its power" (v. 17). The combining of "wisdom," "cross," and "power" lead directly to the following two paragraphs that constitute our text.

The cross, more specifically Jesus' crucifixion, is either foolishness or God's power, depending on whether one looks at it from the perspective of unfaith or faith. To the unbelieving world the cross is an expression of an itinerant preacher's failure to gather a sufficiently strong following to protect him from execution.

PERHAPS NO SINGLE PASSAGE FROM THE NEW TESTAMENT DEFINES THE DISTINCTIVENESS OF THE CHRISTIAN FAITH AND THEOLOGY MORE PRECISELY THAN THIS TEXT.

Further, for Christians to connect his crucifixion with God's will is downright foolish, because such teaching testifies to God's weakness, and the failure is not only that of Jesus but of God as well.

Both Jews and Gentiles had a history with wisdom. Indeed, wisdom was an international movement whose purpose was to make sense of the world and to participate accordingly. Deciding for the opposite—foolishness—meant chaos and led such a fool to the snares of death. Some theological paths within the wisdom movement led to the conviction that knowing the world meant knowing its Creator.

Clearly the apostle drew the lines between the ways of the world and the ways of God. By human standards God is known through signs and wisdom, making the cross a stumbling block and foolish. By God's standards, however, the cross is God's power and God's wisdom. Through the cross on which Jesus, God's Son, died, God had accomplished exactly what God had planned, namely, the salvation of humanity from its sin. In fact, "God was pleased" (RSV) to use the cross as the means by which to save humankind. The cross, therefore, has power.

As for the cross as "the wisdom of God," consider the lofty goal of the wisdom teachers. Wisdom was the means by which people could come to know God. Paul thus blatantly flies in the face of the Gentiles/Greeks who consider the cross to be "folly" and of the Jews who consider it "a stumbling block, a scandal" (see Isa. 8:14; Jer. 6:21). Against this background Paul interprets the cross to be a scandal for unfaith and the means of salvation for faith, a notion he asserts again in Gal. 5:11.

The same understanding of wisdom and power led Paul to speak of the church in Corinth. Just as God chose to use the folly and stumbling block of the cross to serve as divine wisdom and power, so God chose for membership in this congregation the foolish to shame the wise, the weak to shame the strong, the lowly to bring to nothing what is. Clearly such a congregation has nothing to brag about. What gives them and all Christians the right to boast, however, is the identity of Christ as our wisdom, our righteousness, our sanctification, and our redemption. Only God's gift on the foolish and scandalous cross is the basis for our boasting.

Responding to the Text

The truth of this text flies in the face of preachers every day who would soften the message so that Jesus has more appeal to those accustomed to find success in this world by the use of power and to find peace in the attainment of intellectual superiority or meditative bliss. Strikingly, the message of the cross exerts its power not by lifting one's eyes heavenward to the realm of spiritual peace but by forcing us to stare at the crass and ugly reality of a typical Roman execution. The cross contrasts, therefore, not only with the world's ways but also with the focus of religion itself. Far from centering on the ways in which we come to God (religion's goal), the text proclaims how God comes to us in down-to-earth but anti-worldly ways.

While a religious approach might ask about what we can do to please God, this text is one of several in the New Testament that announces a surprise: what pleases God is what God gives to us. While the NRSV of v. 21 focuses on God's "decision" to use the cross for human salvation, the Greek word (and English translations such as the RSV) provides the shocking news that it is God's "pleasure" to work through this foolish and powerless means to accomplish that goal. Other uses of the same Greek verb demonstrate that God is pleased to give us the kingdom (Luke 12:32), to reveal Christ to Paul so that the gospel might be preached among the Gentiles (Gal. 1:16), and to dwell in Christ so that all things might be reconciled to God (Col. 1:19). What pleases God is acting in Christ and through Christ in order to bring the world to himself. With that goal in mind, even the cross on which Jesus was crucified gives God pleasure. How unreligious of God!

Further, Paul admits that God plays a rather worldly hand in redefining wisdom as Christ crucified. When we want to disparage the success of a person whom we think did not deserve an award or a promotion or tickets to a playoff game, we often say, "There it is again. It's not *what* you know that counts; it's *who* you know." Paul turns that worldly annoyance of getting somewhere through a personal connection into a divine act by which God saves us from our own sin by providing us a connection with his crucified Son. Wisdom is not a body of knowledge but a body of flesh and blood hanging on a cross, and that particular body is God's Son. Through that Wisdom we come to know God—or rather God comes to reveal himself to us and to make us his children.

THE GOSPEL

JOHN 12:20-36 (RCL);
JOHN 12:37-38, 42-50
  or MARK 11:15-19 (BCP);
JOHN 13:21-33, 36-38 (RC)

Interpreting the Text

John 12:20-36 brings to a conclusion the so-called Book of Signs (chapters 2-12) that began with Jesus' changing water into wine at the wedding feast in Cana. The end comes rather unceremoniously as the verse following our text announces, "Although he had performed so many signs in their presence, they did not believe in him" (v. 37). Indeed, vv. 37-38 explain this unbelief on the basis of the prophecy in Isa. 53:1, and in vv. 44-50 Jesus explains both the judgment of God on such unbelief and the authority of his own teaching as resting in the Father who sent him to be the light (BCP).

Surprisingly, the final two paragraphs of the Book of Signs (12:20-36) do not specifically contain the word "sign." The last "sign" Jesus accomplished was the raising of Lazarus from the dead, an act described in some detail in chapter 11 and remembered editorially at 12:1 and 12:17-18, where the miracle is described as "this sign." But our text offers two signs (without mentioning the word) that provide a turning point for the Fourth Gospel: first, Jesus' interpretation of the visit from the Greeks and, second, the means by which he will die.

The Greeks were in Jerusalem, as Jesus was, for the Feast of the Passover. Not unexpectedly they approached Greek-speaking Philip to express their wish "to see Jesus" (v. 21). Philip, along with Andrew, reported the visitors' presence and request to their master. To Jesus the presence of the Greeks was the sign that "the hour has come for the Son of Man to be glorified" (v. 23). The statement is truly a turning point. Indeed, common in the Book of Signs is Jesus' or the author's announcement that the hour had "not yet come." Jesus himself said it to his mother at the wedding at Cana (2:4), and the author narrates the same concern as the reason Jesus had not been arrested earlier (7:30; 8:20). On two occasions Jesus said "the hour is coming, and now is" (4:23; 5:25). The framing of the specific words at the beginning and at the end of the Book of Signs, however, draws particular attention to the contrast: "My hour has not yet come" (2:4) and "The hour has come for the Son of Man to be glorified" (12:23). What triggers the arrival of the hour is the visit of the Greeks who wish to see—perhaps, believe in—him. Apparently it was "too light a thing" that Jesus should have come for the people of Israel alone; God sent him into the world as "a light to the nations, so that my salvation may reach to the end of the earth" (Isa. 49:6). The realization that "the hour has come" leads Jesus to speak about death and life. The means by which a grain of wheat bears fruit is by entering the ground where it dies. So shall his disciples find life—by hating their life in this world. In words similar to those in Mark 8:34-38, Jesus here indicates the cost of discipleship in terms of service. Here, however, Jesus goes beyond the similar words in Mark by specifying the outcomes of faithful serving: eternal life (v. 25) and honor from the Father (v. 26). The latter is particularly striking. Throughout the scriptures believers honor and praise God for creating the universe, for saving the people of Israel from bondage, and for delivering individuals from their lamentable situations. Now, Jesus announces, God will honor those who serve him, and in the context of the Greeks' visit, the honor extends not only to Israelites but also to all people who "wish to see Jesus."

The second sign of this text is the cross on which Jesus would die. Strikingly "the cross" does not appear directly in the passage. It occurs indirectly in the author's comment on Jesus' saying, "when I am lifted up from the earth" (v. 32): "He said this to indicate the kind of death he was to die" (v. 33). This "sign" is couched in Jesus' speech about the personal agony he faces. "Now my soul is troubled" (v. 27) sounds like the Synoptic announcement in Gethsemane, "I am deeply grieved, even to death" (Matt. 26:38; Mark 14:34; see also Heb. 5:7).

Yet Jesus demonstrated publicly that beyond his own fear and agony lay his faithfulness to the mission on which God sent him: "No, it is for this reason that I have come to this hour" (v. 27). He announced to the crowd that the time had come for the ruler of this world to be driven out and that, through his death, he would draw all people to himself (vv. 31-32). The saying confused the crowd, for they were under the impression that the Messiah would stay forever and here Jesus talked about dying. Their question allowed Jesus the opportunity to speak about their taking advantage of the light, that is, himself, while it still shines among them, so that they themselves might become "children of light" (v. 36). The expression here focuses on the disciples continuing in their lives the light that is Jesus. Indeed, the reader of this Gospel will recall Jesus' earlier words "I am the light of the world" and promising his followers "the light of life" (8:12). Clearly here the "children of light" are those who follow the light that is Jesus.

Responding to the Text

Certainly, this text could force us to preach on the cost of discipleship, on hating life in this world, and on following and serving Jesus. Those themes jump out of the verses like the "to do" list stuck on the refrigerator door.

Suppose instead that we fix our stare on what God through Jesus is promising us in these verses. Staggering is Jesus' promise that "the Father will honor anyone who serves me" (v. 26). While we honor God with praises and thanksgiving, with contributions to church and charity, with the commitment with which we do our work in the world, and with our attempts to conduct our lives consistent with God's will, how does God honor us? The text suggests, first, that God honors us by placing us at Jesus' side for all eternity: "where I am, there will my servant be also." God provides the place of honor where we can know the presence of the Lord and his love without end. Not unlike Jesus' later promise "to prepare a place for you" in "my Father's house" so that "where I am, you may be also" (14:2-4), here Jesus speaks of his own death and resurrection as the means by which his disciples may join him eternally.

Second, God honors us by providing the means by which we attain the status of "children of light." That honor, we saw in the first reading, God had given centuries earlier to the servant of the Lord, probably Israel (Isa. 49:6; see also 42:6). What was honorable about the title was God's election of the servant to serve the divine purpose of reaching out to the world, to the nations. The point is significant. The honor of that election lies not in the privileged status of the servant people but in the universal mission on which God was sending them. What truly stands out as honorable with this title, however, is that in John's Gospel the light is the Incarnate Word, Jesus Christ. The beginning of the prologue turns our attention to the light (see 1:4-9), and Jesus claims the title "light of the world" for himself at 8:12 and less explicitly in our text at vv. 35-36. To be "children of light" is to belong to Jesus and to participate in his mission to shine in the darkness of human existence.

> THE HONOR OF THAT ELECTION LIES NOT IN THE PRIVILEGED STATUS OF THE SERVANT PEOPLE BUT IN THE UNIVERSAL MISSION ON WHICH GOD WAS SENDING THEM.

Third, God honors us by sending to us the word who "became flesh and lived among us" (1:14). That human nature of Christ literally screams out in our text as Jesus admits the trouble in his soul (v. 27). If Jesus were a phantom or a hologram or some other disembodied spirit, he would have had no fear of pain. He would have shed no tears at the tomb of Lazarus, and he would not have agonized over his own imminent execution. He was, however, one of us, knowing our grief, our pain, our fear, even our thirst from the cross. That God would go to such lengths for our sakes truly honors us as human beings.

With all those honors divinely given and promised, Jesus calls us to discipleship. The call is radical, but it is also one more expression of good news. That message is clear. God enables disciples to put life in this world in its place precisely because Jesus has provided a new place for our eternity.

For the Preacher

"Grief teaches the steadiest minds to wander." So wrote Sophocles in his *Antigone* almost two and a half millennia ago. If even Jesus can for a moment experience such mind-shaking grief in his troubled soul, so might all of us who serve as his spokespersons today. Yet like Jesus we turn again to the purpose of our ministry: the glorification of God.

APRIL 7, 2004

REVISED COMMON	EPISCOPAL (BCP)	ROMAN CATHOLIC
Isa. 50:4-9a	Isa. 50:4-9a	Isa. 50:4-9
Psalm 70	Ps. 69:7-15, 22-23	Ps. 69:8-10, 21-22, 31, 33-34
Heb. 12:1-3	Heb. 9:11-15, 24-28	
John 13:21-32	John 13:21-35	Matt. 26:14-25
	or Matt. 26:1-5, 14-25	

God's glory is at stake in the events of this Holy Week. It is not the first time a god's honor depended on the fate of a son. In Homer's *Iliad* the battle for the city of Troy pitted hero after hero against one another. Some of these legendary warriors were the offspring of sexual affairs between gods and attractive human women. At several points in the story, Athena challenged Zeus when he was about to take action that would save the life of one of his sons in battle. What stopped such divine intervention was the realization that he would lose his honor among the gods if he saved his own offspring. To be sure, Jesus was not a warrior in battle, and Jesus was not the offspring of a sexual affair between God and Mary. Jesus was God's only Son, begotten through the Holy Spirit. Nevertheless, Jesus knew that his death, not his rescue, would honor and glorify his Father, and so we proceed with the events as Jesus himself allowed and directed them toward that end.

FIRST READING
ISAIAH 50:4-9a (RCL, BCP, RC)

Interpreting the Text

See the comments on this third Servant Song at Passion Sunday, above. Here I focus on a specific portion of the text that bears relevance to Wednesday in Holy Week.

Verses 7-9a portray in the servant's own words the confidence the servant places in the Lord's help in the face of adversity. Though the servant has endured beating, shame, and mockery, faith in the Lord sustains him. Everything follows from the words "For the LORD GOD helps me" (v. 7). Once the servant utters that faithful realization, one implication after another leaps off the page:

therefore I have not been disgraced;
therefore I have set my face like flint,
and I know that I shall not be put to shame.

The conviction of the Lord's help enables the psalmist to withstand whatever evil-doers might plan. So confident is the servant in the Lord's help that he actually challenges his adversaries to "stand up together" and to "confront me" (v. 8), even to "declare me guilty" (v. 9).

Such is the confidence with which the servant faces those who would smite him and those who would insult him and spit on him. "It is the Lord God who helps me" (Isa. 50:9a).

Responding to the Text

The servant's trust and confidence in the Lord comes to the surface in the response of Jesus to the betrayal by Judas reported in the Gospel. That Jesus could so instruct Judas to accomplish quickly his act of betrayal reflects his confidence that no matter what humans do to him, even governing authorities, God will have the last word. Even though that betrayal will lead quickly to accusations of his guilt before religious and civil rulers, Jesus knows that God will help him.

In that conviction Jesus not only demonstrates anew the faith of a confident believer. He testifies as well to his own identity as the true servant of the Lord, no matter who might have carried that identity six centuries prior to his own sufferings.

RESPONSIVE READING

PSALM 70 (RCL);
PSALM 69:7-15, 22-23 (BCP);
PSALM 69:8-10, 21-22, 31, 33-34 (RC)

A reader poring over the psalms in their canonical sequence would at this point encounter a déjà vu experience. All of Psalm 70 has already appeared as vv. 13-17 of Psalm 40. The people of biblical days seem to have spent more time feeling Godforsaken than overwhelmed by divine presence. Why after all are there more psalms of lament and cries for help than any other kind of psalm? The repetition of Psalm 70 might, therefore, have more to do with human experience than scribal plagiarism.

The psalmist states his plea immediately. In v. 1 the cry for deliverance jumps to the fore, and for good reason: haste is required. The problem is more typical of such psalms than unique. The worshiper faces enemies "who seek my life" (v. 2a), "who desire to hurt me" (v. 2b), and "who say, 'Aha, Aha!'" (v. 3). Suddenly the psalmist turns to the recognition that not only himself but also others in the faithful community can "rejoice and be glad in you" and "say evermore, 'God is great!'" (v. 4). Having stated the blessings for all who seek the Lord, the worshiper returns to his own situation once again. Confessing that he is "poor and needy," the psalmist returns to his plea for a hasty deliverance (v. 5).

Identifying himself as "poor and needy" virtually guarantees the Lord's prompt attention. Throughout the psalms and everywhere in the prophetic books the Old Testament witnesses repeatedly recognize that while God loves all people, when push comes to shove, God takes the side of the poor and needy. The reader need only consult Prov. 22:22; 23:10-11; Exod. 22:22-24; Ps. 72:2, 12-14. Eventually Jesus will so profoundly identify with the poor that judgment on the last day will be determined by how well the nations have cared for "me" (Matthew 25). The knowledge of God as one responds to the cries of the poor and needy assures this petitioner of Psalm 70 that the Lord will come hastily to deliver.

Psalm 69, used by BCP and RC, contributes to the abundance of psalms of lament, demonstrating again the preponderance of the feeling that God is absent from the people's daily troubles and they have become weary of waiting (v. 3). Like many of the laments in the book of Jeremiah, this one contains a number of expressions that place the reason for suffering and persecution on the worshiper's own devotion to the Lord (vv. 7, 9-11). Like most laments, this one includes the dreaded isolation of the worshiper from friends, even from the immediate family (v. 8). The suffering worshiper, like the one using Psalm 70, counts himself among the oppressed and needy and relies on God to hear these pleas (vv. 32-33).

Unique in this lament are the words describing the action of the foes: "They gave me poison for food, and for my thirst they gave me vinegar to drink" (v. 21). These words contribute, of course, to the story of Jesus' crucifixion (Matt. 27:34, 48; Mark 15:36; Luke 23:36; and most specifically, John 19:29 where the action is considered a fulfillment of this scripture).

SECOND READING
HEBREWS 12:1-3 (RCL);
HEBREWS 9:11-15, 24-28 (BCP)

Interpreting the Text

The author opened chapter 11 with a definition of faith: "Now faith is the assurance of things hoped for, the conviction of things not seen." Faith, therefore, is a confident hope for that which we do not at the moment experience in our daily lives. From that definition the author paraded his cloud of witnesses, beginning with Abel and continuing through Abraham and Sarah, all of whom "died in faith, without having received the promises, but from a distance they saw and greeted them" (11:13). Then the faith of Abraham, Isaac, Jacob, Joseph, Moses and the slaves of Egypt, Gideon, . . . David, and Samuel contributes to the parade (11:17-32). From there the author speaks of the faith of those men and women who suffered persecutions and executions (11:33-38). The reason they "did not receive what was promised" was due to the promise that only the present generation would experience "perfection" (11:39).

All that background provides the basis for the word "therefore" with which our text begins. Surrounded by those generations of faithful people, even heroes, like so many fans in an Olympic stadium, the present generation is exhorted to dispel the heavy baggage and the curtailment of sin and to run for the finish line (12:1). When the supporting crowds do not provide the motivation for the athletes, those who race can find the support they need in Jesus, "the pioneer and perfecter of our faith" (12:2). With his sight set on "the joy that was set before him," Jesus endured the cross and ended up exalted "at the right hand of the throne of God." In that position Jesus fulfills the "prophecy" about the Messiah promised centuries earlier (Ps. 110:1). His example of humiliation and exaltation will enable the present generation of runners to "not grow weary or lose heart" (12:3).

Responding to the Text

The definition of faith and its role in the generations of witnesses provides hope and strength to people of every time and place. The assertion that faith is based on "the conviction of things not seen" recalls the conclusion of John's Gospel, where Jesus speaks his beatitude: "Blessed are those who have not seen and yet have come to believe" (John 20:29). Once those resurrection appearances established that Jesus was alive, faith in him and belief in who he was/is depend on something other than the seeing that occurred throughout the Book of Signs (John 2–12). Sight is no longer the basis for faith.

ONCE THOSE RESURRECTION APPEARANCES ESTABLISHED THAT JESUS WAS ALIVE, FAITH IN HIM AND BELIEF IN WHO HE WAS/IS DEPEND ON SOMETHING OTHER THAN THE SEEING THAT OCCURRED THROUGHOUT THE BOOK OF SIGNS (JOHN 2–12).

That judgment should not come as a surprise to readers of the Bible. The prophets of ancient Israel used their sight to discern the situations in the life of the people to which God addressed the word. Against what the prophet saw, the Lord provided visions. The distinction between sight and vision has become quite blurred in our day. A thesaurus will provide one as a synonym for the other, and across America shopping malls list among their establishments vision centers that deal only with sight. Biblically, however, sight and vision are not the same. Sight does not lead to faith in Jesus Christ. Sight does not provide for those of us who are running the race "the joy" Jesus envisioned and promised to us. Only vision indicates what glories the finish line holds for those who hold the faith that "is the assurance of things hoped for."

The Gospel
JOHN 13:21-32 (RCL);
JOHN 13:21-35
or MATTHEW 26:1-5, 14-25 (BCP);
MATTHEW 26:14-25 (RC)

Interpreting the Text

The immediate context for John 13:21-32 is the account of the foot washing Jesus performed for his disciples and his teaching about their performing the same kind of loving service for one another (vv. 1-17). That account will serve as part of the Gospel for Holy Thursday and will be discussed at that point.

Strikingly, in the first sentence of our text the writer reports that Jesus was "troubled in spirit" (v. 21). The words are not new. They occurred on Jesus' own lips at 12:27 when, recognizing the coming of the hour of his death in the visit from the Greeks, Jesus portrayed a natural human fear. There at 12:27 and here Jesus was quoting from the lament at Ps. 6:3 to explain his pain over the approaching hour. The reason for his present agony is the imminent betrayal by his disciple Judas. Announcing that "one of you will betray me," Jesus wore his emotional pain on his proverbial sleeve while catching his disciples off guard. The disciples did not know what we readers know about Judas, namely, that he was pilfering the group's funds, because that information appears only in the author's parenthetical narrative at 12:6. While they were wondering suspiciously about one another, an interesting interaction took place between "the one whom Jesus loved," apparently John, and Simon Peter. Since John was reclining directly beside Jesus, Peter—apparently sitting at some distance—motioned to him to ask Jesus about the identity of the traitor. Jesus told the beloved disciple that the betrayer is the one to whom he will give the piece of bread after dipping it into the dish. That turned out, to no reader's surprise, to be Judas.

As soon as Judas took the bread, "Satan entered into him" (v. 27). One would have imagined that receiving food from the one who claimed earlier, "I am the bread of life" (6:35), would effect a conversion experience: from pilfering to philanthropy, from betrayal to loyalty. Instead, the gift of food and the sign to the beloved disciple that Judas was the traitor set in motion the continuation of the tragic drama. That comes as a surprise here. A second surprise is the use by this evangelist of the name Satan. While Matthew, Mark, and Luke mention Satan three, five, and five times respectively, John uses the name only here in his Gospel. Elsewhere he calls the same character "the prince of this world" (12:31; 14:30; 16:11). In the only occurrence of that expression prior to our text (12:31), Jesus had already indicated the prince's expulsion by the upcoming events in Jerusalem. In the texts following our present passage Jesus will likewise assert that the prince's time has come and gone (14:30; 16:11). Within that framework, Satan's entering Judas virtually hastens the end of his own devilish reign over the world. Jesus' subsequent command to Judas to "do quickly what you are going to do," namely, betray his master, only verifies that Jesus, the apparent victim, is completely in charge of the coming events. Judas, even with Satan within him, cannot act any further without Jesus' permission, yes, even command, to proceed with his evil deed.

How interesting that the author reports that, when Judas left the room and went out, "it was night" (v. 30)! Possibly John was concerned only about indicating the time of day when this event occurred, but another possibility seems more likely. Starting with the fourth verse of his Gospel, John announced that with Jesus coming into the world, light appeared. He even reported Jesus' saying, "I am the light of the world," and in the text we discussed for Tuesday in Holy Week, after identifying himself as the light once again, Jesus promised his disciples they would become "children of light." Now with the arrival of Satan in one of Jesus' own disciples, "it was night." Jesus, the light, was about to enter the darkness of the human existence he willingly took upon himself when "the word became flesh and lived among us." Jesus would allow the prince of this world, the ruler of darkness, to have his moment, brief though it would be.

> JESUS, THE LIGHT, WAS ABOUT TO ENTER THE DARKNESS OF THE HUMAN EXISTENCE HE WILLINGLY TOOK UPON HIMSELF WHEN "THE WORD BECAME FLESH AND LIVED AMONG US."

Indeed, at the departure of Judas, while the disciples were baffled that Judas would go shopping at this time of night, Jesus announced the moment for the Son of Man to be glorified and with him for God to be glorified as well. Glorification is a major theme in John's Gospel. At 7:39; 8:54; 12:16, 22, 28; 17:1, 4, 5, it refers to Jesus' resurrection and ascension, perhaps even the resurrection appearances John will report in chapter 20. In 11:4 both the Son of Man and God will be glorified by the appearance of Lazarus exiting the tomb. Jesus promises that his own faithful obedience to God will be the means by which God will be glorified (14:13) and teaches his disciples that their fruitful discipleship will also glorify God (15:8). The resurrected Lord even prophesies that Peter's own crucifixion will glorify God (21:19). In the midst of this continuing and powerful theme, Jesus indicates in our text that the time has come for the Son of Man and for God to be glorified. Indeed, the hour has come for his death, his resurrection, and his ascension—all to the glory of God.

BCP's extension of the text to include also vv. 33-35 leads to consideration of Jesus' "new commandment," a section discussed as part of the Gospel lection for Holy Thursday.

The use of Matthew 26 by BCP (vv. 1-5, 14-25) and RC (vv. 14-25) takes the Gospel message in quite different directions from the insights in John. The text of Matthew 26 also focuses on the betrayal by Judas, but many of the details vary from John's account. The opening verses of chapter 26 present the forthcoming arrest and crucifixion as a prophecy uttered by Jesus to his disciples. Immediately following his words, the author narrates the action as already taking place in the plans of the Jewish leaders. Their only hesitancy at this point is the potential rioting among the people if they pursue their evil plot during the time of the Passover when so many folks are in the city. When the action picks up in v. 14, we see Judas approaching the chief priests with his offer to betray Jesus for a price. They paid him thirty pieces of silver, the amount of money Zechariah the prophet was paid for playing his divinely appointed role as "the shepherd of the flock doomed to slaughter" (Zech. 12:1-13). The connection with the thirty pieces of silver in Zechariah's story seems all the more likely since Matthew (following Mark 14:27) quotes at 26:31 the passage from Zech. 13:7 about striking "the shepherd, that the sheep may be scattered." The use of such "prophecy" in the telling of Jesus' betrayal by Judas interprets the events of our text as fulfillment of ancient God's word rather than as arbitrary acts on the part of humans, Judas and the chief priests notwithstanding.

Matthew, unlike John, specifies that the meal at which these events take place is the Passover meal. Indicating in terms similar to those in John that "my time is near" (v. 18), Jesus instructs his disciples to go into the city to locate the place for the meal, and immediately the disciples get busy preparing the Passover meal. In the course of eating the meal, Jesus announces "one of you will betray me," and while that prediction sets off a buzz among the disciples, one after another asking, "Surely not I, Lord?" Jesus assures them that prophecy, not Judas, will determine his own fate, but the traitor will come to wish he had never been born. At that threat, Judas adds his deceitful question, "Surely, not I, Rabbi?" This time Jesus responds affirmatively.

Responding to the Text

Recognizing the control of Jesus over the events of his death, even over the details of Judas's timing for his betrayal, focuses our theological attention on the plan and purpose of God in sending the eternal Word to become incarnate and live among us. The evangelist John's interpretation that the crucifixion of Jesus is God's act recalls other writings in the New Testament. Following Mark, even Matthew, who is sometimes criticized for anti-Jewish tendencies, quotes the Lord's words from Zech. 13:7 in his rendition of his disciples' imminent desertion: "I will strike the shepherd, and the sheep of the flock will be scattered" (Matt. 26:31). The apostle Paul presents a variety of expressions to indicate God was the actor in bringing about the crucifixion of Jesus "whom God put forward as a sacrifice of atonement by his blood" (Rom. 3:25). This proclamation of the New Testament enables preachers of every age to announce again and again that the crucifixion was God's deliberate and purposeful act, not a divine resignation to the failure of humans to accept his Son. Focusing on that theological insight so evident in our text renders completely inappropriate and horrendously wrong any attempt to blame Judas or the Jewish people or any other group for the death of Jesus. They were simply the instruments in God's plan to effect the salvation of the world, and they were able to complete their awful deeds only by the permission and even at the command of Jesus himself. His own motive was not a suicidal desire but a faithful commitment to fulfill his goal that God be glorified.

THIS PROCLAMATION OF THE NEW TESTAMENT ENABLES PREACHERS OF EVERY AGE TO ANNOUNCE AGAIN AND AGAIN THAT THE CRUCIFIXION WAS GOD'S DELIBERATE AND PURPOSEFUL ACT, NOT A DIVINE RESIGNATION TO THE FAILURE OF HUMANS TO ACCEPT HIS SON.

The timing of Judas's betrayal of Jesus might be described in that proverbial opening of a novel, "It was a dark and stormy night." (Those words are actually the opening line of *The Last Days of Pompeii*, by Bulwer-Lytton.) That "it was night" not only contrasts with the light theme running throughout this Gospel; it enables us to recognize that through the events that followed, Jesus had entered into the night as well. Far from simply designating the chronological time of the betrayal and what ensued, the author makes a theological point of demonstrating that Jesus was entering the darkness of human existence. It is precisely this point that comforts many listeners of our preaching, especially those who for reasons such as death of a loved one, their own failing health, an unresolved separation or divorce, the loss of a job, or the stress of parenting can barely see light at the end of their tunnels. Recognizing that Jesus knows the darkness, too, enables us to recognize that it is precisely when we feel most forsaken by God that we are closest to the crucified Christ (Luther).

The use of Matthew 26 in the telling of this event focuses on none of the above themes discussed in terms of John's account. Matthew's frequent use of prophecy, however, even in the words of Jesus, "as it is written of him" (the Son of Man) in v. 24, forces the reader to focus on the theological motive for Judas's betrayal and Jesus' subsequent death: God is fulfilling the prophecies in order to accomplish the divine purpose promised long before. Then Matthew, unlike John, refuses to let Judas off the hook—or more appropriately, the rope (27:5).

For the Preacher

Admitting with the psalmist, "I am poor and needy," gives us the freedom to set aside all our self-allusions. Martin Luther's similar words "We are beggars, that is true" enable us to come before God completely dependent on divine grace as we, with Judas, go out into the nighttimes of life.

MAUNDY THURSDAY / HOLY THURSDAY

APRIL 8, 2004

REVISED COMMON	EPISCOPAL (BCP)	ROMAN CATHOLIC
Exod. 12:1-4 (5-10) 11-14	Exod. 12:1-14a	Exod. 12:1-8, 11-14
Ps. 116:1-2, 12-19	Ps. 78:14-20, 23-25	Ps. 116:12-13, 15-18
1 Cor. 11:23-26	1 Cor. 11:23-26 (27-32)	1 Cor. 11:23-26
John 13:1-17, 31b-35	John 13:1-15	John 13:1-15
	or Luke 22:14-30	

How utterly astonishing that the biblical reports of outstanding events take such ordinary forms! The celebration of the Lord's salvation of the people of Israel from their bondage in Egypt involves not thunder and lightning bolts or magnificent edifices or majestic crowds but lambs and bread and family gatherings. The New Testament witnesses describe the means by which Christians remember the death of Christ the Savior with bread and wine and foot washing. What transforms such common elements into extraordinary meaning are ordinary words.

Through the ordinary God makes extraordinary. That transformation is precisely what any reader of the New Testament would expect when the eternal and divine Word became flesh and lived among us. Yet, much to our surprise, by such ordinary means God transforms individuals into community and calls us to act in most extraordinary ways. The community involved in the Passover is the family, gathered around a meal that identifies each generation with the one of the past that God brought out of the land of Egypt. The community gathered around the Lord's Supper—ever since Jesus established it—foretastes the future meal when generation after generation dines together at the eschatological banquet.

FIRST READING

EXODUS 12:1-4 (5-10), 11-14 (RCL); EXODUS 12:1-14a (BCP); EXODUS 12:1-8, 11-14 (RC)

Interpreting the Text

The Passover ritual described in this text appears to derive from another world. Its description of the details for serving size, qualifications for the lamb, cooking directions, and dress code contribute to the apparent irrelevance of the whole text for twenty-first-century preaching. Not to get lost in these details, however, is the meaning of the event. The Passover is the means by which Israel will celebrate the Lord's saving event from the land of Egypt, an event with which every Jew from generation to generation will consider themselves part by saying, "It is because of what the Lord did for me when I came out of the land of Egypt."

In another sense, the instructions for the supper prepare for a horrific act of God. The Lord will pass over the homes of the Israelites who have smeared the lamb's blood on the lintel and doorposts. In the homes and pens of the Egyptians—unprotected by the blood—the plague will kill the firstborn of humans and animals. Even the plethora of gods in Egypt will fall victim to the Lord's judgments: "I am the LORD" (v. 12). Indeed, it is the identity of Israel's God that has been the guiding principle in the narratives about the plagues thus far. Pharaoh himself said, "Who is the LORD that I should heed him and let Israel go? I do not know the LORD, and I will not let Israel go" (Exod. 5:2). In order to answer that question for Pharaoh, the Lord brought upon the land of Egypt one plague after another (see 7:5, 17; 8:22; 9:14; 29; 10:2); the salvation event at the sea is the climactic moment for this lesson in identity (14:18). The issue at stake is not simply a matter of the Lord's self-introduction to the rulers and people of Egypt; it is matter of demonstrating who is God around here.

The means by which the Lord will bring the decisive judgments is a "plague to destroy" (Heb: *negef l'maschît*, v. 13). Only a few verses later, the instrument of destruction takes on a more personal form when it is described as "the destroyer" (Heb.: *hammaschît*, v. 23), virtually a demon under the power of the Lord. In either case, the presence of the sacrificial blood on the doorposts of the Hebrew slaves will keep the destroyer away. By that means the Lord will save the people from the awful night and take them out of the land of their bondage.

Responding to the Text

In his book, *The Old Testament and the Literary Critic,* David Robertson compared the story of Exodus 1–15 with Euripides' tragedy *The Bacchae.*[2] Robertson employed the commonly accepted literary definitions of comedy and tragedy: a comedy is a story that ends with the hero incorporated into the community to which he or she rightfully belongs, while a tragedy is one that ends with the hero cast out of the community to which he or she belongs. Those definitions apply respectively to Exodus 1–15 and to *The Bacchae,* two stories that possess a similar plot: a little known god asserts divinity by unleashing mighty power against a stubborn unbeliever. The comedic nature of Exodus 1–15 diminishes any sympathy for the villain (the Pharaoh), while the tragic nature of *The Bacchae* develops a tension around the person of the unbeliever Pentheus.

Robertson's intriguing study highlights an issue that bothers many Christians. Why did God not find another way to free the Hebrew slaves without murdering so many innocent Egyptians and their undiscerning livestock, what we today call collateral damage? Recall the position of the Passover. Until this point the people of Egypt have been inconvenienced by blood in the river, frogs in their beds, flies in their soup, locusts in their fields, and so on. Until this final plague not one Egyptian had died. Only now, when all else has proved futile, does God act to bring death.

THE KILLING OF THE FIRSTBORN COMES ONLY AS A LAST RESORT.

The killing of the firstborn comes only as a last resort.

The final result of the story is a rite by which the people of Israel, family by family, celebrate with a meal the Lord as their Redeemer and the Exodus as the salvation act that defines them as a people.

RESPONSIVE READING

PSALM 116:1-2, 12-19 (RCL);
PSALM 78:14-20, 23-25 (BCP);
PSALM 116:12-13, 15-18 (RC)

If the psalms of lament focus on the apparent absence of God in the midst of personal and communal struggles, Psalm 116 gives the Lord thanks for having heard the voice and supplications of the petitioner. As one of the "Hallel psalms," Psalms 113–118, this song of praise played a significant role in such festivals as Passover. After the opening in which the psalmist expresses love for the Lord because of the longed-for response (vv. 1-2), the psalmist asks the rhetorical question regarding an appropriate response for the Lord's bounty (v. 12). The verses that follow virtually describe the details for a *tôdâ* ("thanksgiving") meal. Among the key elements of the meal are the cup of salvation, the paying of vows, a sacrifice of *tôdâ*, the presence of the congregation, and the courts of the house of the Lord (vv. 13-19). Essentially the action runs as follows: after deliverance from a lamentable situation, the delivered one invites family, friends, and other members of the congregation into the courts of the temple for a celebration meal, a *tôdâ*. There the delivered one lifts "the cup of salvation" and hosts a party to offer the Lord thanks (see also Ps. 22:26).

In its totality Psalm 78 (BCP) demonstrates the disunity that existed between the northern kingdom of Israel and the southern kingdom of Judah. Setting the whole history of Israel in the context of a wisdom instruction (vv. 1-4), the teacher from Judah reiterates the traditions the northerners held dearest, those of the Exodus and the wilderness. The teacher describes the grace of God through one act of goodness after another for the people and simultaneously the people's rejections and rebellions against this gracious Lord.

On this Holy Thursday the psalm points to the "bread of angels//the grain of heaven," namely, the manna that God provided for the nourishment of the people in the wilderness, even in the midst of their rebellion. Such grace spills over to every generation of believers for whom God supplies the Lord's Supper for life's journey through the wilderness, even as we continue our own rebellions against our God.

SECOND READING

1 CORINTHIANS 11:23-26 (RCL, RC);
1 CORINTHIANS 11:23-26 (27-32) (BCP)

Interpreting the Text

Paul introduces the words of institution by stating unabashedly that he is simply passing on the tradition he himself had received. It is a device Paul uses again in 15:3 where he summarizes the gospel about the death and resurrection of Jesus, along with resurrection appearances, as the body of tradition he received. In our text he states that the source of his revelation is the Lord. The words of Jesus that Paul reports are similar to the words in the Synoptic Gospels (Matt. 26:26-29; Mark 14:22-25; Luke 22:15-20), but they are not identical. In spite of minor differences, there are such obvious similarities among all four versions that we are able to conclude that the basic elements of the words have their origin in Jesus. Above all, there is in Paul, Matthew, and Mark a connection between the cup and the covenant. Paul's terminology about "the new covenant in my blood" calls to mind the eschatological prophecy of the new covenant written on the hearts of the people in Jer. 31:31-34. The "new covenant" in the words of institution indicates that with the death of Jesus the kingdom of God dawns and that we will enjoy its fullness in the banquet at noon.

Responding to the Text

The connection between blood and covenant-making is rare in the Old Testament. At the foot of Mount Sinai, God made a covenant with the people of Israel through the ritual of throwing the blood of a sacrificed animal on the altar of the Lord and on the people while announcing the words "the blood of the covenant" (Exod. 24:8; see also Zech. 9:11) The unique expression "in *my* blood" (Matt. 26:28; Mark 14:24) is the means by which Jesus speaks of his impending death. It points directly to the uniqueness of what is about to transpire in Jesus' crucifixion and to its consequences.

The device that Paul uses in this text is instructive for the church of every generation. What the church teaches and preaches is not an invention of human origin but a tradition that has defined the church from one century to the next and has its origin in Jesus. The sacrament of the Lord's Supper is clearly, then, a profound gift that Jesus Christ left to the church. In his popular book *Joshua*,[3] Joseph Girzone concludes his story of Jesus' revisiting us in our own time by leaving only his sandals. In our text, however, Jesus leaves the meal as the means by which the Lord's death is proclaimed again and again until he comes again. The words that accompany the meal enable the church of Jesus Christ to focus on the heart of the gospel and to reap its benefits. They also indicate the promise that the Lord will indeed come again and that he gives us the meal as the sign.

THE SACRAMENT OF THE LORD'S SUPPER IS CLEARLY A PROFOUND GIFT THAT JESUS CHRIST LEFT TO THE CHURCH.

THE GOSPEL
JOHN 13:1-17, 31b-35 (RCL); JOHN 13:1-15 or LUKE 22:14-30 (BCP); JOHN 13:1-15 (RC)

Interpreting the Text

The first verse of John 13 provides the stage on which the remaining drama will be enacted. In spite of various modern translations, including NRSV, only one finite verb appears in the verse. It occurs in the final words of the verse: "he loved them to the end." The significance of the verb lies in its tense: the aorist in Greek indicates a single act. "He loved" can only refer to the sacrificial act of love Jesus is about to make on the cross. This definitive single act of love is distinguished from the continuing love Jesus has shown for his disciples, the kind described by the participle in the same verse: "having loved his own who were in the world." That was the love Jesus had been showing his disciples ever since he called them to follow him. This initial verse virtually serves as a heading for everything that follows, defining every forthcoming act of Jesus as a sign and expression of the cross. That this love will extend "to the end" (Greek: *eis telos*) is verified by Jesus' final words in John's Gospel: "It is finished" (Greek: *tetelestai* at 19:30).

At supper, probably the evening prior to the Passover meal, Jesus took off his robe and tied a towel around himself, taking on the appearance of a servant. The author sets this act within the context of forthcoming events, telling us that Jesus was aware that (1) "the Father had given all things into his hands" and (2) "he had come from God and was going to God" (v. 3). The latter indicates Jesus' knowledge of his divine origin and of his imminent exaltation through his arrest and subsequent death. Like the reference to the single act of love in the first verse, this comment places the action of the foot washing in the context of his death. Even the verbs describing Jesus' actions with his clothes appear to point beyond the immediate scene to the coming one. Taking off (Greek: *tithēsin* = "laying down") his robe and taking (Greek: *labōn*) a towel, Jesus girded himself. The same Greek verbs appear in Jesus' own teaching at 10:17-18 in terms of his laying down his life and taking it again.

After washing the feet of some or all of the disciples, Jesus came to Peter who objected to the protocol of the moment. Jesus the master should not be washing his feet. Jesus' response is classic: "You do not know what I am doing now, but later you will understand" (v. 7). John the Evangelist repeatedly indicates that only after the death, resurrection, and ascension of Jesus will the disciples understand things Jesus said and did during his ministry (see 2:22; 12:16). For the moment, Jesus instructed Peter that if he did not wash him, the disciple would "have no share with me." With that comment, Peter volunteered for a bath. A bath, however, was not offered. Instead, after washing the feet of all the disciples, Jesus indicated "not all of you" are clean, referring of course, to Judas rather than to each one's anatomy.

Jesus asked if they knew what he had done to them. We can assume they did not understand. Jesus' question has no meaning at all if he is only talking about washing their feet. The question has more to do with what the action means. Since they cannot possibly understand the full significance until after his glorification, he provides them here with a partial object lesson: "You also should do as I have done to you" (v. 15). Yet, the following verse seems to hint at a larger assignment than foot washers: servants, perhaps even slaves, and messengers (Greek: *apostolos;* v. 16). Recognizing that the slave is not greater than his "lord" and that the messenger is not greater than the one who sent him, establishes the foot washing as an illustration of servanthood and apostleship.

> RECOGNIZING THAT THE SLAVE IS NOT GREATER THAN HIS "LORD" AND THAT THE MESSENGER IS NOT GREATER THAN THE ONE WHO SENT HIM, ESTABLISHES THE FOOT WASHING AS AN ILLUSTRATION OF SERVANTHOOD AND APOSTLESHIP.

Knowing all these things is one thing; doing them brings the servant blessing. In fact, Jesus promises a beatitude on those who follow the lead of Jesus not merely to foot washing but to sacrificial service and love. Like the beatitudes of Matt. 5:3-11 and Luke 6:20-22, the one offered here and in John 20:29 are possible only because the coming kingdom of God is already breaking in to human history in the death and resurrection of Jesus. Because the hour has come for the Son of Man to be glorified, disciples who act as servants and messengers can already know the future of God's blessings.

The addition of vv. 31b-35 provides the second bookend with which to enclose the library of Jesus' teachings about sacrificial love and service that he began in v. 1. Judas's exit into the night to continue his treason enables Jesus to talk about glorification. He had already defined the coming of the Greeks as the hour for his own glorification (12:23), but in our text he introduces the same theme with "now." Judas's betrayal provides the immediacy of the more general "hour." Several key insights develop in vv. 31-32 in regard to glorification. In the first place, Jesus declares that "the Son of Man has been glorified, and God has been glorified in him." The use of the past tense here implies that the death and resurrection sequence have already been set in motion and that the entire act is as good as done. Jesus has spoken on several occasions about his being lifted up (see, for example, 3:14), a description that seems to refer first to his crucifixion and then to his resurrection/ascension. That both the suffering and the resurrection/ascension serve as his exaltation probably came into the tradition of Jesus and the early church from the first verse of the Servant Song of Isa. 52:12—53:12.

> See, my servant will prosper;
>   he shall be exalted and lifted up,
>   and shall be very high.

Jesus the servant is exalted in his imminent and inevitable crucifixion and, therefore, he "has been glorified." Likewise, Jesus taught, the Father has been glorified in him, for "through him the will of the Lord shall prosper" (Isa. 53:10b). Further, Jesus speaks here not only of the completed glorification but of the future as well, just as the voice of God uttered at 12:28: "I have glorified it (God's name), and I will glorify it again." The future glorification points to the eternal honor due God and God's Son through the resurrection/ascension that the church will celebrate throughout the earth.

With that critical teaching stated, Jesus turns to his "new commandment," and here the text comes full circle: "that you love one another. Just as I have loved you, you also should love one another" (v. 34). Again, as at v. 1, the aorist of the verb is used to describe Jesus' love for his disciples, and that once-for-all event can only refer to the cross. Here, however, Jesus adds a new twist, similar in style to the follow-the-teacher method at v. 15: "You love one another" in the same way that "I have loved you"—sacrificially, unconditionally, responsively. So critical is this teaching that Jesus will repeat it before the evening is over, even prefacing his love for them with the news that "the Father has loved me" (see 15:9-12). In fact, Jesus indicated the powerful opportunity for witnessing to the world: the disciples will have no credibility as his disciples unless they "have love for one another" (v. 35).

That Jesus "has loved his disciples to the end" provides both the foundation for his washing their feet and the motivation for his disciples to love and serve one another. By their modeling of the Teacher, the world will know whose they are.

The church of every generation has in one way or another focused on the lifestyle and teachings of Jesus as the model for the Christian life. Yet, from the time of Jesus to the present time, disagreements among Christians that split us apart are precisely those about lifestyle and teachings. What gets lost in the midst of intra- and inter-denominational squabbles is the new commandment that Jesus offers to his disciples in this text: "Love one another, as I have loved you."

A profound ethical principle is developed in Christianity on the basis of "old" commandments: "You shall love the Lord your God," and "You shall love your neighbor as yourself." The two appear side by side in the Synoptic Gospels in essentially the same context (Matt. 22:37-39; Mark 12:30-31; Luke 10:27). They are not new commandments but quotations from the Law of Moses (Deut. 6:4 and Lev. 19:18 respectively). Apart from that single context in which the two commandments appear, the love of neighbor alone becomes the commandment that sums up the whole law (Rom. 13:9; Gal. 5:14; James 2:8). If only we would demonstrate our love for the Lord our God by loving our neighbors as ourselves (see 1 John 4:20-21)! Heeding those commandments of old would make the world more loving, more just, more peaceful.

The new commandment that Jesus teaches in our text, however, pushes the envelope considerably further. Loving one another even within the church on the model of the love Jesus gave to us on the cross requires more than loving others as ourselves. It means surrendering ourselves for the sake of others. The story "No Greater Love," written by John Mansur, provides a powerful image of this love.[4] A young Vietnamese boy named Heng offered to give blood so that one of his friends wounded in a bombing of an orphanage might live. After the needle was inserted into his arm, young Heng began to cry. Neither the doctor nor the nurse could understand why. When a Vietnamese nurse talked with Heng, she learned that he thought the giving of his blood would kill him. When asked why he would assent to this act under those circumstances, Heng said, "She's my friend."

Even the sacrificial love that Jesus commands us to give to one another is not exclusively a Christian responsibility. Yet, as Jesus indicated to his disciples, that kind of love will send a message to the world that we are his disciples, and that message would be a far cry from the one we send by our blatant disagreements over lifestyle and teachings.

For the Preacher

"As the members of the congregation are united in body and blood at the table of the Lord so will they be together in eternity. Here the community has reached its goal. Here joy in Christ and his community is complete. The life of Christians together under the Word has reached its perfection in the sacrament."[5]

GOOD FRIDAY

APRIL 9, 2004

REVISED COMMON	EPISCOPAL (BCP)	ROMAN CATHOLIC
Isa. 52:13—53:12	Isa. 52:13—53:12	Isa. 52:13—53:12
	or Gen. 22:1-18	
	or Wis. 2:1, 12-24	
Psalm 22	Ps. 22:1-21	Ps. 31:2-6, 12-13, 15-16,
	or 22:1-11 or 40:1-14	17, 25
	or 69:1-23	
Heb. 10:16-25	Heb. 10:1-25	Heb. 4:14-16; 5:7-9
or 4:14-16; 5:7-9		
John 18:1—19:42	John (18:1-40); 19:1-37	John 18:1—19:42

Out of the story of this entire week, this is the day on which Christianity is defined. Good Friday is the day of the cross, the day on which laments abound and hopes are assured. The texts for the day enable us to know that only by walking in our shoes straight to death can Jesus accomplish what God sent him to do. In the midst of what appears to be a failure, God was performing a great injustice: to give us what we do not deserve and what we could never earn.

FIRST READING
ISAIAH 52:13—53:12

Interpreting the Text

Like the first Servant Song at 42:1-4, this fourth song begins with, "Behold, my servant." The connection of the two songs is significant. In the first one the Lord introduces the servant, reports the commissioning, and identifies the servant's purpose, while the same introduction in the fourth song leads to the Lord's pleasure at the servant's accomplishments. The end result of the servant's mission turns out to be quite different from the original job description of establishing justice for the nations.

The structure of this lengthy song offers the reader a variation in speakers and in the content they present. The speakers fluctuate between the Lord (as in the first song) and some other party, a community that appears as "we," "us," and "our."

Specifically, the Lord speaks at the beginning and the end (52:13-15 and in 53:11b-12), providing the framework for the community's report about their responses to the servant's experiences and their benefits due to his accomplishments (53:1-11a).

In the framework, the Lord promises and pronounces the exaltation of the servant (52:13) and thereby offers a sharp contrast to what any observer could have imagined (52:14-15). Indeed, many people who saw the servant were so utterly appalled at the sight of him that they would do anything not to look in his direction. The Lord promises that just as people had been appalled at such a humiliating sight, now the world—nations and their kings—will be startled at the report they will hear: the humiliated one has been exalted. Unheard of! The end of the framework at 53:11b-12 moves the reader's understanding even beyond the servant's own transition from humiliation to exaltation. The Lord announces the benefits the servant's sufferings accomplish for "many," indeed, "for the transgressors": he shall bear their iniquities, make intercession for them. With those words the Lord announces that the sufferings previously described by the servant himself at 49:4 and 50:6 bear significance far beyond the fate of a divine commissioning (as with Moses, Jeremiah, Ezekiel). Here they carry vicarious significance. They accomplish redemption and righteousness for others.

In the intervening report of 53:1-11a the community attests to the truth of everything the Lord uttered in the framework. From his youth the servant's appearance was downright disgusting, and many did indeed turn their eyes away from him. Not only did others despise him but even "*we* held him of no account" (53:3b). Further, *we* regarded him as "struck down by God, and afflicted" (v. 4b), as people in ancient times did when affliction struck a person. How blind *we* were, the reporter confesses, that *we* were not able to recognize that the servant was suffering for *us,* he was bearing *our* transgressions, and his bruises were the means by which God was healing *us* (vv. 5-6). The servant endured his suffering without complaint (no lament on his lips!), was taken away "by a perversion of justice." Though completely innocent, the servant was executed and buried (vv. 7-9). The reporter asks appropriately, "Who could have imagined his future?" (v. 8b) and then answers that rhetorical question in the conclusion of the report: he shall see light and find satisfaction, having become the instrument through which the will of the Lord shall prosper (vv. 10-11a).

Responding to the Text

Jesus' brutal beatings, the miscarriage of justice, the rejections and denials, along with imagery of the sacrificial lamb and the results for transgressors—they all appear prefigured in the divine and human sections of this song. What astonishes me is how seldom the New Testament writers quote or allude to the actual words of this Servant Song and how they use these words when they do cite them. Granted, the author of 1 Peter summarized the essential elements of the song and applied them to Christ's own sufferings and their effects (1 Pet. 2:22-24) in order to encourage patient suffering at the hands of others. Granted, too, the author of Luke-Acts used Isa. 53:7-8 as the quoted scripture by which the apostle Philip was able to define Jesus Christ as the suffering servant to the Ethiopian eunuch (Acts 8:32-33). Apart from these precise usages of the song, however, the New Testament writers use the words of Isa. 52:13—53:12 in surprisingly less significant ways. See the use of Isa. 52:15 at Rom. 15:21; Isa. 53:1 at John 12:38 and at Rom. 10:16; Isa. 53:4 at Matt. 8:17; Isa. 53:12 at Luke 22:37.

All these rather feeble quotes and allusions to this text in the New Testament do not detract, however, from the song's powerful impact as we hear it on Good Friday. Its words challenge us to focus on God's pleasure in the servant Jesus to forgive our sinfulness in this most unheard of way and on God's surprise to move far beyond what is just to give us generously what we do not deserve.

> ALL THESE RATHER FEEBLE QUOTES AND ALLUSIONS TO THIS TEXT IN THE NEW TESTAMENT DO NOT DETRACT FROM THE SONG'S POWERFUL IMPACT AS WE HEAR IT ON GOOD FRIDAY.

The alternate reading from Gen. 22:1-18 for Good Friday (BCP) reports the Lord's command to Abraham to sacrifice Isaac in the land of Moriah on one of the mountains. Strikingly, in the Septuagint, Isaac is three times called "the beloved son" in exactly the same Greek words used for Jesus at his baptism (Matt. 3:17; Mark 1:11; Luke 3:22) and at his transfiguration (Matt. 17:5; Mark 9:7; see also Mark 12:6//Luke 9:13). Since the words appear nowhere else in the Septuagint except at Gen. 22:2, 12, 16 and in the New Testament only for Jesus, it appears that the expression is limited to a son about to be sacrificed. The remarkable news on Good Friday is that while God spared Abraham's "beloved son" at the last moment, God did not spare his own "beloved son" from death.

Still another alternate reading (BCP) is the apocryphal Wisd. of Sol. 2:1, 12-24. Wisdom was written rather late, possibly even during the last half of the first century A.D. The verses of this text describe the unjust sufferings and death of a righteous person who might represent either righteous people in general or a specific righteous one persecuted by the wicked. The language here and at 5:1-8 recalls the imagery of the suffering Servant Song of Isa. 52:13—53:12. The author's point is that the wicked who pursue such persecutions do not have a clue about the danger they are in because of contradicting the way of the Lord or his secret purposes.

RESPONSIVE READING
PSALM 22 (RCL);
PSALM 22:1-21 or 22:1-11 or 40:1-14
or 69:1-23 (BCP);
PSALM 31:2-6, 12-13, 15-16, 17, 25 (RC)

According to Mark and Matthew, Jesus spoke only one "word" from the cross: the opening verse of Psalm 22; neither Luke nor John shows any knowledge of this saying of Jesus. While the discussion of Psalm 22 might carry more impact if the Gospel for the day were from Mark or Matthew rather than John, the content and structure of the psalm, as well as its use in the New Testament, deserve attention here nevertheless.

Like most psalms of lament, this individual lament consists essentially of two parts: lament and praise. The lament proper appears here in vv. 1-21, while vv. 22-31 articulate the praise a worshiper offers when God has resolved the once lamentable situation. In this case, the psalmist's lament, mixed with expressed trust, repeats itself through three well-structured stanzas. In the first stanza, the lament over God's apparent absence (vv. 1-2) is balanced by the recognition of the Lord's holiness and praiseworthiness, justified by the Lord's response in days of old to the cries of the ancestors (vv. 3-5). The second stanza offers the lament in terms of the worshiper's scorn and mockery by others (vv. 6-8), followed by the brief history of the relationship between God and worshiper that began at the human's birth; the section ends with a plea for God's presence (vv. 9-11). In the third stanza the psalmist first identifies the enemies in such terms as bulls, a lion, and dogs while admitting to the physical, emotional, and spiritual effects their persecutions are having (vv. 14-18); the stanza concludes with a series of petitions for divine presence (hastily!), for deliverance "from the power of the dog" and salvation "from the mouth of the lion" (vv. 19-21).

The response of praise in vv. 22-31 begins with the announcement that the previously afflicted worshiper will praise the Lord for having appeared and listened and with the subsequent invitation to others of the household of faith to do likewise (vv. 22-24), even in the context of a *tôdâ* meal (vv. 25-26). Then the praise turns to some astonishing implications. The saving act of the Lord to this worshiper's lament will result in the conversion of the whole world to the Lord (27-28), and that new worshiping community will consist not only of those who have already died (thus resurrection?) and those who have not yet been born (vv. 29-31). The Lord's act carries universal and eternal implications.

Psalm 40:1-14 (BCP), like Psalm 22, balances praise and thanksgiving on the one hand and petitions for deliverance on the other. Here, however, the two parts are

reversed, the praise and trust (vv. 1-10) preceding the pleas (vv. 11-17). The worshipers who used Psalm 40 for thanksgivings and petitions indicated that they interpreted God's response to their sorrows in the past to be nothing short of divine vic-
tories. Their reports of such acts of deliverance were like those of heralds from the
field of battle to anxious waiters (see 2 Sam. 19:19, 20, 22, 25, 26, 27, 31).

For an interpretation of Psalm 31 (RC) the reader can refer to the discussion in
the Palm Sunday texts. Psalm 69 (BCP) has been discussed among the texts for
Wednesday of Holy Week.

SECOND READING
HEBREWS 10:16-25 or 4:14-16; 5:7-9 (RCL);
HEBREWS 10:1-25 (BCP);
HEBREWS 4:14-16; 5:7-9 (RC)

Interpreting the Text

At this point in the epistle the author has made clear his proclamation
that Christ has not only offered the pure and perfect sacrifice; he has also ascended
to the right hand of God's throne where he serves as the high priest of the heavenly sanctuary. The text here follows immediately upon the distinction between
priests who offer sacrifices daily for sins that can never be taken away and the single event of Christ's sacrifice that accomplished the forgiveness of our sins (see vv.
1-15 in BCP). Having accomplished that forgiveness "for all time," "he sat down at
the right hand of God," following the order of the priest-king Melchizedek and
waiting "until his enemies would be made a footstool for his feet" (Ps. 110:1).

For the second time the author uses the quotation from Jer. 31:31-34 (see 8:8-
12) regarding the new covenant (vv. 16-17). The prophecy enables the author to
connect the new covenant written inwardly on human hearts and the eschatological forgiveness of sins. The once-and-
for-all event of Christ's sacrifice ends the
need for further offerings for sin. The word
"therefore" moves the reader to the result of
that sacrifice to end all sacrifices. We can
confidently enter the heavenly sanctuary,

> JEREMIAH 31:31-34 ENABLES THE AUTHOR TO CON-
> NECT THE NEW COVENANT WRITTEN INWARDLY ON
> HUMAN HEARTS AND THE ESCHATOLOGICAL FORGIVE-
> NESS OF SINS.

just as those who are washed in the blood of the Lamb can enter the new creation
temple in the Bible's final vision (Rev. 21:22-27). That freedom to "approach the
throne of grace," however, is in Hebrews not simply a future hope but a means
here and now by which every Christian can receive mercy and "find grace to help
in time of need" (4:16). The approach runs through the curtain that had previ-

ously separated the believers from God's throne (see also 6:19-20). That same curtain had been ripped down the middle when Jesus cried out from the cross and yielded up his spirit (Matt. 27:51).

The author then offers three exhortations consistent with his overall purpose of awakening a lapsing faith so that his readers might be prepared for the inauguration of the new age. First, "let us approach with a true heart in full assurance of faith" (v. 22). Second, "let us hold fast to the confession of our hope without wavering" (v. 23). Third, "and let us consider how to provoke one another to love and good deeds" (v. 24). The basis for that mutuality is the act of worshiping together. Worship and praise of God as a community of faith is the sign that the kingdom of God has dawned (Rom. 15:7-13).

The alternate reading of 4:14-16; 5:7-9 (RCL) or 4:14-16; 5:5-9 (RC) contains some emphases similar to the preferred reading. A different point, however, that deserves attention on this Good Friday is the notion that Jesus, the Son of God, our high priest, is one who knows our weaknesses and temptations, yet did not sin. Worshiping such a high priest enables us to obey the exhortations offered here, namely, to "hold fast to our confessions" (4:14) and to "approach the throne of God with boldness, so that we may receive mercy and find grace to help in time of need" (4:16). This Jesus did not appoint himself but was appointed to his priestly office by the God who addressed him directly: "You are my Son" (what God said to the Davidic king on the day of his coronation at Ps. 2:7) and "You are a priest forever" (what God said to the Davidic king according to the order of Melchizedek, probably also on coronation day at Ps. 110:4). Further, as illustration of Jesus' knowing our weaknesses, the author writes of his agony voiced in prayer "with loud cries and tears" (5:7; see also Matt. 26:38-39; Mark 14:34-36; Luke 22:42-44; John 12:27). Jesus' obedience, in spite of his agony, made him "perfect" and "the source of eternal salvation for all who obey him" (5:9).

Responding to the Text

The alternate reading from chapters 4 and 5 demonstrate in no uncertain terms what the sufferings and death of Jesus and his subsequent exaltation to God's right hand mean for us. That we have a high priest who traveled the road of human weakness removes all kinds of barriers between him and us and provides a hospitality that welcomes us into the presence of the throne. There is something of an analogy with Mark Twain's *The Prince and the Pauper* in that the lordly one becomes an understanding ruler by taking the place of an impoverished look alike. Here, however, the one who takes on our human condition is the Son of God, and his exaltation following death provides untold benefits for those who believe in him, both here and now in terms of accessibility to God and eternal salvation in the future.

Many of the same themes in the preferred reading from chapter 10 lead to some further benefits. The bases for the exhortations focus on the cleansing of our sins to make us free, the faithfulness of God to promises, and the emphasis on the coming Day. Note once more how the action of God precedes and provides the impetus for the exhortations: God's cleansing us enables us to approach the sanctuary with full assurance of faith; God's faithfulness enables us to hold fast to faith; God's promise of the coming Day encourages the mutual and reciprocal love in community over against the privacy of much contemporary piety. Without God's act

on this Good Friday, our deeds are nothing more than humanitarian goodies.

GOOD FRIDAY

APRIL 9

WITHOUT GOD'S ACT ON THIS GOOD FRIDAY, OUR DEEDS ARE NOTHING MORE THAN HUMANITARIAN GOODIES.

on this Good Friday, our deeds are nothing more than humanitarian goodies. Because of God's act on the cross, our deeds become the means by which we act in faith and in thanks to God.

THE GOSPEL
JOHN 18:1—19:42 (RCL, RC);
JOHN (18:1-40); 19:1-37 (BCP)

Interpreting the Text

As soon as Jesus had finished his profound and moving prayer (chapter 17), he went across the Kidron Valley to an unnamed garden. There, John reports, without any delay—not even time for Jesus to pray—Judas brought the soldiers, some chief priests and Pharisees, to arrest Jesus. Identifying himself as the Jesus of Nazareth whom they were seeking, he calmed down the wrath of the sword-wielding Peter, and placed the entire scene under his control with his words, "Am I not to drink the cup that the Father has given me?" (cf. Matt. 26:39; Mark 14:36; Luke 22:42). Willingly, then, Jesus was taken before Annas, then to Caiaphas, the high priest that year. While Jesus was being questioned by them, Peter was fulfilling Jesus' prophecy about his denying the Lord three times, clearly not the fisherman's finest hour. The religious leaders took Jesus to Pilate, the Roman governor, who stated three times that he could find no case against him, but granted nevertheless that he should be crucified with the label "King of the Jews." At the Place of the Skull called Golgotha, the soldiers crucified him along with two others (not called "thieves" by John). When the Jews present realized the Sabbath was drawing near—what an offense to have these bodies hanging around!—they asked the soldiers to break the legs of the victims so they could suffocate and be taken down before sunset. Jesus was already dead and had no need of such select treatment. Suddenly we readers meet Joseph of Arimathea, one of Jesus' disciples, who along with Nicodemus, known to us from chapter 3, buried Jesus in a never-before-used tomb located in the same garden where he was crucified.

Several key points along the way deserve some discussion. First, the evangelist reports two conversations between Jesus and Pilate. The first one begins with Pilate's question about Jesus' reputation as king of the Jews (18:33) and concludes with another question, namely, "What is truth?" (18:38). Between those two questions Jesus told Pilate that his kingship "is not from this world . . . not from here" (v. 36). Jesus takes the opportunity to distinguish between what the world knows of kings and armies and what he represents. Admitting kingship, even of another realm, Jesus finds the need to say more, and so he tells Pilate about the reason he came into this world: to testify to the truth (18:37). When Pilate asks the famous question, "What is truth?" he does not know what the readers of this Gospel know, namely, that truth is standing in front of him. The prologue to the Gospel announces that the Word of God who became flesh and lived among us was "full of grace and truth" (1:14). On one of his trips to Jerusalem Jesus taught his followers that continuing in his word makes them his disciples, "and you will know the truth, and the truth will make you free" (8:32). In the same conversation only four verses later, Jesus says, "So if the Son makes you free, you will be free indeed" (8:36). The two statements make clear that the truth and the Son are one and the same: Jesus is the truth. Finally, at 14:6 Jesus announces to his disciples in terms of one more "I am" saying, "I am the way, and the truth, and the life." Unfortunately, Pilate never got the chance to read the book, and so his question went unanswered while we know exactly who—not what—truth is.

The next time Jesus and Pilate converse, Pilate begins by asking Jesus where he came from (19:9). Again, readers of the Gospel know the answer. He is the Word who was with God in the beginning; indeed, he was God (1:1). In the nocturnal conversation with Nicodemus, that Pharisee confessed that Jesus was "a teacher who has come from God" (3:2), an insight that led Jesus to talk about the need to be born "from above," apparently connecting his own origin with that of new birth for others. In front of Pilate, however, Jesus gave no answer to the question, and so the governor still did not know what we do. When Pilate brought up the question of authority, however, Jesus gave him a lesson in creation theology. "You would have no power over me unless it had been given you from above" (19:11). As Creator of the world, God had the authority to use earthly rulers in whatever ways God chose. Pilate was simply one more government official (like Nebuchadnezzar at Jer. 27:6 and Cyrus at Isa. 45:1; see also Rom. 13:1-7) whose authority came from God and who would now be used to accomplish God's purpose for the world through the death of his innocent Son.

Second, God's purposes and plans through this entire event become evident in the author's announcement that scripture is being fulfilled. The treatment of Jesus' clothing by the soldiers happened, the evangelist writes, to fulfill the scripture of Ps. 22:18. Interestingly, while Mark's narrative of the account of the crucifixion oozes with allusions to Psalm 22 and places the first verse of that psalm on Jesus' lips, this quotation at John 19:24 is the only hint of that psalm in the entire narrative. The report about Jesus' dying prior to the breaking of his legs is stated to be the fulfillment of the prophecy at Ps. 34:20, a psalm of praise for God's deliverance (19:36). Immediately, the author cites Zech. 12:10 as the prophecy fulfilled by the piercing of Jesus' body. The purpose of all these scriptural quotations demonstrates in one more way that the events surrounding Jesus' arrest and death are part of the divine plan.

> THE PURPOSE OF ALL THESE SCRIPTURAL QUOTATIONS DEMONSTRATES IN ONE MORE WAY THAT THE EVENTS SURROUNDING JESUS' ARREST AND DEATH ARE PART OF THE DIVINE PLAN.

Third, the same purpose is evident in two of the three sayings Jesus uttered from the cross. His last words, according to John, begin with his redefining the relationship between his mother and the beloved disciple: "Woman, here is your son" and, "Here is your mother" (19:26-27). The words echo those from the Synoptic tradition by which Jesus defines as his mother and brothers "those who hear the word of God and do it" (Matt. 12:46-50; Mark 3:31-35; Luke 8:19-21). His disciples enter into a relationship not only with Jesus but also with the family that he creates by his teaching of the word (the Synoptics) and through his death (John). The second word from the cross in our text is "I am thirsty" (19: 28), specifically stated to be the fulfillment of another scripture. The only possibility is Psalm 69, a psalm of lament in which the worshiper reports, "for his thirst they (his foes) gave him vinegar to drink" (Ps. 69:21; see the discussion on Wednesday in Holy Week, BCP). Like most such psalms, this one concludes with praise and thanksgiving, not only by the worshiper but also by the whole creation (v. 34). The third word is simply "It is finished" (one Greek word, *tetelestai*). The word appears throughout John's Gospel, even on Jesus' lips, to teach that he has "accomplished the works" that the Father sent him to do (4:34; 5:36; 17:4). That Jesus uses the word here again indicates that everything happening to Jesus this day is the culmination of the divine plan that has been in place and that defined his reason for coming into the world.

The narrative about the burial, therefore, is not read with dismay and a sense of failure on the part of believers. Rather, the involvement of Joseph of Arimathea and the return of Nicodemus signal the accomplishment of the work that God sent Jesus to do and the anticipation of concluding the lament with praise and thanksgiving.

Responding to the Text

That Jesus not only speaks the truth but also is the truth carries profound significance for the effect his coming and dying have for us. Influenced as we are by the more Greek understanding of the word "truth," we tend to regard even the words about truth in John's Gospel as pertaining to the accumulation of knowledge and to a statement supported by evidence, even in a court case: "Do you promise to tell the truth and nothing but the truth, so help you God?" Some colleges, even church-related colleges, use as their motto Jesus' words from John 8, "You will know the truth and the truth will make you free," and the same words appear inscribed in stone over some courthouses across our country. In both cases, the intent is laudable, but the words of Jesus and the testimony of John's Gospel that Jesus is "the truth" have nothing to do with those applications. As the truth, Jesus is the means by which we come to the knowledge of God, knowledge in the Semitic

> AS THE TRUTH, JESUS IS THE MEANS BY WHICH WE COME TO THE KNOWLEDGE OF GOD, KNOWLEDGE IN THE SEMITIC SENSE OF PERSONAL AND INTIMATE RELATIONSHIPS.

sense of personal and intimate relationships. The author of John's Gospel repeatedly makes the connection between knowing Jesus and knowing the Father and, while the ancient notion of wisdom might provide the more common way to explain how people come to know God, the use of truth in that regard is virtually synonymous. (See the discussion on wisdom in 1 Cor. 1:18-31 under the section on Monday in Holy Week.) What an advantage we have over Pilate, for whether he knew it or not, Jesus is the truth that brings us into the eternal love of God. What a difference that can make in our lives when we know it!

Jesus' words "I am thirsty" must have taken by surprise some of the people at the foot of the cross, as they startle those of us who read the words almost two thousand years later. Jesus is the one who said to the woman at the well in Samaria that he was the source of living water, that whoever drinks of his water will never thirst, that it will become water welling up to eternal life (3:10-14). Jesus was citing imagery from the scriptures, particularly from Jer. 2:13 and Zech. 13:1; 14:8. What irony here that the one who promised water that would prevent the drinker from thirst now says from the cross, "I am thirsty." And to think that both the discussion at the well and these words from the cross are unique to John! It appears that the author was willing to risk the apparent contradiction in order to focus on using the lament of Psalm 69. That reference accomplishes two things for us readers and hearers today. First, it demonstrates how thoroughly Jesus "became flesh and lived among us" (1:14). His expression of thirst from the cross announces in one more concrete image that Jesus was one of us, that he experienced our pains and sorrows, and that he was therefore just as capable of lamenting as we are. Recognizing his involvement in our humanity from this side of Easter provides us with the comfort that our risen Lord knows intimately our sorry conditions and with the hope that we can walk through the darkness with him to emerge with him into eternity.

Second, the citing of the lament of Ps. 69:21, as we have seen, places the entire crucifixion in the context of God's will and purpose for humanity. Recognizing that larger picture can enable us to come to terms with the extent of God's love for us. Jesus died, not because of his failure to convince a sinful humanity, even his own people, but to become God's success story in which "the will of the Lord will prosper in his hand" (Isa. 53:12).

For the Preacher

"When sorrows come, they come not single spies, but in battalions."[6] So said Claudius to Gertrude. The statement was certainly true for Jesus on this day. Since he knew the rejections, the betrayals, the beatings, the nails, and the death, we can find strength when sorrows come to us as we worship a Lord who faced the battalions for our sakes.

THE GREAT VIGIL OF EASTER / HOLY SATURDAY

APRIL 10, 2004

REVISED COMMON	EPISCOPAL (BCP)	ROMAN CATHOLIC
Service of Readings		
Gen. 1:1—2:4a	Gen. 1:1—2:2	Gen. 1:1—2:2
Gen. 7:1-5, 11-18, 8:6-18; 9:8-13	Gen. 7:1-5, 11-18, 8:6-18, 9:8-13	Gen. 22:1-18
Gen. 22:1-18	Gen. 22:1-18	Exod. 14:15—15:1
Exod. 14:10-31; 15:20-21	Exod. 14:10—15:1	Isa. 54:5-14
Isa. 55:1-11	Isa. 4:2-6	Isa. 55:1-11
Prov. 8:1-8, 19-21; 9:4b-6 or Bar. 3:9-15, 32—4:4	Isa. 55:1-11	Bar. 3:9-15, 32—4:4
Ezek. 36:24-28	Ezek. 36:24-28	Ezek. 36:16-17a, 18-28
Ezek. 37:1-14	Ezek. 37:1-14	
Zeph. 3:14-20	Zeph. 3:12-20	
Second Lesson		
Rom. 6:3-11	Rom. 6:3-11	Rom. 6:3-11
Psalm 114	Psalm 114	
The Gospel		
Luke 24:1-12	Matt. 28:1-10	Luke 24:1-12

What irony that in the darkness of this night while Jesus lay in the tomb, people of faith have for almost two thousand years expressed their confidence in a God committed to life. And while the attention is focused on Jesus, there is no denying that our own self-interest plays a significant role. The morning for which we wait determines not only Jesus' fate but our own.

SERVICE OF READINGS

Interpreting and Responding to the Texts

The many and various texts that form this moving Service of Readings actually focus on the will of God. They serve on this Easter Vigil to assure believers that the God we worship and for whom we wait to act in Jesus' tomb is committed to life and salvation and that God will accordingly have the last word.

God's Commitment to Created Life

The so-called Priestly account of creation (Gen. 1:1—2:4a) places the entire universe under the governance of God the Creator. When God had finished building the neighborhood, God decided to make humanity, bestowing dignity on each and every human being by making us "in the image of God." Finally, on the seventh day God set aside the day when each week the creation might praise its Creator through the Sabbath observance. When the wickedness of this humanity became so grave that God decided to send the flood, God made immediate plans through the agency of Noah to rescue a sufficient number of humans and other creatures so that creation might begin anew (Gen. 7:1-5, 11-18; 8:6-18; 9:8-13).

> WHAT IRONY THAT IN THE DARKNESS OF THIS NIGHT WHILE JESUS LAY IN THE TOMB, PEOPLE OF FAITH HAVE FOR ALMOST TWO THOUSAND YEARS EXPRESSED THEIR CONFIDENCE IN A GOD COMMITTED TO LIFE.

In time God entered directly into the realm of history by calling Abraham and Sarah that their descendants would be a blessing for all the families of the earth. No sooner was their first descendant born than God tested Abraham's faith by asking him to sacrifice this promised child, Isaac. God interrupted the action of faithful obedience by supplying a ram as a substitute for the child so that Isaac might live and the promise for blessing all the earth might be fulfilled (Gen. 22:1-18). When even the extended family of Abraham and Sarah seemed to thwart rather than advance the Lord's purpose for life and blessing, the Lord threatened judgment on the people. Yet true to his word, the Lord promised a new creation for the remnant that would survive the judgment (Isa. 4:2-6).

God's Commitment to Life through Salvation (The First Exodus and the Second)

In order to preserve the lives of many people in a time of famine, God sent Joseph and then Jacob's whole family down to the land of Egypt where they were enslaved for four hundred years. The Lord brought them out by the saving event at the Red Sea. The people of Israel "need only to keep still" while the Lord does all the necessary work. They responded in faith and broke out in songs of praise (Exod. 14:10—15:1, 20-21). Many centuries later, after the people had been sent into exile in Babylon because of their sins, the exiles considered their hope in God gone, their own spirit dried up, and their existence like that in Sheol. God restored them to life by the prophetic word and promised to return the people to their own land (Ezek. 37:1-14), cleansing them with a new heart and new spirit

(Ezek. 36:24-28). The surety that they will never experience such divine absence again is as solid as the promise God made long ago to Noah (Isa. 54:5-14). To support that promise for new life, God offered the exiles a warm invitation to receive food and milk without money and divine grace without condition, and he assured the people of the effectiveness of the word (Isa. 55:1-11). Blending that promise of restoration to the land with the familiar prophetic vision of a new day, God promised to appear on behalf of the people of Israel as a divine warrior, saving the afflicted, restoring the people from foreign lands to their own land, and establishing the divine reign over all (Zeph. 3:12-20).

God's Commitment to Life through Teaching

In addition to these great savings acts in the exodus from Egypt and the new exodus from Babylon, the Lord offered daily ways for the people to find life. One of these ways is through the instructions of the wisdom teachers, even the teaching of Wisdom herself. Like the Lord's invitation to food and to life at the beginning of Isaiah 55, Wisdom offers a similar invitation to dine, indicating that her teaching is the way to life (Prov. 8:1-8, 19, 21; 9:4b-6). In time, the teachers developed the notion that the wisdom in which the people of Israel could find life is the torah that the Lord gave the people years earlier (Bar. 3:9-15, 32—4:4).

> WITH THAT STORY OF GOD'S COMMITMENT TO LIFE THROUGH CREATION, SALVATION, AND INSTRUCTION, CHRISTIANS WAIT CONFIDENTLY DURING THIS EASTER VIGIL FOR GOD TO CONTINUE THAT PROMISE OF LIFE THROUGH THE MIRACULOUS AND HITHERTO UNKNOWN EVENT OF RAISING JESUS FROM THE DEAD.

With that story of God's commitment to life through creation, salvation, and instruction, Christians wait confidently during this Easter Vigil for God to continue that promise of life through the miraculous and hitherto unknown event of raising Jesus from the dead.

SECOND READING
ROMANS 6:3-11

Interpreting the Text

Paul's teaching in this text leads us once more to recognize God's commitment to life. Now, however, that divine commitment focuses on the death and resurrection of Jesus Christ. The death of Jesus is the means by which "Christ redeemed us from the curse of the law by becoming a curse for us" (Gal. 3:13). The shedding of his blood on the cross is God's way of justifying sinful humanity "by his grace as a gift" (Rom. 3:24), accomplishing for us reconciliation now and promising salvation from the wrath to come (Rom. 5:9-11). The resurrection of Jesus is the means by which God became victorious over death and raised Jesus to the status of Lord (Rom. 1:3; 10:9). Christ's death and resurrection together comprise "the gospel: it is the power of salvation to everyone who has faith, to the Jew first and also to the Greek" (1:16). That larger context is critical as we examine our text.

The issues Paul raised in the previous chapter also pave the way into this text. There he discussed how sin came into the world through Adam and spread universally by all of humanity contributing generously. That sin led to death; more specifically "sin exercised dominion in death" (5:21; see also vv. 14, 17). The new Adam, Jesus Christ, however, is the means by which "the grace of God and the free gift in the grace of the one man, Jesus Christ, abounded for the many" (5:15). This "one man's obedience" becomes the act of righteousness that leads to justification and life for all (5:18). In sum, Jesus Christ ushers in a new dominion or reign—a reign of life—that replaces the reign of death and sin caused by Adam's rebellion.

Our text tells how Christians leave the old reign and become part of the new: through baptism. Being baptized into Christ Jesus means being baptized into his death and buried with him. Until baptism sin and death were our masters; we were "enslaved to sin" (v. 6), an image the author of John's Gospel used years later: "everyone who commits sin is a slave to sin" (John 8:34). Death is the way we finally rid ourselves of sin's reign over us, and baptism into Christ's death is the death that sets us free. That is good news.

> DEATH IS THE WAY WE FINALLY RID OURSELVES OF SIN'S REIGN OVER US, AND BAPTISM INTO CHRIST'S DEATH IS THE DEATH THAT SETS US FREE. THAT IS GOOD NEWS.

But the good news gets even better. Dying with Christ is the means by which we also rise with him to life. Since sin and death have no power over us, we enter a new reign—that of Christ, in which we will, like him, live and "walk in newness of life" (v. 4). While the resurrection to eternal life is still in the future, the newness of that life begins here and now, made possible by the sacrament of baptism. On the basis of that new freedom Paul exhorts his readers to "consider yourselves dead to sin and alive to God in Christ Jesus" (v. 11).

Responding to the Text

During this Easter Vigil the realization of our baptism takes paramount importance. Because we have been baptized into Christ's death, we await the light of the new day both to experience his resurrection to eternal life and ours as well. By having already joined Christ in his crucifixion and burial, we look forward to joining him in life. His Easter is our Easter.

On Saturday afternoons during football season more than 100,000 Pennsylvanians flock to the center of the state to watch the Nittany Lions of Penn State play their rivals. The town of State College lies in what is called Happy Valley. Many of those loyal fans drive from the east along a very dangerous route. One section of that route has come to be known as Death Valley. A sign along the road announces, "To get to Happy Valley you must drive through Death Valley." In one sense, the message is obvious: death is the way to life. Yet our text and this entire Easter Vigil make clear that life is not the obvious result of death. It is death and burial *with Christ* that leads to life with Christ now and forever, and our incorporation into his death and resurrection happens through our baptism.

In addition to solving the problem of our eternal mortality, rising to newness of life with Christ makes a difference in the way we live even now. Surely the apostle did not intend to suggest that because of our baptism we live sinless lives. Paul did not understand sin to be a moral path that we could travel or avoid. He interpreted sin as a power that seeks to reign over us and is ever struggling to enslave us. Against that hostility Paul defined the gospel of Jesus Christ as "the power of God for salvation to everyone who has faith." Through the power of that gospel conferred by the Holy Spirit at our baptism, we are saved for life and live under the reign of God. So saved and so freed, we are enabled to consider ourselves "alive to God in Christ Jesus."

THE GOSPEL
LUKE 24:1-12 (RCL, RC); MATTHEW 28:1-10 (BCP)

Interpreting the Text

The final verses of Luke 23 are necessary to provide the context for our text and to identify the women who appear suddenly as "they" in 24:1. At 23:55 they are called "the women who had come with him from Galilee." It was they who followed Joseph of Arimathea to the tomb where Jesus' body was laid. Since the Sabbath was about to begin, however, the women could not anoint his body at that moment, and so they returned, prepared spices and ointments, and then "rested according to the commandment" (23:56). These final words of chapter 23 identify the women not by name (that will come in 24:10) but by their origin in Galilee and by their devotion to the Jewish law. Clearly they were not rebels who would invent stories that might undermine the very faith they so devoutly professed.

That the Easter scene begins with the words "at the break of day" might simply be a way of indicating the women went out to fulfill their responsibility to Jesus' body as early as possible. However, the indication of time might be a clue to hearers and readers alike that a divine victory was now to be revealed. The divine act that destroyed the Egyptian armies and enabled the Israelites to cross the sea floor on dry land, happened "in the morning watch" (Exod. 14:24). In the psalmic celebration of God's victory over the chaotic waters that threaten Jerusalem, the worshipers sing that God will help Jerusalem "at the break of day" (Ps. 46:5). A biblical story that begins with the words "at the break of day" offers the reader hope for something more than the illumination of sunshine.

When the women arrived at the tomb and found the stone rolled away, they were perplexed over the disappearance of Jesus' corpse. Suddenly two men in dazzling apparel appeared and asked them, "Why are you seeking the living among the dead?" (v. 5). The men reminded them of the words Jesus taught them in Galilee about dying and then rising on the third day (vv. 6-7). Then they remembered and apparently began to grasp what had happened. This entire sequence is reminiscent of the narrative about Jesus' youth, told only by Luke (2:41-51). Only "after three days" did his parents find their missing son in the Jerusalem temple. After Mary scolded their preteen for his thoughtlessness, Jesus asked, "Why are you seeking me?" Strikingly, the author reports, "And they did not understand the saying that he spoke to them." The author of Luke appears to be establishing a framework between the second chapter and the twenty-fourth, between Jesus early visit to Jerusalem at the Passover festival and his final one. In each case, the episode focuses on the inability of those around Jesus to understand where he is and on the utter waste of time in looking in the wrong places.

> THE EPISODE FOCUSES ON THE INABILITY OF THOSE AROUND JESUS TO UNDERSTAND WHERE HE IS AND ON THE UTTER WASTE OF TIME IN LOOKING IN THE WRONG PLACES.

The men immediately announce in words that are quite similar to those in Matthew and Mark that Jesus "is not here, but has been raised!" The use of the theological passive here indicates that Jesus did not raise himself from the dead, but God did. God is the actor. God is the victor. Nevertheless, Jesus did tell about it in advance. While Matthew makes this assertion with the words "as he said" (28:5), Luke makes a more complete statement by having the two men remind the women that in Galilee Jesus had spoken of his arrest, his crucifixion, and his resurrection (active voice). That prophecy appeared in Luke's Gospel at 9:22 ("be killed" rather than "be crucified," and the passive voice for "raised) and in somewhat different terms in 13:32-33. That Jesus spoke in advance about what would happen might point more to his divinity than to his prophetic ability, for in the preaching of Second Isaiah, it is precisely the ability of the Lord to speak of forthcoming events that distinguishes the Lord from the idols of Babylon.

Remembering those earlier words of Jesus, however, apparently does not enable the women to believe. Now identified—Mary Magdalene, Joanna, Mary the mother of James, and some unnamed women—they did manage to return to the Eleven to report what they had experienced. The ever-uncomprehending apostles regarded their story as "an idle tale, and they did not believe them" (v. 11). We can hardly blame them, for nowhere in the scriptures is the issue of resurrection clearly attested, least of all in connection with the Messiah. Even the commonly used "after three days" in Jesus' teaching has roots only at Hos. 6:2 where the object of the Lord's resurrection will be "us" and the death from which the community hopes to be raised is God's judgment for their apostasy. Resurrection also occurs, of course, at Dan. 12:2, but there again the object is the people, and the timing is fixed at the time of the apocalyptic end. That Jesus was raised within the context of human history is as unheard-of as the exaltation of the humiliated servant of Isa. 52:13—53:12. While disbelieving, Peter nevertheless runs off to the tomb himself. Finding nothing but the linen cloths, "he went home, amazed at what had happened" (v. 12). We do not know whether Peter believed or what he thought happened.

Responding to the Text

Many of us Christians today tend to assume more than this text says, and as a result, we might miss the opportunity to stand in the sandals of the women from Galilee and those of Peter. At the conclusion of the text all that the women knew was that the tomb was empty and that two smartly clad men told them by implication that Jesus was alive, just as he said in his earlier prophecies. We all have seen enough mystery movies and TV criminal trials to know that thus far we have only circumstantial evidence and the testimony of two strangers whose credentials have not been established. (According to the men Jesus later met on the road to Emmaus, the women had interpreted the identity of the two men as angels, but we are not told what led them to that conclusion; see 24:23.) On the basis of that flimsy case, what jury would be convinced that Jesus was raised from the dead? If the deciding panel were to function on the basis of reason and reasonable doubt, surely the report of the women was "an idle tale." Perhaps the word to describe the reported event is "preposterous"! It defies logic. It did not make any more sense in the culture of the first century than it does in ours two millennia later. Is it any wonder that the disciples in this text were "perplexed . . . terrified . . . did not believe . . . amazed"? Can any of us truthfully deny that in their sandals we would have responded the same way? Perhaps many of us do even today.

Think, too, of the unfruitfulness of witnessing in this text. The two men *told* the story, but with no unambiguous result, for while the women remembered Jesus' words, they did not necessarily believe at this point that Jesus was raised and now alive. The women *told* the story to the apostles, but they clearly did not believe them. While telling the story, the gospel story, is the means by which people come to believe and thus are saved (so Paul at Rom. 10:14-17), such witnessing here falls on disbelieving hearts.

In teaching the meaning of the Third Article of the Apostles' Creed, Martin Luther asked his customary catechetical question "What does this mean?" He began his explanation with these words: "I believe that by my own reason or strength I cannot believe in Jesus Christ, my Lord, or come to him. But the Holy Spirit has called me through the Gospel, enlightened me with his gifts, and sanctified and preserved me in the true faith." The gift of the Spirit came early in John's Gospel, already later on Easter Day (John 20:22). In Luke the disciples will wait for another fifty days until the Spirit comes (Acts 2).

In the meantime, however, Jesus made several resurrection appearances, even here in Luke. The remainder of this chapter tells of several appearances: to the two disciples on the Emmaus road (vv. 13-31), to Peter (v. 34), and to all of them, exhorting them to be his witnesses to all nations (vv. 36-49). While Matthew will report different appearances (28:16-20) and John will offer two in chapter 20 and another in the epilogue, chapter 21, Paul will describe more appearances, even to himself (1 Cor. 15:5-8).

At this Easter Vigil, however, we are not at the point of the gift of the Holy Spirit who enables people to believe the absurd news. We are not even in the midst of resurrection appearances that brought the disciples to faith. Yet we are beyond the announcement that the jury is still out. We are waiting confidently for some clearer sign that the hearsay from the two strange men and the emptiness of the tomb really mean what they promise. And so we can spend this vigil identifying with the women in their perplexity and with Peter in his amazement, waiting for the morrow when the Son shall rise.

For the Preacher

In the darkness of this night we find hope for humanity in these words of Douglas John Hall: "A faith that knows failure (that begins in failure) can touch the lives of many today who otherwise do not have the courage to have failed."[7]

Notes

1. *The Riverside Shakespeare* (Boston: Houghton Mifflin, 1974). See *Henry V,* 4, prologue, 30–41.

2. David Robertson, *The Old Testament and the Literary Critic* (Philadelphia: Fortress Press, 1977), 16–32.

3. Joseph E. Girzone, *Joshua: A Parable for Today* (Garden City, N.Y.: Doubleday, 1994).

4. William J. Bennett, ed., *The Moral Compass: Stories for a Life's Journey* (New York: Simon & Schuster, 1995), 466–67.

5. These are the final words of the meaningful and widely read text by Dietrich Bonhoeffer, *Life Together,* trans. John W. Doberstein (New York: Harper & Row, 1954), 122.

6. *Riverside Shakespeare, Hamlet,* 4.5.78-79.

7. Douglas John Hall, *Lighten Our Darkness: Toward an Indigenous Theology of the Cross* (revised ed.; Lima, Ohio: Academic Renewal Press, 2001), 2.

NOVEMBER 2003

Sunday	Monday	Tuesday	Wednesday	Thursday	Friday	Saturday
						1
2	3	4 Election Day	5	6	7	8
9	10	11 Veteran's Day	12	13	14	15
16	17	18	19	20	21	22
23	24	25	26	27	28 Thanksgiving	29
30 1 Advent						

DECEMBER 2003

Sunday	Monday	Tuesday	Wednesday	Thursday	Friday	Saturday
	1	2	3	4	5	6
7	8	9	10	11	12	13
2 Advent						
14	15	16	17	18	19	20
3 Advent						
21	22	23	24	25	26	27
4 Advent			Christmas Eve	Christmas Day	Boxing Day (Canada)	
28	29	30	31			
Christmas 1 / Holy Family			New Year's Eve			

JANUARY 2004

Sunday	Monday	Tuesday	Wednesday	Thursday	Friday	Saturday
				1 Name of Jesus New Year's Day	2	3
4 Epiphany	5	6	7	8	9	10
11 1 Epiphany	12	13	14	15	16	17
18 2 Epiphany	19 Martin Luther King Day	20	21	22	23	24
25 3 Epiphany	26	27	28	29	30	31

FEBRUARY 2004

Sunday	Monday	Tuesday	Wednesday	Thursday	Friday	Saturday
1 4 Epiphany Presentation of Our Lord	2	3	4	5	6	7
8 5 Epiphany	9	10	11	12	13	14
15 6 Epiphany	16	17	18	19	20	21
22 7 Epiphany	23	24	25	26	27	28
29 1 Lent			Ash Wednesday			

MARCH 2004

Sunday	Monday	Tuesday	Wednesday	Thursday	Friday	Saturday
	1	2	3	4	5	6
7	8	9	10	11	12	13
2 Lent 14	15	16	17	18	19	20
3 Lent 21	22	23	24	25	26	27
4 Lent 28	29	30	31			
5 Lent						

APRIL 2004

Sunday	Monday	Tuesday	Wednesday	Thursday	Friday	Saturday
				1	2	3
4 Palm Sunday	5 Monday in Holy Week	6 Tuesday in Holy Week	7 Wednesday in Holy Week	8 Maundy Thursday	9 Good Friday	10 Holy Saturday Vigil of Easter
11 Easter Sunday	12	13	14	15	16	17
18	19	20	21	22	23	24
25	26	27	28	29	30	